D1203698

Arab-Israeli Wars

A.J. Barker

HIPPOCRENE
BOOKS, INC.

First published 1980

Published by Hippocrene Books
171 Madison Avenue
New York, N.Y. 10016

All photos unless otherwise credited are courtesy of Israeli Govt. Press Office and the *Israeli Sun.*

PRINTED IN THE U.S.A.

Contents

Prologue

Historical tragedies are not caused by right clashing with wrong; they arise from right clashing with right. This is how it is in the Middle East where the conflict between Israel and the Arab states has been raging since 1948.

How did it begin? Simply that a large number of Jews tried to recreate a state of their own in a land that had been occupied by Arabs for centuries. Hitler's systematic extermination policy lent an added impetus to their efforts, which reached a climax at the very moment when the Arab peoples were beginning to discover their own national destinies. Thus there was a head-on clash between Arab and Jewish nationalism in Palestine and the war which has been raging for over 30 years between Israel and her Arab neighbours is the result of this clash.

The Holy Land has in fact been the breeding ground for more violence than any other region on earth. Wars have been waged there since the dawn of Western civilisation, and because Palestine is the birthplace of Christianity and sacred to Islam bitter hatreds and violent passions have been a feature of them all. But never more so than in the current Arab-Israeli conflict, where both sides regard their rights and claims as self-evident as well as being morally and legally justified. With the passage of time the stance of both Arabs and Israelis has hardened, and their attitudes have become increasingly irrational. Neither side can now distinguish clearly between responsibility and guilt; both sides have done things which the other finds difficult to forgive let alone forget. Arabs and Israelis alike are implacably committed to their claims; both sides are inherently suspicious of the others' intentions and it has not so far been possible to break the impasse with a lasting peace settlement.

All this suggests, perhaps, that there is no solution to the Arab-Israeli problem and that the five wars described in the following pages are merely progressive eruptions in a historical encounter that is nothing less than a protracted war which is doomed to continue until it is resolved in a catastrophic holocaust.

I Background

The earliest organised claim of Jews to Palestine goes back to 1897. In that year the first World Zionist Congress met at the initiative of Theodor Herzl, an Austrian journalist. Herzl had already published a book, *The Jewish State*, in which he urged the settlement of Jewish agriculturists and artisans in Palestine. These pioneers, he hoped, would realise an ancient Jewish dream — the re-establishment of a Jewish homeland in the Promised Land and the gathering together of the Jewish people from their 2,000-year long Diaspora. At that time Palestine was under control of the Ottoman Turks and inhabited by about half a million Arabs and some 50,000 Jews. No Arab voice was raised in protest against the Zionist proposal and the Sultan of Turkey, the sovereign master of Palestine, far from taking umbrage, received Theodor Herzl to discuss the idea before politely rejecting it. Herzl and his colleagues tried to persuade the Turkish government to change the attitude expressed by the Sultan but their efforts proved to be of no avail until World War I broke out.

Meantime, responding to Herzl's vision and reacting to anti-semitic programmes in Russia and Poland several thousand Jews had emigrated to Palestine and set up Jewish settlements on land purchased from absentee Arab landlords by wealthy philanthropists like Baron de Rothschild or with money collected by the Zionist organisation. By 1914 almost 100,000 acres of Palestinian land had been purchased and 60,000 Jewish emigrants had settled on it.

World War I transformed the Zionists' prospects. When Turkey joined Germany and Austria against Britain, France and Russia, its defeat was expected to bring about the collapse of the Ottoman Empire and end Turkish domination of Palestine. Before this actually happened, however, the Zionists put pressure on the British who were bearing the brunt of the fighting in the Middle East and who in the past had expressed some sympathy for the idea of a Jewish homeland. In 1917, thanks to the efforts of Chaim Weizmann, a fervent Zionist, the British Foreign Secretary, Lord Balfour, issued a proclamation that was to authenticate Herzl's dream with a British pledge:

'His Majesty's Government views with favour the establishment in Palestine of a national home for the Jewish people, and will use their best endeavours to facilitate the achievement of this object, it being clearly understood that nothing shall be done which may prejudice the civil rights of existing non-Jewish communities in Palestine, or the rights and political status enjoyed by Jews in any other country.'

This pledge, known more generally as the 'Balfour Declaration', was eventually approved by Britain's allies and subsequently incorporated in the terms of the League of Nation's Mandate over Palestine granted to Britain in 1922.

Arab nationalists and some historians now regard the Balfour Declaration as the root-cause of the Arab-Israeli conflict, and it is certainly true that without it there could not have been Zionist settlement in Palestine on a large scale. Understandably enough the Palestinian Arabs became increasingly uneasy about the growing influx of Jewish immigrants. During the 1930s when Hitler's persecution of European Jews gathered momentum, Jewish immigration into Palestine soared dramatically. By 1937 their numbers had risen to about 400,000 — almost one third of the total population of Palestine. Meantime the Arab population had become increasingly alarmed; hostility grew and bitterness developed between the Arab and Jewish communities. Acrimony had first given way to violence in 1921; another conflict broke out in 1929 and there was a third protracted period of violence between 1936 and 1939. The British, trapped between the undertaking they had given in the Balfour Declaration on the one hand, and pledges and promises made to the Arabs on the other, tried to temporise. Ultimately the Arabs were placated when the British promised to impose a ceiling on Jewish immigration.

British troops attempted to keep the Arab and Israeli communities from each others' throats, whenever violence erupted. But their efforts were only partially successful and the Jews had concluded that they must develop their own military organisations. The outcome was the formation of the *Haganah* (Defence Movement), the direct fore-runner of today's Israeli Defence Force (IDF).

Left: Israeli settlers of all ages and both sexes were required to play their part in building defensive positions.

Right: Israeli defensive positions, equipment and tactics were conventional and based on British Army practice.

Below: Men of an Israeli Palmach unit manning the defences of a kibbutz, May 1948.

Because the British authorities were reluctant to permit the Jews to build up a private army, the Haganah became a clandestine organisation. However, its numbers grew and in the years between 1936 and 1939 — the period known in British circles as the 'Arab Revolt' — when the Arabs launched an all-out effort to prevent the Jews from moving any further towards creating a Jewish homeland, the Haganah made dramatic progress.

With the manpower and resources of the British garrison in Palestine stretched to the limit by the concerted efforts of the Arab rioters, the British authorities turned a blind eye on the Haganah, which rapidly built up into a 3,000-strong force. Most of the Haganah units were deployed in the agricultural settlements with orders to fight only if attacked. But this policy began to change when the British formed the Jewish Settlement Police — a small force for guard duties, with a few mobile units whose task was to maintain communications between the isolated settlements. (Besides attacking the settlements and creating disturbances in the towns, the Arabs attempted to disrupt road communications throughout the country. Beginning with such simple devices as nails strewn on the roads their efforts escalated to attacks on passing vehicles — British, Jewish, or on occasions even Arab.) Officers of the Jewish Settlement Police were all British but many of the NCOs and other ranks were Haganah officers.

The next Haganah development came when a young British officer, Captain Orde Wingate, was appointed to command a mixed British-Jewish unit known as the Special Night Squad charged with the protection of the Iraq Petroleum Company's oil pipe-line to Haifa — regarded then as a life-line of the British Empire. Wingate, an unconventional and enigmatic character, was to have a lasting impact on the military doctrine and tactics of the embryo Israeli army. Initiative, discipline, surprise, mobility and ideological motivation were the important aspects of warfare which Wingate imparted to the Night Squad. Wingate did not believe in waiting for the Arabs to attack, his tactics were aggressive and his influence can be traced in all the Israelis' subsequent campaigns. At this point mention must also be made of Wingate's Jewish counterpart, Yitzhak Sadeh, a Russian Jew who had served as an officer in the Soviet Army before he emigrated to Palestine. In 1948 Sadeh was appointed Chief of Staff to the Israeli Army that had been spawned by the Haganah.

British-Jewish military cooperation came to an abrupt halt in May 1939 when the British Government issued a

Below: Most of the Israeli army's transport consisted of requisitioned kibbutz and commercial vehicles.

policy statement which came to be known simply as the 'White Paper'. Its issue followed a conference in London to which representatives of the then independent Arab states as well as the Palestinian Arabs and representatives of World Jewry were invited to discuss a settlement of the 'Palestine problem'. By that time it was apparent that Britain was almost certainly going to become embroiled in a war with Germany and some kind of decision on Palestine was imperative. A Royal Commission had recommended partitioning the country into an Arab State, a Jewish state and a British enclave, and the Zionist leaders had accepted the proposal — albeit reluctantly. The Arabs, on the other hand, had vehemently rejected the idea, and insisted that the Arabs' right to the whole of Palestine should be recognised. So a conference was called. With the Arabs refusing even to sit together with the Jews the dicussions got nowhere, and the British government tried to compromise. Assuming that the Jews would resist Nazism to their utmost and believing that Arab good will was essential to the British and French effort, Chamberlain's government published its White Paper of May 1939, announcing a change in policy which virtually over-turned the Balfour Declaration. The Jewish settlements in Palestine would be frozen at their existing level and an independent Palestinian state would be created in which an Arab majority could dominate the constitution.

It was now the turn of the Jews to pass to defiance and resistance. Illegal immigration and settlement was stepped up and sabotage teams were organised and trained for the day when more offensive action would be possible. However when World War II broke out the Jews felt that disruption of one of Britain's main bases could not be justified until Germany was defeated. Thus in the early years of the war resistance was limited to evasions and violations of the terms of the White Paper restricting land purchase and immigration. But military preparations continued and the idea of resistance to the White Paper was fostered.

During the war years many Jews acquired military experience while serving in the British forces. (For example three of the early commanders of the Israeli Air Force, Aharon Remez, Dan Tolkovski and Ezer Weizman, flew with the RAF, and two others, Chaim Lazkov and Shlomo Shamir, served in the British Army.) Some wholly Jewish units were also raised and trained by the British; these were known as *Palmach* (so-called because the word is formed from the initials of the Hebrew words for 'striking companies') and when war ended four Palmach battalions were in being. To preserve their existence these battalions promptly went underground when the fighting ceased in Europe, the battalions being split up into platoon units most of which were stationed in the agricultural settlements *(kibbutzim)*.

After the war, when the British Government tried to enforce the policy outlined in the May 1939 White Paper the Jews set about showing the rest of the world that they were not prepared to tolerate such treatment. Because of the terrain classical warfare was hardly possible — there were no forests in which to hide, while the more remote and hilly districts were populated by the Arabs. In the open countryside guerilla operations were possible only at night and in consequence most of the Haganah raids on British installations were staged at night. Nearly all the acts of urban terrorism which took place in this period were the work of two independent organisations, the dissident Stern Group and the Irgun Zvai Leumi (IZL) led by Israel's current prime minister, Menahem Begin. (Both of these organisations operated independently and outside the strategy laid down by the official leaders of the Jews in Palestine, but the Haganah maintained a liaison link with them until July 1946.) Meanwhile, in defiance of the British administrations' orders the Haganah was busy shipping Jewish refugees from Europe and the setting up of new settlements.

Haganah attacks were confined to targets which were clearly vulnerable but which generally entailed little military risk, such as the railway and isolated bridges and police posts. But the IZL was more ambitious and the Jewish anti-White Paper campaign came to its climax on 22 July 1946, when an IZL Assault Group blew up Jerusalem's King David Hotel, the British military headquarters.

For the British, Palestine had become an intractable problem by the end of 1946; they had tried to suppress resistance and play for time in the hopes of finding a solution to the Palestine question in the context of a broader settlement of their Middle East problems. But the US was pressing for the immediate admission of 100,000 Jews from Europe while the Arabs were demanding a total ban on immigration. Tension inside the country was increasing and the burden of keeping an army of 100,000 men in Palestine — in the face of equally pressing commitments elsewhere in Europe — was becoming intolerable. So the British decided to turn the whole Palestine question over to the United Nations.

Early in 1947 a specially constituted UN commission (UNSCOP) — whose members supposedly had little or no interest in Palestine — visited the Middle East and examined the alternatives. Eventually the majority of the commission recommended the partition of Palestine into two states — one Arab and one Jewish — with Jerusalem held as trustee of the UN (The minority of the commission advocated a federal state with autonomous Arab and Jewish provinces). The Jewish state would have 55% of the land and a 58% Jewish population; the Arab state 45% of the land and a 99% Arab population. This partition plan was eagerly welcomed by the Jews and denounced with equal fervour by the Arabs.

Right to the very last moment the representatives of the Arab countries and the Palestine Arab leadership opposed both plans. When they decided to opt for a federal state it was too late. When the General Assembly put the issue to a vote on 29 November 1947, the majority of its members voted for the partition plan. Those who supported the Jewish cause — especially the Zionists who had packed the spectators' gallery — were ecstatic. But the Arab delegates walked out of the General Assembly, declaring that their governments would not be bound by the UN decision.

The die was now cast: both Jews and Arabs realised that the issue would now be put to the test of strength through force of arms.

2 The War of 1948

In 1947 the leader of the Jewish settlers in Palestine was David Ben Gurion, who had emigrated from Poland in 1906. No single leader represented the Arabs, but the most influential men were Haj Amin el-Husseini, the Grand Mufti of Jerusalem, Azzam Pasha, the secretary-general of the Arab League, King Abdullah of Transjordan, and Glubb Pasha, the commander of Transjordan's British-trained Arab Legion. The Grand Mufti — who had been in Germany during World War II, helping the Nazis plan a 'final solution' of the Jewish 'problem' — was an ambitious man. For this reason he was distrusted by the other Arab leaders.

Both Ben Gurion and the Grand Mufti appreciated that the UN vote in New York was no guarantee that a Jewish state would ever come into being. Between the debate on 29 November and the expiration of the British mandate — scheduled for May the following year — was a time-span that might well be decisive. So the two leaders immediately began to prepare for the forthcoming conflict. In Jerusalem and elsewhere in Palestine there were violent clashes between rival Arab and Jewish demonstrators the day after the UN vote. The Jews were afraid that Arab resistance might deprive them of the fruits of the partition vote; the Arabs were furious about a decision which in their view deprived them of their patrimony. On both sides it seemed there was no time to lose.

Procuring arms with which to strengthen their forces was now the prime concern of Arab and Jewish leaders alike. And here the Jews were at a disadvantage. The right to buy arms openly on the international arms market was the prerogative of sovereign states. Lebanon and Syria — countries which had been granted independence in 1943 and 1946 respectively — were both able to purchase arms for the Arabs, while the Jews had to resort to clandestine means of buying.* Furthermore the Jews were prohibited from importing or even possessing weapons while the British were still administering the territory. To overcome these problems the Haganah bought up wartime surplus stocks of American arms and equipment destined for the scrapyard. The equipment was then broken down into component parts, and shipped to Palestine in random bits and pieces with other miscellaneous machinery — under official import licences describing the shipments as textile or agricultural machinery.

Meantime the British had started the count-down to the end of the Mandate by pulling their troops out of the more remote areas of the country, prior to falling back on Haifa, where the last British troops would embark. The British authorities proclaimed that during the interim period, they proposed to act with strict neutrality. The troops would react only if they were attacked or if anyone tried to interfere with their preparations for departure. In the opinion of the Jews however, the British discreetly gave the Arabs considerable assistance, and to substantiate their case they recall that the British naval blockade — aimed not only at stopping Jewish immigrants entering Palestine but also to prevent those who were there getting any arms — continued to the very end of the Mandate. Yet nothing was done to halt Transjordan's Arab Legion — organised, commanded and trained by the British — when it embarked on offensive operations before the Mandate ended. Yet, however it may have seemed to both sides, the British troops — who in fact did on occasions intervene to prevent wholesale massacres — tried to maintain a neutral attitude. But after two years' of terrorism and relentless vilification it is small wonder that the attitude of most British soldiers was pro-Arab and no doubt this influenced their behaviour on occasions and they turned a blind eye on Arab activities.

In the middle of April, with the days of the British Mandate numbered, the first phase of what the Israelis now call the War of Liberation opened. Up to then and with the limited resources available Jewish policy had been to fortify every settlement. Most of the settlements were in the coastal plains, Galilee and the northern Negev — isolated enclaves in Arab territory. In theory the roads were under British control but individual vehicles travelling to the settlements were often ambushed by the Arabs. To resolve this problem the Haganah organised convoys and, having no armoured vehicles of any kind, commercial vehicles were pressed into service. Two layers of steel plates were fixed to the chassis of such vehicles and concrete poured

**As an example: Syria's Minister of Defence ordered 10,000 rifles direct from the Czech armaments firm Waffenwerke Brunn AG, in Brno. Israel was eventually allowed to buy some old fighter aircraft from the Czechs but only because the political scene changed, and the Israelis who were sent to ferry the aircraft back to the Middle East were segregated from the Czech Air Force personnel at the Czech base when the planes were handed over.*

Right: Palestinian refugees in Galilee, October 1948.

Below: Jeep driver, October 1948.

Below right: Wireless operator, November 1948.

between them. This crude makeshift armour resulted in the vehicles being dubbed 'sandwich' cars.

The ban on Jews possessing weapons was still being enforced during this 'unofficial' phase of the war and the Jewish convoys were halted by the British and searched for arms. To overcome this, Palmach girls rode in the convoys with grenades and dismantled Sten guns hidden under their skirts. British gallantry was such that the women were rarely searched.

As the British withdrawal progressed the tempo of the fighting increased, and in the last week of April the Jews undertook three key operations. The aim of the first, Operation Nahshon, was to re-open the road to Jerusalem which had been under siege for some weeks and whose Jewish population was short of both food and water. Unfortunately, in the first stages of the fight for the road IZL men raged through a village called Deir Yassin, killing women and children as well as Arab combatants. This further embittered the Arabs who took their revenge a few days later when they trapped a convoy on its way up to the Jewish university on Mount Scopus outside Jerusalem. The Jews now launched an all-out attack to open the Tel Aviv — Jerusalem road. A force of 1,500 men, the largest ever assembled by the Haganah, advanced up the road. Heavy fighting took place for possession of a hill called Castel which dominated the twisting road, and the Arab commander of the Jerusalem area, Abdul el Husseini — a cousin of the Mufti — was killed in the action.

The second Haganah operation was intended to open the road linking Haifa and the all important agricultural region known as the Valley of Jezreel. The main battle was fought on the site of the legendary Armageddon, near the excavated fortifications of King Solomon. Partly because of its historic connections the region had been used by the Haganah as a training ground and the Jews who staged the action knew the ground well. The result was a resounding victory for the Haganah who captured a welcome number of guns and mortars together with a quantity of small arms and ammunition.

The Jews now turned their attention to the 'mixed' city of Haifa — populated by 70,000 Arabs and an equal number of Jews — where there had been a good deal of sniping. General Sir Hugh Stockwell, the British commander, announced on 21 April that he would hold only the port area for the evacuation of the remaining British troops, and this announcement signalled the start of a fight for possession of the urban area. It also marked the start of the Palestinian refugee problem — a problem that continues to haunt the Middle East. Following radio broadcasts by the Mufti, instructing all Arabs to get out of the way until his armies pushed the Jews into the sea, entire Arab families in Haifa rushed to the coast to board fishing smacks, rowing boats and indeed anything that floated. They fled across the bay to Acre, and up into Lebanon and Syria.

Above: Palestinian villagers being marched off, following the capture of Ramle on the Tel Aviv-Jerusalem road.

Left: Many of the important villages were dominated by fortress-style police stations — a legacy of the British administration. This one at Safed near Haifa was captured by the Haganah after bitter fighting.

The subsequent battle for Haifa was short and sharp. The Jews had the advantage of being above the old town in the new suburb they had created on the heights. Flaming tar barrels were rolled down the hillside on buildings which the Arabs were holding, and although the Arabs fought bravely they were quickly overwhelmed.

Operation Hametz, the third important offensive undertaken by the Jews was to secure and clear the Jaffa — Tel Aviv area. From the minaret of a Jaffa mosque snipers had been picking off people in the streets below and skirmishes in the slum area between the two cities had became a regular feature of life. IZL gunmen had already gone on to the offensive when the Haganah launched Operation Hametz. Five days of bitter fighting followed and then British troops moved in, and a truce was arranged. As at Haifa a large number of the Arab population of Jaffa fled and the Jews took over. Thus on 13 May, the eve of the British departure, the Jews were occupying or controlling northern Galilee, Haifa, the Arab city of Jaffa and parts of 'New' Jerusalem. They had also managed to import about 10,000 rifles and 4,500 light machine guns together with large quantities of ammuniton, and these weapons had been distributed to Haganah units. Meantime Jewish workshops and garages were turning out a Jewish version of the Sten gun, and homemade 'Davidka' mortars — so-called after the name of the designer.* A good deal of reorganisation had also taken place. The Palmach's four battalions had been expanded to 10 battalions grouped into three brigades, some Haganah units had been brigaded, and men too old or boys too young to serve in the Palmach or Haganah had been enrolled into a Home Guard. The question now was whether all the feverish preparations they had undertaken would be enough to enable the Jews to withstand the full scale war that was clearly about to erupt.

Before it did so Ben Gurion sent Golda Meir on a peace mission. Disguised as an Arab woman Mrs Meir travelled to Amman for a secret meeting with King Abdullah of Transjordan to discuss how it might be possible to prevent a collision. The king proposed that the Jews should give up the idea of a separate Jewish state, and suggested Palestine should be administered by a parliament composed equally of Arab and Jewish members. Unless the Jews were prepared to accept these conditions, the king said, war was inevitable. Mrs Meir replied to the effect that there could be no question of giving up the idea of a Jewish state, and added that if it did come to war then the Jews would fight as long as their strength lasted. Thus this final attempt to stave off the catastrophe ended in failure.

Two days after Mrs Meir's return to Tel Aviv, at 4pm on 14 May 1948, and two hours before the termination of the British Mandate, Ben Gurion read Israel's Declaration of Independence to a Jewish audience gathered in Tel Aviv's museum of art. That night Eygptian aircraft bombed Tel Aviv; the second phase of the war of 1948 had started. In world terms it was a 'small' war and because it was fought in spasms cannot be regarded as a conventional war. Officially it lasted about eight months, from 15 May — when Israel was simultaneously invaded by armies from Egypt, Transjordan, Syria and Lebanon — until January 1949 when Egypt sued for an armistice. Actual fighting took place in four phases during only about one quarter of those eight months, however, and the course of the war is best described by reference to each of these phases separately.

Phase 1 started with the Arab invasion. The plan was that the Egyptians would sweep up the coast. Short of the

Below: Major phases of the War of Liberation, 1948-1949.

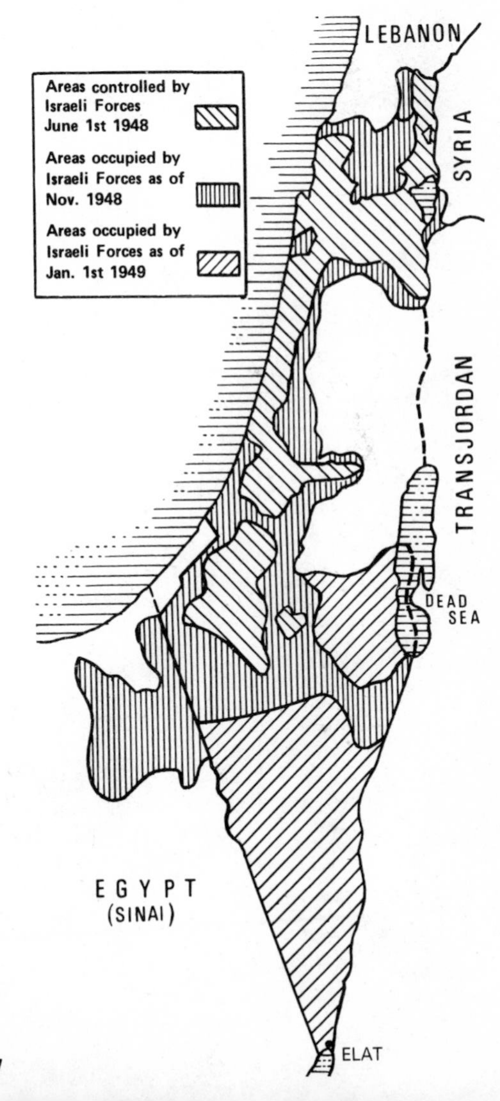

**This weapon fired an outsize bomb; it was not very accurate but the bombs detonated with a great roar which had a tremendous psychological effect on the Arabs. First used in Jerusalem, some of the Arabs there thought it to be an atomic bomb.*

Left: These pictures, showing Israeli troops in action, give some idea of the terrain in Galilee.

Right and below: The Israelis had very little heavy equipment in the early days of the 1948 war. This 75mm howitzer was probably of Czech origin.

Jaffa-Tel Aviv region their invasion army would split into two, with one force going on to seize and occupy Tel Aviv while the other headed east to link up with King Abdullah's Arab Legion coming from Jordan. The juncture was to be in Jerusalem. Meanwhile Iraqi troops advancing from Jordan would link up with what was left of the Palestinian force after its defeat by the Haganah in the Haifa region, and then cut across the narrow waist of Palestine to the coast, slicing Israel in two. In the north the Syrian and Lebanese objetive was Haifa and Galilee. According to their timetable the Arabs reckoned that the Jews would be wiped out within two weeks. Arab commanders had earmarked the houses they would take over in Tel Aviv, and the troops had been promised the usual spoils of war — women and loot.

The total of the invading Arab armies was approximately 23,500 men; they had an overwhelming superiority in firepower, were much better organised, supplied and equipped than the Israelis, and they had the strategic initiative. Moreover the Israelis, poorly equipped in comparison with their enemy, were overawed by the tanks, artillery and aircraft deployed against them.* Six months of fighting the 'unofficial' civil war had also exhausted the Palmach units. Nevertheless the Arabs were not able to implement their plan; Tel Aviv and Haifa were not occupied and none of the Arab troops enjoyed the spoils of war they had been promised.

The Egyptians crossed the Sinai Desert and did not run into any real difficulty while they advanced through territory populated by Arabs. However when they came up

**The Israelis put about 17,000 men into the field (of these about 14,000 had had very little training). They had 10,000 rifles, 3,600 sub-machine guns, a few bazookas and four ancient cannons smuggled in from Mexico; they had two tanks — snatched from a British Ordnance Depot at Haifa in April 1945. (They were acquired by the Haganah in a daring raid in which British soldiers — two of whom deserted to the Israelis — collaborated.) Neither of these tanks was deployed in the operations.*

Right: Palmach briefing before an advance.

Below: Loading a convoy for Jerusalem.

Bottom: A convoy on the Jerusalem-Tel Aviv road, October 1948.

against the first Israeli defence line at one of the isolated kibbutzim the invaders from the south were halted and a ferocious battle ensued. Following a heavy artillery bombardment the Egyptians attacked with tanks, armoured cars and a brigade of infantry, but after five hours the defenders were still holding firm. Two Egyptian tanks had been knocked out, with the only bazooka in the settlement, another had been set ablaze by a Molotov cocktail, and two other tanks had lost their tracks when they attempted to charge across the minefield enclosing the settlement. The Egyptians eventually managed to push on until they were finally stopped at Ashdod 35km from Tel Aviv. But this particular action could be said to illustrate the pattern of the battles elsewhere. The Israelis fought bravely and generally managed to deal with critical situations with little more than dash and tactical initiative while the Arab commanders — with the sole exception of those with the Arab Legion — generally displayed timidity and lack of imagination. There can be no doubt that the Arab armies could have swept through Palestine at this stage and achieved all they had set out to do if they had shown a little more verve, coordinated their battle plans and pursued them with determination. But it was not to be.

With the Egyptian drive on Tel Aviv held up, their second column's drive on Jerusalem was halted as well. This was the force which was to have linked up with the Arab Legion in Jerusalem. In fact the Legion's own time-table had been upset by fierce fighting in the Old City, which the Jews had attempted to seize as soon as the Mandate terminated. In the north where they failed to break through the ring of the Israeli settlements on the road to Haifa the Syrian and Lebanese time-table was also upset. At Degania, near the southern end of the Sea of Galilee, an Iraqi armoured column was halted by settlers hurling Molotov cocktails. That night the Israelis staged a deception operation. Trucks and tractors with headlights blazing were repeatedly driven down the road towards the kibbutz and then driven back without headlights. Believing that vast Israeli reinforcements had arrived the Iraqis pulled out at first light and did not attempt to resume their advance.

The fiercest fighting took place in Jerusalem where the Jewish quarter of the Old City was completely gutted and its inhabitants compelled to surrender to the Arab Legion. In the 'New City' of West Jerusalem King Abdullah's Legionnaires were less successful. Even so the Israelis there were brought near to capitulation because their water supplies had been cut off and very little food was reaching them from the coastal plain. Relief came when a month long truce was arranged by the United Nations. When it started on 11 June Israel held nearly the entire area marked as Jewish on the UN partition map and although the invading armies had occupied most of the portions of Palestine allocated to the Arabs and the Arab Legion had a stranglehold on Jerusalem, they had failed to attain their objectives. They had not destroyed the Israeli forces and their efforts to strike at the heartland of the Jewish state in the coastal plain, Jezreel and the upper Jordan valley had all been frustrated.

During the truce neither side was supposed to bring in arms and United Nations mediators were sent in to monitor the activities of the belligerents. In fact both Arabs and Jews used the four weeks lull to reorganise and reinforce their troops, replenish their supplies and deploy better equipment. In this the Israelis did better than the Arabs. For one thing they were much more adept at smuggling in men and equipment under the noses of the UN monitoring teams than were the Arabs. For another, they had assembled men and equipment abroad* while the Arab reserves were low. (Poor administration was primarily responsible for the Arab armies running short of ammunition — a situation exacerbated when Britain acceded to a UN request to discontinue the supplies she had made under her treaties with Egypt, Iraq and Jordan.) The effect of these factors showed when the fighting was resumed.

The second phase of the official war started at midnight on 11 July and lasted for ten days. It was characterised by an Israeli pre-emptive strike against the Arab Legion — a form of action that would be repeated in the Sinai campaign in 1956 and in the Six Day War 11 years later. During these days the embryo Israeli Air Force made its debut. Aircraft flown to Israel from Czechoslovakia and manned by Jewish volunteer pilots from the US, Britain, South Africa and France — flew in support of the Israeli ground troops, and with transport planes even attempted some retaliatory bombing missions on Cairo and Damascus. (Tales are still told of how bombs were simply rolled out of the open hatches of the Dakotas.)

The Egyptians in the south and the Syrians and Lebanese in the north were held at bay, while the Israelis concentrated on lifting the siege of Jerusalem. The operation was relatively successful, and although the Arab Legion escaped destruction it came under very heavy pressure from which it was delivered only by a second cease-fire imposed by the UN. In the south the Egyptian Army, the most powerful of the invading forces, was still intact.

The second cease-fire had no time limit; it was supposed to lead to a permanent truce during which the conflict could be settled by diplomatic means with the help of a United Nations Mediator, Count Folke Bernadotte. (In the event fighting broke out again on 10 October.) Once again the Israelis made good use of the breathing space afforded by the truce; more immigrants and heavy equipment were brought in, and the Israeli Army, now some 60,000 strong, was reorganised yet again. From this time on King Abdullah's troops and their Iraqi allies operating alongside on the Jordan-Jerusalem front were preoccupied with consolidating their positions and incapable of initiating any large scale offensive operations.

When the cease-fire came into operation on 19 July, besides relieving besieged Jerusalem the Israelis had made other minor territorial gains. They had captured Lydda, Ramle, Nazareth and had cleared Lower Galilee Elsewhere the Syrians retained the small bridgehead they

**Apart from the huge manpower pool in Displaced Persons camps in Europe, Jewish volunteers — mostly ex-servicemen from the USA and South Africa — flocked to Israel. Much of the equipment came from Czechoslovakia, paid for with dollars raised by Jewish organisations in the USA.*

Left: **Action in the hills above Jerusalem. The rocky terrain increased the lethality of mortar bombs.**

Above: 'O' Group. Lt-Col Moshe Dayan before the spectacular capture of Lydda by his 'jeep cavalry'.

Right: The first Israeli resupply convoy for the Negev settlements cut off by the Egyptian Army.

had gained in eastern Galilee, and the Lebanese and a force of Palestinian guerillas were occupying a sizeable stretch of terrain in central Galilee.

Hostilities began again on 10 October. This was the final phase of the war, and it was preceded by an ugly incident. On 17 September Count Bernadotte, the UN mediator, was killed when terrorists stopped his car in Jerusalem and fired a burst of shots into it. The terrorist Stern Group had been disbanded but ex-Sternists claimed responsibility for the murder. They had executed Bernadotte, the assassins said, because the UN mediator intended to recommend to the United Nations that the Holy City should be turned over to the Arabs.

But it was not the situation in Jerusalem that led to the break down of the second truce. When the cease-fire was arranged the Israelis had been given the right to send food at certain times on certain roads to settlements cut off in the Negev behind the Egyptian lines. Whether the Israelis adhered to the conditions applying to these re-supply

The Battle for Beersheba

Above: This scene is clearly a re-enactment; notice the Piper cub.

Left: After the battle, Egyptian prisoners.

Right: Israeli troops cleaning up.

operations, or whether they deliberately broke the truce agreement is arguable. In the event the Egyptians responded to what they considered provocation by shooting up Israeli convoys. The Israelis replied with a brief lightning campaign that had obviously been carefully planned. Their aim was to secure control of the Negev and they succeeded. There was some heavy fighting, but the Israelis enjoyed the elements of surprise and initiative. Within a week the Egyptian front had been shattered, most of the Negev had been occupied, one third of the Egyptian army — including the 4th Egyptian Brigade in which a certain Major Gamal Abdul Nasser was serving — was trapped and the biblical town of Beersheba had fallen to the Israelis. (Nasser's encircled battalion held out for a few days but the future Egyptian leader had to surrender in the end.)

One week after the Negev offensive the Israelis struck at the Arab guerilla forces in northern Galilee. In a campaign which lasted only 50 hours they chased the Arab Liberation Army commanded by the Syrian ex-Major Fawzi-al-Kaoudjki out of Palestine and went on to occupy some Lebanese villages. Whilst this was happening and earlier, when the Egyptians were being mauled, the other Arab armies made no move to come to the assistance of their allies. Neither Jordan or Iraq had much stomach for further fighting, the Syrians were in no position to do much anyway and the Lebanese were on the run. The Arab coalition had disintegrated.

During December 1948 the fighting flared up again and lasted about two weeks. On 16 November the UN Security Council had ordered all those involved in the conflict to conclude armistice agreements. When the Egyptians refused the Israelis launched an offensive, Operation Horev, the aim of which was to destroy the Egyptian invasion army by a flanking movement through the Sinai desert up to the coast at El Arish. As in the previous campaigns the Israelis set the scene for their attack by provoking the Egyptians and the Egyptians obliged by responding and giving the Israelis a legitimate excuse for breaking the truce. Again, as in the previous phase also, the other Arab armies sat still whilst the Israelis concentrated their whole weight against the Egyptian front. Israeli mobile columns, moving along uncharted desert tracks broke through the Egyptian lines and circled round to enclose the Egyptian army in a great pocket extending from Gaza to El Arish. With no avenue of retreat now open to them the Egyptians did some of their best fighting in the entire war. Nevertheless they would almost certainly have been wiped out if their government had not agreed to conclude an armistice to end the war.

The fighting stopped on 7 January 1949 and in February the Egyptians signed an armistice agreement with Israel. With the exception of Iraq the other Arab governments followed suit: Lebanon in March 1949, Jordan in April and the Syrians in July. Iraq simply pulled out of Palestine without concluding an armistice. However while the armistice negotiations were still under way the Israelis staged a final operation. On 10 March two Israeli brigades motored down to Negev the secure the Elat coastal area opposite the Jordanian port of Aqaba on the Red Sea gulf of Elat.

Thus at the end of the first Arab-Israeli war the Israelis had gained possession of the whole of Galilee, a section of central Palestine connecting the coastal area with Jerusalem, and the whole of the Negev; Jerusalem was a divided city. The entire area controlled by Israel was marginally larger than had been allotted to the Jews in the UN partition resolution of 1947. So it may seem that the Arab invasion had benefited the Jews. But the conflict had displaced a million Arabs who had fled to Syria, Jordan and the Egyptian-controlled Gaza Strip as refugees. From their midst would rise the *Fedayeen* and the Palestinian freedom fighters — the Palestine Liberation Front, who would maintain that Israel had deprived them of their homes and their homeland. Thus the war of Liberation left a festering sore which was to have far reaching consequences in the whole of the Middle East.

Below: Egyptian Bren carrier captured at Beersheba (displayed in Tel Aviv).

3 The Second Arab-Israeli War and the Suez Crisis of 1956

Despite the armistice agreements in 1949 it was quite obvious that the War of Independence had not been the end of the Palestine conflict. On the Arab side the plight of almost a million refugees constituted a constant reminder of the alien Zionist presence. No matter how conciliatory Israel's policy would be, the very presence of these refugees made the Jewish state a standing provocation in the eyes of the entire Arab world. For their part the Israelis were afraid of allowing the refugees to return to their former homes. There were only 700,000 Israelis and an influx of one million Arabs would threaten the security of the new state. So most of the wretched refugees lingered in camps in Jordan, Lebanon, Syria and the Egyptian-controlled Gaza Strip; and the Arab governments openly declared that they would not rest until Israel had been wiped out. At the same time large numbers of Jews were driven out of Iraq, Yemen, Egypt and Morocco.

During the early 1950s clashes between Arab and Israelis on Israel's borders increased and Egypt began to develop the Gaza Strip as a base for guerilla raids by detachments of *Fedayeen** commandos; as time passed these raids steadily increased in scope and intensity.

In 1952 Gamal Abdel Nasser became president of Egypt and under his direction anti-Israel activities were stepped up. The Suez Canal was barred to Israeli shipping and in 1953 the ban was extended to non-Israeli ships carrying cargoes to Israel. This left the Israelis with only one port with access to the Red Sea — Elat on the Gulf of Aqaba — and in late 1953 Nasser began to restrict Israeli commerce through the Straits of Tiran. Subsequently the blockade was broadened and Israeli aircraft were forbidden to overfly Egyptian territory. Meantime Fedayeen activities against Israel had been steadily increasing in ferocity and frequency and the Israelis in turn had responded with reprisal raids similar in pattern to the British operations on the North-West Frontier of India in the days of the British Raj. The first sizeable raid of this type which was mounted against Gaza in February 1955 resulted in 38 Arabs being killed; as a result Nasser decided that he must have more arms. Following a United States refusal to upset the Arab-Israeli balance of strength he turned to Russia, and on 27 September 1955 announced to the world that he had concluded an arms deal with the Soviet bloc. The implications of open hostilities were obvious and Israel now began to watch the deliveries of Soviet weapons to their self-professed enemies with growing anxiety. After her appeal to the United States for supplies of modern weapons to counter the threat had been rejected for the same reasons as had been given to Egypt, Israel turned to France who agreed to supply aircraft and tanks to correct the military balance.

At this juncture the Arab-Israeli conflict blended into a broader confrontation between Arab nationalism and the Western World. The cause is attributable to two great engineering structures, one in existence and the other projected — the Suez Canal and the Aswan High Dam. Nasser saw the former as a post colonial relic and the latter as a modern pyramid, which, when built, would be seen as a symbol of resurgent Arab nationalism.

The United States had agreed initially to help finance the Aswan Dam but Nasser's arms deal with the Soviet bloc in 1955 and his recognition of Communist China a year later led to a renegation of the agreement, Nasser, furious, then announced the nationalisation of the Suez Canal, in which Britain and France had a considerable financial interest. The stage was now set for another conflagration in the Middle East.

Britain and France decided on a show of force against Nasser and began to prepare for military action. Meantime a new government committed to pro-Egyptian and anti-Western policies had come to power in Jordan — policies which included a more belligerent attitude towards Israel and union with Egypt and Syria. On 24 October a military pact between Egypt, Jordan and Syria was proclaimed; a unified command — an 'Arab Entente Militaire' — with the Egyptian Commander-in-Chief, General Amer, as Supreme Commander was to be established immediately. Jordan had thrown her lot in with Egypt; when they were ready three Arab armies under a combined Egyptian command would march against Israel.

*Fedayeen *means self-sacrifice. The men were recruited mainly from Palestine Arabs, many of whom were pathetically eager for a job which would pay well enough to take them out of their refugee existence, as well as to express the hatred of the Jews; recruitment was undertaken by special units of the Egyptian Army Intelligence Corps. A successful raid was rewarded by a cash bonus as well as military honours; success was often rated by the production of 'trophies' such as an ear or finger. Their bases were located in the Gaza Strip and just across the Jordanian frontier. The Israeli Government claimed that there were more than 3,000 raids in the seven years between 1949 and the end of 1956.*

To Israel this was the final straw. Although no immediate aggression might be contemplated it was only a matter of time before Egypt would strike. If any advantage was to be gained from the Anglo-French rumblings over the Suez Canal, now was the time to undertake the preventive war that members of the Israeli Government Opposition and indeed some of Mr Ben Gurion's Government, had been advocating ever since the announcement of Nasser's arms deal. Anglo-French preparations for an operation of sorts against Egypt were nearing perfection and little military genius was needed to deduce the form which such an operation would take. The Anglo-French plan was to occupy the Canal Zone, splitting Egypt's forces and so cutting communications and isolating her Sinai army. As Nasser had already withdrawn a considerable number of units from Sinai for the defence of the Canal and to supplement the mobile reserve which would operate only on orders from Cairo, Sinai probably now had little more than 30,000 troops to garrison it. The odds would never be better; now was the time to act.

The mobilisation order in the early hours of Friday the 26th was conducted with the maximum secrecy that such an event can allow. Israel's standing army was relatively small and relied on conscription, as now — the 11,000 strong regular cadre normally being supplemented by about 40,000 conscripts, who serve for two and a half years before being relegated to the reserve. Her population then totalled about 1,800,000 however, and in an all-out mobilisation the standing army could be expanded to about 250,000 in about 48 hours (men and women, since women are also conscripted); on this occasion, about 100,000 reservists were called up, so producing a total of about

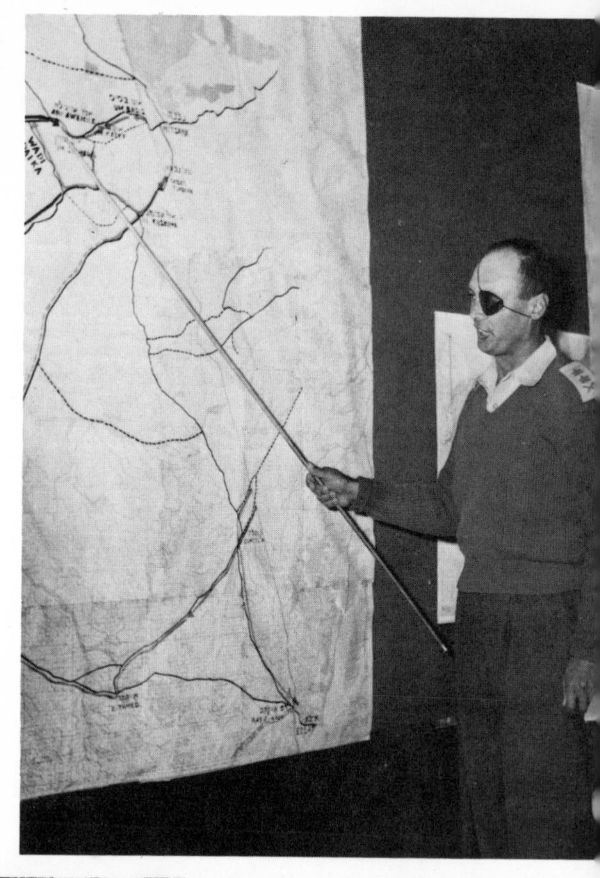

Above: Moshe Dayan, Chief of the Israeli Defence Staff, at a briefing before the operation commenced.

Left: Briefing at a lower echelon prior to an attack.

Top right: North American P-51 Mustangs on an IAF airstrip in Sinai, 1956. */ via Jackson*

Centre right: Gloucester Meteor F8 — the IAF's first jet combat aircraft.
/ Peltz via Jackson

Right: Dassault Mystère IVA.
/ Peltz via Jackson

150,000 men and women under arms. The standing army normally provided a field force of 16 brigade groups, some of which were considered as 'armoured' formations; the role of the reservists was to bring these brigades up to war establishment, strengthen the line of frontier posts and fortified settlements which were Israel's first line of defence, and form additional brigades. The call-up followed lines which had been well rehearsed. There was no general proclamation but key personnel were summoned by telephone and telegram; the remainder being notified by word of mouth. On the Friday morning, key men were rapping on the doors of those for whom they were responsible; cars were stopped at street corners and their owners given cards which directed them to assembly points; the cars were parked, the men quietly collected their kit and reported for duty. In less than 12 hours, 12 brigades were ready for action and on Israel's airfields fighter aircraft were standing ready. Some of these aircraft were old US piston-engined P-51 Mustangs but the majority were Meteors and French Mystères — considerably more of the latter than the single squadron that France was supposed to have delivered. Even so, numerically, Israel's Air Force was greatly inferior to that of Egypt but the Israelis were better trained, and their pilots were of better quality and knew their machines better than the Egyptians.

The operation which was now launched was called 'Kadesh' — a biblical reference of thanksgiving and prayer deriving from the wanderings of the children of Israel in the Sinai desert. It started with a feint towards Jordan. On the Friday night Colonel Ariel Sharon's airborne brigade, less one battalion, ostentatiously trundled north, away from the Sinai border towards Ein Quesib in the north-east corner of

the Negev; at the same time a curfew was imposed on the frontier region bordering Jordan.* Like the rest of the operation, the feint worked well and right until four days later when the operation began in earnest the Egyptian High Command appears to have assumed that the threat was directed towards Jordan. In any case Sinai could be assumed to offer little prospect of a successful campaign. Not only were the Egyptians confident that their defences were strong enough to withstand any attack, the country itself was thought to present the biggest obstacle to any sustained offensive. Known as the 'landbridge' between Africa and Asia, Sinai is 24,000 square miles of rugged nothingness. Flanked on the north by the Mediterranean, in the south by the Red Sea, the Canal and Gulf of Suez in the west, and the Gulf of Aqaba to the east, it is mostly barren desert which is virtually economically valueless and almost uninhabited. In the north the wandering Bedouin who are compelled to live there follow the strict code of desert hospitality, which allows the throats of any strangers not under their direct protection to be cut without compunction. Southern Sinai where the rolling seas of sand give way to a

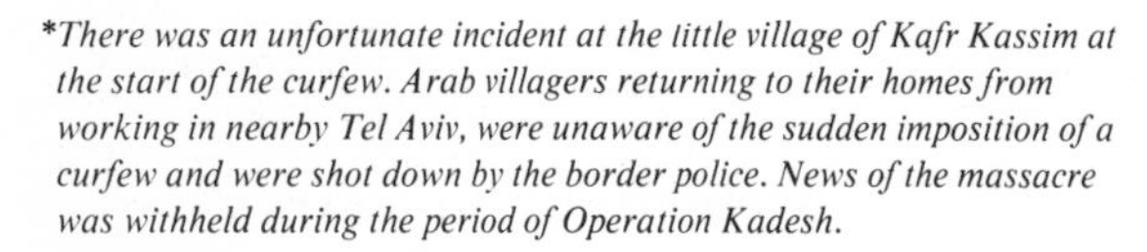
There was an unfortunate incident at the little village of Kafr Kassim at the start of the curfew. Arab villagers returning to their homes from working in nearby Tel Aviv, were unaware of the sudden imposition of a curfew and were shot down by the border police. News of the massacre was withheld during the period of Operation Kadesh.

Above left: Israeli commando.

Left: Jeep mounted recce group — the eyes of the Israeli Army.

Above: Into battle; H-hour D-Day.

more mountainous form of desert is rich in the relics of ancient civilisations but the country is no less forbidding. Communications were poor; there were only two main roads and a railway line running east to west, although over most parts it was feasible for vehicles to move across country and for light aircraft to land on flat stretches of sand. The northern route from Egypt into Sinai was a vehicle track which ran alongside the railway from Kantara on the canal, to El Arish, connecting there with a metalled road which continues on to Gaza. In the centre the main road between Ismailia and Abu Ageila was the best route; its first-class classification being attributable to its being a relic of British administration. Finally, there is a southern route from Suez to Aqaba. This, which is often referred to as the 'Pilgrims' Way', passes through a number of narrow rocky defiles, of which the Mitla Pass is the most important; the state of going on this route was not so good.

Since the war of Independence the Eyptians had maintained and developed the roads from Egypt into Sinai in order to make the area of eastern Sinai ready to serve as their openly declared 'invasion springboard'. And, as has already been mentioned, there were about 30,000 Egyptian troops in Sinai at the end of October 1956. Force headquarters were in Ismailia; the 8th Infantry Division occupied the Gaza Strip and the 3rd Infantry Division, of three infantry brigades and one armoured battalion, was deployed between defences in the Rafa, El Arish, Jebel Libni, Abu Ageila and Kuseima areas. Two battalions of the Desert Frontier Force guarded the southern route and two infantry battalions with various ancillary units known as the Red Sea Force, were stationed near Sharm-El-Sheikh, whose coast defences controlled entry to the Gulf of Aqaba. A single battalion only was responsible for the road from Kuntilla to Mitla and this was split between El Thamed and El Nakhl with but one company at the vital pass. In the Canal Zone immediate Egyptian reserves comprised the 2nd Infantry Division and an armoured brigade; behind them lay the 1st Infantry Division and the 4th Armoured Division near Cairo. Of the troops actually deployed in Sinai the 3rd Infantry Division was probably the best formation. Its rank and file were conscripts but its officers were regulars and it was organised on British lines. Compared with the 3rd Division, the 8th, which had a National Guard brigade in and around Gaza itself, a Palestinian brigade at Khan Yunis and a reserve brigade in the southern part of the Gaza Strip, subsequently showed that it had much less fire in its belly, despite that fact that its volunteer National Guardsmen were said to have a fanatical fervour and its locally recruited Palestinians might have been expected to exhibit a particularly bitter hatred of the Israelis.

On Sunday, 28 October, Israel's mobilisation could no longer be considered secret and the whole country was anxiously waiting for something to happen. In fact, a striking force had formed up in the Negev by this time; vehicles of one of the armoured brigades at Elat on the extreme southern tip of the Israeli border being plainly visible to men of the 10th Hussars in the British base at Aqaba just across the Jordan border. Next day was D-day

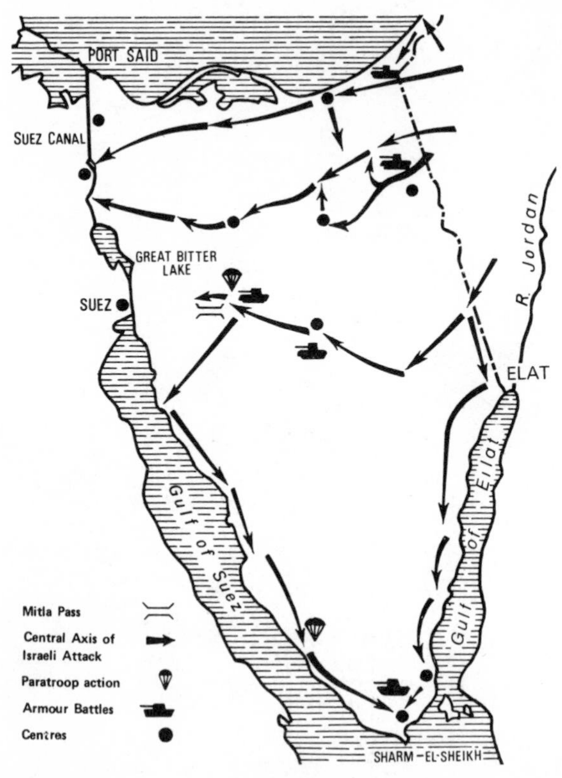

and at about 1600hrs, with an hour and a half to go before darkness fell, the advance guard of Sharon's brigade crossed the frontier into Sinai at Suweilma; an hour later his parachute battalion was dropped about 15 miles east of the Mitla Pass. The first phase of Operation Kadesh and of the 1956 'Suez' War had begun.

Operation Kadesh had been planned to permit the Israeli Government to pause after the opening phase — to enable them to review its scope, and, if necessary, to adjust it. The hope was that some tangible success, which would boost the morale of the Israeli nation and cause the Arabs to reconsider their aims, would result; one suitable prize in this category would be the capture of the Gaza Strip since this would liquidate the main fedayeen base; another would be the capture of Sharm-El-Sheikh as this would enable the Gulf of Aqaba to be opened to Israel's shipping. For real success and an absolute victory the defeat and routing of the Egyptian Army in Sinai was necessary. If, during the operation, the Egyptian Army proved more formidable than had been anticipated, however, or the Great Powers intervened, it might be preferable to call it off and its first

Left: Main lines of attack during the Sinai Campaign, 29 October-5 November 1956.

Below: Sinai dust — caked on the faces of this jeep patrol.

Below right: Replenishing ammo for Israeli Shermans.

phase could then be held to have constituted a reprisal raid. With this background a plan was devised in which a four-phase operation using three main axes of advance was envisaged. In the first phase a parachute battalion would be dropped in the Mitla area; this would be quickly reinforced by an armoured brigade advancing up the Kuntilla road. At the same time another force would cross the frontier and capture the road junction at Kuseima;* from Kuseima this force then had a choice of two roads by which, if the worst came to the worst, it could go to the assistance of the parachutists at Mitla. The second phase was the pause; before 24 hours had elapsed a decision would be taken as to whether to continue with the two remaining phases or withdraw. Then, if the operation was to become a full-scale campaign, the next phase would be a thrust southward from Elat down the Gulf of Aqaba to capture Sharm-El-Sheikh, whilst the forces from Mitla, advancing along the Gulf of Suez road would converge on the same area. At the same time the force which had taken Kuseima would attack the Abu Ageila complex of defences where another fresh task force would link up with them after it had captured Rafa.

Finally, in the fourth phase, when Abu Ageila and Rafa had been secured, the key Egyptian defence point at El Arish would be captured. This would seal off the Gaza Strip and make it possible to exploit the Kantara road, to the Canal.

**In the event this column moved up the desert road from Kuntilla and attacked Kuseima from the south.*

Returning to the first phase: Sharon's column reached their first objective at Kuntilla about an hour after crossing the border and the garrison of a single infantry platoon was overrun after only about 20 minutes' fighting. Continuing the advance, the column then swept on to Thamed. Here the Egyptians had two companies of infantry in defences on the fortified cliffs overlooking the village, together with a platoon in the village itself. They did not hold out for long; and at a cost of three Israeli dead and six wounded, Thamed was captured shortly after dawn on the 30th. The column now halted to await a re-supply by air of petrol and ammunition and whilst they waited the wounded were evacuated in a Piper Cub which landed close by the village. During this interval, six Egyptian MiGs flew in to strafe and bomb Sharon's men and caused a number of casualties; a similar attack took place about three hours later when four Egyptian Vampires flew in at ground-level and again inflicted casualties on the resting column. By now a message from the parachute battalion 15 miles east of Mitla in the area of Parker's Memorial* to the effect that they were being shelled and also had suffered casualties from air strikes, made it essential that Sharon should press on and he decided to move without any further delay; his decision was reinforced by a Piper Cub reconnaissance which reported an Egyptian column seen to be advancing towards Mitla from Suez. By 1630hrs the advance guard of his force was within small-arms range of the El Nakhl defences. Here, the rest of the Egyptian battalion which had

**A stone monument to a former British administrator.*

Top right: Wrecked Egyptian vehicles on one of the roads south into Sinai.

Centre right: MiG fighter also abandoned by the Egyptians.

Below: Archer SP gun abandoned by the Egyptians.

Far right: The Egyptian destroyer *Ibrahim-el-Awal* **being towed into Haifa after being boarded.**

defended Kuntilla and Thamed were expected to put up a spirited resistance. Surprisingly, after only a brief artillery bombardment from a battery of Israeli 25-pounders, the Egyptians evacuated their positions however, leaving Nakhl with all of its wealth of stores, ammunition and food, to Sharon. By nightfall he had linked up with the parachutists and the following day after a stiff battle, Mitla Pass, only 12 miles from Suez, was occupied. The first round of the Sinai campaign was over.

Meanwhile, at dawn on the same day (30th) two brigades, one armoured (Colonel Ben-Avi) and one infantry (Colonel Harpaz), had moved in past Kuntilla and drawn blood at the defences of Kuseima. After less than an hour's fighting, Kuseima fell to Harpaz's infantry and Ben-Avi's tanks took the lead in the advance to Abu Ageila, the key position of the Egyptians' Sinai defence system — a complex which consisted of three fortified sand ridges garrisoned by two brigades, one armoured and one infantry. As the vehicles of Ben-Avi's advance guard approached the defences, they fanned out to locate the Egyptian flanks; at this moment they ran into a force of Egyptian armour and a tank battle which lasted for the next 16 hours developed. However, as the Egyptian T-34s shot it out with Ben-Avi's Shermans and AMXs, the Israeli brigade's reconnaissance company which was mounted in jeeps, managed to slip round to a position behind the rearmost fortified ridge. There, on the Ismailia road it effectively blocked all Egyptian rear communications. Then, after dark, a detachment from Harpaz's brigade succeeded in linking up with Sharon at Nakhl so that by dawn on the Wednesday morning — D+2 — the whole of the southern Sinai had, in effect, been cut off.

This was the time for the Israeli pause and their first official announcements were couched in the planned cautionary terms by which the invasion could, if necessary, be interrupted as a retaliatory raid. 'Units of the Israeli defence forces have penetrated and attacked fedayeen commando bases... This operation was necessitated by the continuous Egyptian aggression... the purpose of which was to deprive the people of Israel of the possibility of peaceful existence.' To this, the Egyptians replied with an airy communué implying that all was well: 'We have annihilated the invasion forces'. Nasser was aware of the success of the Israeli opening moves however and it seems somewhat surprisng that Egyptian reactions were not quicker off the mark. Not until the Tuesday morning did the Egyptian Air Force go into action; then only a limited number of planes were used and no attempt was made to bomb Israeli cities. The potential Anglo-French threat can hardly have been the reason for keeping the Egyptian aircraft on the ground since Nasser himself had declared that he did not believe that the British would make any military move. His miscalculation on this score was to come as another shock later that day (30 October) when he received the cable telling him of a joint British-French ultimatum requiring both Egypt and Israel to stop all military operations and withdraw to lines 10 miles from the Canal. When, eventually, the Egyptian Air Force did go into action it was not particularly successful; in dog fights over Sinai the Israelis claim to have shot down four MiGs and three Vampires for the loss of only two Mustangs.

Meanwhile, at sea, Nasser's Navy had attempted to show its worth. The destroyer *Ibrahim el Awal** made a

**The* Ibrahim el Awal, *armed with 4.4inch guns, was the ex-British Hunt class destroyer* Cottesmore *launched in 1940 and transferred to Egypt in July 1941. After this action she was recommissioned into the Israeli Navy as the* Haifa.

single attempt to shell Haifa, although most of her 160 shots fell well short of the target as she opened fire beyond the maximum range of her guns. Chased by an Israeli destroyer of the same vintage as herself and attacked by rocket-firing aircraft the crew attempted to scuttle her after their ship had received several direct hits. Their efforts were abortive as they were unable to find keys to fit many of the seacocks and it was not long before a white flag was run up. An Israeli boarding party quickly went to work on the pumps and by keeping them at full pressure were able to tow the *Ibrahim* into Haifa harbour. There, she was proudly exhibited as war booty.

To return to the land battles. At first light on the morning of the 31st, Colonel Yoffe's 9th Motorised Infantry Brigade crossed into Sinai at Ras el Nagb and set off down the long difficult coastal track which runs along the Gulf of Aqaba towards the southern tip of the peninsula. It took the brigade four days to reach the outer defences of Yoffe's objective — Sharm-El-Sheikh — and during the march it was supplied by sea from Elat, the landing craft performing this service having been transported overland from Haifa. In the north the fighting continued for Abu Ageila. This was the most promising area for the Egyptians to defend and to reinforce their position there; an infantry brigade with an armoured regiment was despatched from Ismailia. Most of these reinforcements got no further than Bir Gifgafa, 20 miles up the road. Spotted by Israeli Mystères soon after leaving Ismailia the Israeli Air Force successfully put in a number of damaging air strikes which scattered the column, despite the air cover which was provided by MiGs and Egyptian

Above: Egyptian officer surrenders near Gaza.

Left: Egyptian prisoners at Gaza — not all of them appear to be soldiers.

Right: Israelis 'mopping up' in El Arish.

Vampires. Those vehicles which did get beyond Bir Gifgafa and tried to get through to Abu Ageila were held up by troops from Ben-Avi's force, who by now had infiltrated round Abu Ageila and were across the road in some strength. Meantime, another column of Egyptian reinforcements comprising a weak armoured brigade which half-heartedly attempted to recapture the Mitla Pass position was repulsed; after a short time it withdrew, being followed up by Israeli patrols which probed almost as far as the Canal banks. By now, Abu Ageila was virtually surrounded, although the Egyptians were still fighting back hard — certainly with considerably more skill and courage than they had shown in 1948. And, when the Israelis attempted to tighten the encirclement, the Egyptians launched a strong armoured counter-attack — their one major counter stroke of the campaign. The Israeli infantry was pinned down by artillery fire and at dusk the battle was still raging with the battlefield littered with the wrecks of burning tanks. Ignoring this battle next day (Thursday, 1 November), a fresh task force of an infantry brigade (Colonel Givly) and an armoured brigade (Colonel Barlev), under Brigadier Laskov, the Israeli Armoured Corps commander, bypassed Abu Ageila by driving westward round the defences to strike at Rafa, near the southern end of the Gaza Strip. Rafa had been heavily bombarded during the night by French naval units and its defences were soon overrun by Laskov's men who now turned west down the coast road towards the next important Egyptian post at El Arish.

Meantime, the Abu Ageila battle was still raging, the Israelis finding that they were unable to make little progress, although by now they were using captured T-34s to supplement their losses in armour. That the position in this sector was causing the Israeli High Command some alarm may be deduced from the fact that their Chief of Staff, General Moshe Dayan, flew to the scene and assumed command. Under his direction a fresh assault was launched and by dusk the Egyptian defences had been breached, although the two main defended ridges were still held. When dawn broke the following morning, it was realised that most of the Egyptian garrison had evacuated the area during the night and the rest of that day was spent by Harpaz's troops mopping up the few remaining pockets of resistance; by nightfall the whole of Abu Ageila had been captured. Few prisoners were taken by the Israelis as a result of this action, most of the Egyptians allowed to escape to make their own way back to the Canal across the inhospitable desert. Meanwhile, while Harpaz's men mopped up what remained of the Abu Ageila garrison, Ben-Avi collected his brigade and advanced towards Ismailia. Brushing aside a weak resistance at Bir Gifgafa he raced down the road halting only about ten miles from Ismailia.

On the northern coast route, Brigadier Laskov had closed in on the remaining stronghold of El Arish. Garrisoned by an Egyptian brigade, the El Arish area contained an airfield, huge petrol dumps, stores and supplies — a rich prize for the Israelis. As many of the Egyptian garrison had fled during the preceding night it was occupied with little difficulty and a large number of prisoners were taken here despite Israeli preference otherwise, since those who escaped relieved them of the

Above: 'Go Slow' (in Arabic) sign near the Suez Canal.

Above right: Norwegian UNEF officers in Gaza when the armistice came into effect.

Right: Egyptian PoW in an Israeli hospital.

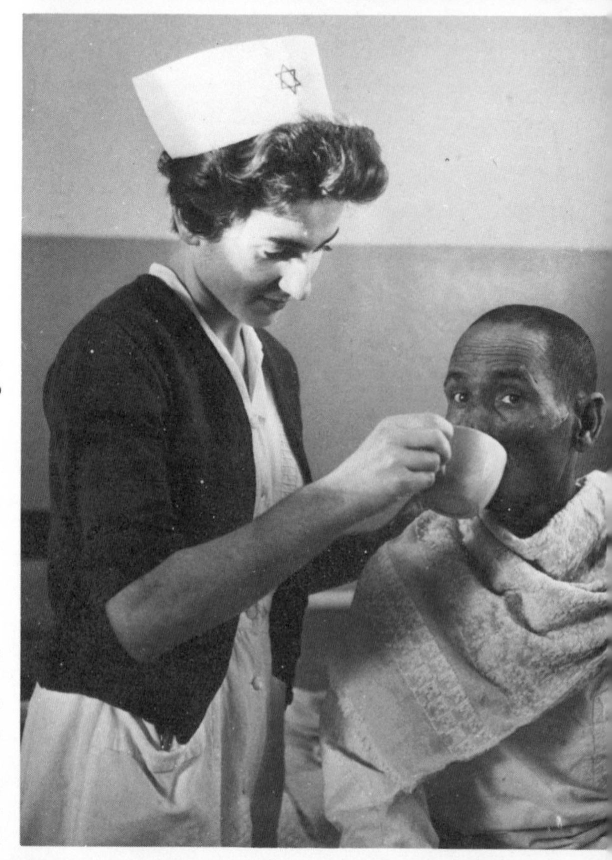

embarrassment and problems in feeding and guards. With El Arish in their hands, units of Laskov's column were soon speeding westwards to Kantara and by dusk they too had occupied positions about ten miles from the Canal. Thus, by Friday evening, Israeli troops were occupying positions at three separate strategic points astride the roads into Sinai and well within striking distance of the Canal. That night an army spokesman in Tel Aviv proudly announced: 'We have conquered the bulk of Sinai'. But for the restriction imposed by the Anglo-French ultimatum he might well have been able to say that Israeli troops were fighting in the town of Ismailia.

Operation Kadesh may be said to have ended with the fall of the ancient city of Gaza, although the southern operations at the mouth of the Gulf of Aqaba continued for another two days after this. Supposedly garrisoned by two brigades, the Gaza Strip which was crammed with Palestinian refugees was doomed when Laskov occupied El Arish. Gaza itself had been left to the last and the decision to occupy it was not taken until after the capture

Above: The Israelis pulled out of Sinai on the understanding that the UNEF would prevent fedayeen raids from Jordan and the Gaza Strip and that Israeli shipping would not be interfered with in the Gulf of Aqaba.

of Rafa. A fresh infantry brigade was moved into position opposite the town and at dawn on the Friday morning the Israelis forced their way through its defences and the town was formally surrendered at 1000 hours. The surrender document was signed by an unhappy Governor-General who now handed over the responsibility for 325 square miles of land and a quarter of a million ragged, ill-fed, ill-housed and ill-fated refugees whose very presence obviously had helped to bring about the surrender.

To complete the story, mention must be made of the exploits of Yoffe's brigade which had started out for Sharm-El-Sheikh on the Wednesday. The state of the road which he was compelled to follow was such that it was Friday before they had arrived at Ras Nasrani; this was the site of the Egyptian outpost opposite the island of Tiran from which coast guns prevented entry of Israeli ships into the Gulf of Aqaba. After a brisk action the garrison withdrew south on to their main defences of Sharm-El-Sheikh and Yoffe paused to take stock of the situation. His brigade was tired, the Egyptians and Sharm-El-Sheikh were expecting him and the campaign having gone as it had, there was now less urgency to complete his mission. He was opposed by an infantry battalion which occupied well-prepared defences, including a number of anti-aircraft guns and the garrison could be expected to put up a spirited resistance. Nevertheless after a short respite the offensive was resumed on the 3rd; by which time his men were refreshed and two AMX tanks, which Yoffe had considered would be necessary to break the outer defences, were on their way from Elat in the landing craft. (They arrived too late to take part in the action.) Preceded by an air strike, the Israelis attacked the Sharm-El-Sheikh perimeter and opened up a route to the main positions; the battle continued until the position had been completely overrun and most of the garrison taken prisoner — those who managed to get away escaping across the water to Saudi Arabia. Then, on Sunday morning (4 November) the island of Tiran surrendered and the final action of the Sinai campaign took place on the Monday with an amphibious landing on the neighbouring fortified island of Sinafar. With its capture the entrance of the Gulf of Aqaba was at last open to Israeli shipping and Yoffe signalled to General Dayan: 'It is finished . . .'

It was. On 5 November, in less than a week, a third of Egypt's army had been defeated, the Egyptian Air Force had been destroyed, Sinai was in the hands of its most hated enemies, and its capacity to resist the Anglo-French invasion was crippled. At midnight on Tuesday the Israeli official communiqué announced: 'The Campaign in Sinai is over . . . and there is no more fighting.'

At that moment an Anglo-French assault force was on its way to Port Said, but the following day 6 November, Britain and France yielded to pressure by the United Nations and their war — which lasted barely a day — was terminated.

For a time it seemed that the Israelis would hold on to the territory they had over-run, but they now came under strong American pressure to withdraw, and on 15 November soldiers of a United Nations Emergency Force (UNEF) began to replace the Israeli troops. However only an explicit American guarantee that their ships would enjoy the right of free and uninterrupted passage in the Gulf of Aqaba persuaded the Israelis to evacuate the Gaza Strip and the east coast of the Sinai Peninsula down to the Straits of Tiran. By March 1967 they had given up all their territorial gains on the undertaking that the UNEF would prevent fedayeen raids from Jordan and the Gaza Strip.

The 1956 Israeli campaign in Sinai may be compared with Wavell's 1940 campaign in the Western Desert. At a cost of less than 200 killed and only four taken prisoner — one of whom was the pilot of a Piper Cub which crash-landed behind the Egyptian lines — in four days the Israelis routed at least 50,000 Egyptians, occupied the whole of the Sinai peninsula and captured much rich and welcome military booty. The Egyptian Army defeat was even more humiliating than that of 1948 and at this time there was no King Farouk or corrupt Pashas to blame. Its failure may be attributed to the poor morale of the troops and the poor qualities of leadership shown by the officers; certainly there was no lack of equipment, it was well organised and the Egyptian fieldworks, which followed German patterns, had been well prepared. There were many reports — particularly from the Abu Ageila battles — of Egyptian soldiers standing fast to fight bravely and well in small groups or as individuals, but it seems that the esprit de corps which Nasser had been advocating had not yet penetrated sufficiently to inspire the young officers — many of whom were reported to have deserted their men quite blatantly.

Nothing like this could be said of the Israeli army, which had retained much of the ideological background provided by the Haganah in 1948. Despite its increasing professionalism it remained a people's army and the people knew that so far as the Arabs were concerned they faced the problem of survival. Not that such an outlook necessarily made them good soldiers. Israeli leadership in the 1956 war was characterised by 'speed and risk' and such a theme does not alway pay off. If Egyptian morale had been better, so enabling more determined and sustained resistance to be offered, the Israeli attack might well have collapsed. Their vehicles were so unsuitable that about half of them needed base workshop repair by the end of the five days' fighting, and the pace which Moshe Dayan set his commanders strained the logistical support to its absolute limit. But in this campaign of short duration 'speed and risk' worked.

Below: Moshe Dayan with jubilant troops in Sharm-El-Sheikh at the end of the campaign.

4 The Six-Day War of 1967

Once again time did not heal but exacerbate the tensions between the Arab states and Israel, and in the short hot summer of 1967 the conflict erupted yet again. On this occasion it exploded with an abrupt and stunning violence which subsided almost before the shock waves broke. It took just six days to redraw the map of the Middle East as the forces of Israel quadrupled the size of their country in a campaign which is probably the most sensationally swift and complete ever recorded in the annals of war.

Since 1956 deep rifts had appeared in the Arab world on the over-riding question of policy vis-a-vis Israel. But whilst the Arab rulers differed as to the method to be used to annihilate the Jewish state all of them agreed on the common objective: to wipe Israel off the map . . . to cast the Jews into the sea . . . to put an end to Zionist existence. And to attain this objective, they concentrated on preparation for war — largely at the expense of their own national interests. Propaganda campaigns were an essential feature of these preparations, and the 'hate Israel' campaign initiated after 1956 had steadily grown in intensity and virulence. Pamphlets, films, television, radio and even school texts were used to foment the 'ideological' campaign against Israel.

But Arab hostility was not confined to the campaign of words. It was accompanied by an irregular war of familiar style. From the Syrian heights above Galilee the occasional mortar bomb or an artillery shell fell on an Israeli settlement; saboteurs laid mines on roads inside Israel, cut telephone lines, or severed water pipes; whilst terrorist 'commandos' staged night ambushes — killing a solitary farmer here, another there. There were few casualties but the situation was unsettling; moreover it was getting worse. Terrorists of the sinister Fatah (the Arabic word for 'conquest' is formed by the letters FTH, hence *Fatah*, letters which reversed form the Arabic word 'death') organisation operating from Syria were trying to get a foothold in the Arab villages within Israel to establish guerilla bases there. All this was at a time when Israel was suffering an economic depression, and immigration was falling off. US aid had been cut back, Zionist fund-raising organisations were finding it increasingly difficult to obtain money overseas. German reparations had ended, and 10% of Israeli workers were unemployed.

By the beginning of 1967 all northern Israel smarted from the pinpricks of the guerillas and public opinion was demanding military reprisals, against Syria in particular. But Israel's Prime Minister, Levi Eshkol, and his new Foreign Minister, Abba Eban, preferred diplomacy to militant action. Eshkol had plenty of domestic troubles, especially with inflation and unemployment, and he did not want to add to them by provoking war with the Arabs. Nor did he wish to offend the Soviet Union, which was in an anti-Israel mood. Another important reason for treading carefully was Egypt's military strength, which had recently been augmented by large quantities of modern Soviet weapons. So the terrorist raids directed by Syria continued until they reached a stage in April when Eshkol was persuaded to authorise a raid. From then on tempers rose, the tension between Israel and the Arab world steadily increased and President Gamal Abdul Nasser began the brinkmanship in the fatal game which got out of control.

'It was not we who started the crisis', protested Nasser after the war. 'We all know that this crisis began with Israel's attempt to invade Syria . . . in that attempt Israel was not working for itself alone but also for the forces that had got impatient with the Arab revolutionary movement . . .' This was probably what the leader of the United Arab Republic, formed originally 'with the object of liberating the Arab homeland from the Zionist peril', genuinely believed at the beginning of the crisis — that Israel was planning a military strike against Syria which would topple the Baathist government in Damascus and so, perhaps, bring an end to Fatah's operations. Nasser felt that he could not afford to stand by and let this happen; hence the claim that his first moves were merely an attempt to deter the Israelis from attacking Syria.

Thursday, 7 April 1967, may be set as the starting point of the crisis. On that day the Syrian guns opened fire on Israeli farmers working in the border settlements of Haon, Ein Gev and Gadot. The settlements were in a disputed border region, but the Syrians had not previously interfered with their cultivation. Israeli machine guns returned the fire and a battle involving tanks, heavy mortars and artillery rapidly developed. Aircraft of the Israeli Air Force were called into action to silence the Syrian guns, and Syrian jet fighters also appeared. An aerial dogfight ensued, in the course of which six Syrian MiGs were shot down. Some of the Israeli Mirages then flew on the 50 or so miles to Damascus to demonstrate their superiority in Syria's air space. Largely because of this loss of face Nasser sent the commander-in-chief of the UAR Air Force to Damascus to discuss Egyptian cooperation with Syria in any future

Above: Prime Minister Eshkol visiting kibbutzim in Galilee a few days before the outbreak of war.

Right: An example of the propaganda war waged by the Arabs. This painting, displayed at an elementary school in Kahn Yunis, purports to show Israelis attacking Arab women.

incident. As a result of this vital mutual pledges of joint action against Israeli aggression were announced.

The next step up in the crisis came in the middle of May. During the first week of the month the Fatah made two attacks inside Israel which showed a higher degree of professional training and equipment than hitherto. This was noted with concern not only by the Israelis but also by the UN Secretary-General U Thant. During the next few days two developments then combined to precipitate the second phase of the crisis. The first emanated either directly from Moscow or was concocted in the Soviet Embassy in Tel Aviv. According to the Russians the Israeli troops were concentrating on the Syrian border, and this information was duly passed to Cairo. The second development arose from statements made by Prime Minister Levi Eshkol, and General Yizhak Rabin, the Israeli Army's Chief of staff, on 12 and 13 May. Construed by Nasser as confirmation of the Russian reports, the UAR leader decided that an Israeli attack on Syria was imminent.

In the event not only was there absolutely no truth in the Soviet stories, there was also some doubt that either Eshkol or Rabin said what Nasser was told they had said. Both the Israelis and the UN observers on the Syrian frontier denied the existence of any build up of Israeli troops, and Eshkol even invited the Soviet Ambassador to tour Israel's northern border with him and see the truth for himself. In the event the Ambassador declined. But the damage had been done and, despite a statement by U Thant on 19 May to the effect that there was no sign of any of the alleged concentrations of Israeli troops on the Syrian border, Nasser appears to have been convinced that 11 to 13 Israeli brigades were there. In a message to a Palestine Day rally of Arab students in Britain on 14 May his theme was that the 'Arab revolution' was faced with a coordinated conspiracy in which the US and British 'imperialism' was acting together with both Israel and 'Arab reaction'. ('Arab reaction' referred to King Hussein of Jordan, who was at loggerheads with Syria over the activities of the Fatah terrorists, and who refused to allow Egyptian troops to be stationed in his country.)

Against this melodramatic and almost paranoid picture of a powerful imperialist threat to the Arab world, Nasser's reaction to the reports of Israeli troop concentrations was prompt and fateful. Lieutenant-General Mohammed Fawzi, the Egyptian Army's Chief of Staff, who had been nominated to command the joint Egyptian and Syrian forces in the event of hostilities with Israel, was sent post-haste to Damascus to confer with Syrian Ministers and senior Syrian officers. And amid great publicity, on 15 May, large formations of the Egyptian army began to cross the Suez Canal to take up positions in the Sinai desert. Before 15 May there were less than two UAR infantry divisions and only a small amount of armour in Sinai; within a week there were four divisions. Then, on 16 May, a message from Nasser was delivered to Major-General Rikhye the Indian commander of the UN Emergency Force in Sinai and the Gaza Strip: 'I have instructed the armed forces of the United Arab Republic to be prepared for action against Israel the moment the latter carries out an act of aggression against any Arab state. In the light of these orders our forces have been concentrated in Sinai on our eastern frontiers. To ensure the complete safety of all UN forces in observation points along our borders, we request that these forces be removed at once.' UN personnel in Gaza and Sinai should be concentrated in the interior of the Gaza Strip; nothing was said at this stage about the UN posts at Sabha and on Sharm-El-Sheikh, whose guns could command the strait that is Israel's only back door access to Africa and Asia.

Rikhye objected to the demand on the grounds that it was irregular. But he sent it on to the UN headquarters. While it was being considered in New York on 17 May, Egyptian soldiers were trying to jostle the UNEF troops out of their positions and by that evening they had been turned out of their observation post at Sabha. Next day they were evicted from positions near Kuntilla and several other points in Sinai, and the UNEF commander at Sharm-El-Sheikh was brusquely ordered to withdraw his men. Simultaneously with these moves Mahmoud Riad, the Egyptian Foreign Minister, cabled U Thant formally demanding the urgent removal of the UNEF. Anticipating this demand, the UN Secretary-General had already consulted representatives of the countries providing the UNEF contingents, and Canada, India and Yugoslavia had intimated that they would evacuate their men as soon as they were officially asked to do so. Israel had also been asked if she would allow the UNEF to operate on the Israeli side of the frontier, but she had declined. Thus, after voicing 'serious misgivings', U Thant ordered General Rikhye to remove the UN troops and concentrate them in Gaza. Most of them had been withdrawn by the evening of 18 May; only the detachment at Sharm-El-Sheikh remained in position and it too packed up and left on the 23rd.

This sudden and dramatic departure of the UNEF came as a shock to the world in general, and to Israel in particular. Since the Suez debacle in 1956 the presence of the UNEF had succeeded in preventing hostilities between Egypt and Israel. It had also assured the free passage of Israeli and other ships through the Straits of Tiran and the Gulf of Aqaba into Elat, the southern port vital to Israel's economy. Ninety per cent of Israel's oil supply came from Iran in tankers which discharged their cargoes at Elat so the importance of free passage through the Aqaba Gulf could not be overestimated. Whether Nasser was legally within his rights in demanding the withdrawal of the UNEF, and whether U Thant was wise to agree with so little argument is arguable. Nasser himself, who expected to have to bargain and bully over his demand, was taken by surprise when U Thant agreed so readily. In retrospect it seems that legality was on Nasser's side, and from a practical point of view it is quite certain that the UNEF could not have operated without the consent of the Egyptians. Nevertheless, when the UNEF was withdrawn from Sharm-El-Sheikh, and Elat was threatened with strangulation, war between Israel and the UAR became a certainty.

For a few days nothing seemed to happen; to the rest of the world the Middle East was still simmering but it had not yet boiled, and with the moderate and compromising Levi Eshkol in charge of Israel's affairs there seemed to be a good chance of the crisis blowing over. But tension was mounting on both sides. On Monday 22 May, Eshkol told the Knesset that he had authorised a partial call-up of Israeli reservists to meet the 'grave developments' on Israel's southern border. With many men absent from their daily jobs the Israeli public was already aware that their army was mobilising. In Cairo, as Egyptian reinforcements continued to pour into Sinai, the Egyptian Government announced that the UAR was also mobilising, and Ahmed Shukairy told a press conference that his '8,000-strong' Palestine Liberation Army — banned in Jordan — had been placed under the national commands of Egypt, Syria and Iraq. Anxious not to be left out of the drama, Jordan also volunteered to place its armed forces under joint UAR-Syrian command, but Nasser pointedly ignored the offer.

Meantime U Thant had set out from New York to try to persuade Nasser to cool the situation. While he was still on his way to Cairo, the UAR leaders took the fatal step which escalated the crisis into its next phase and made war inevitable. The Straits of Tiran would be closed to ships flying the Israeli flag, Nasser announced. '.... Under no circumstances will we allow the Israeli flag to pass through the Aqaba Gulf. The Jews threatened war. We tell them, we are ready for war. Our armed forces and all our people are ready for war but under no circumstances will we abandon any of our rights. This water is ours...' Legally, this was not true. In 1957 the United States and other Western Powers had supported Israel's contention that the Straits of Tiran were an international waterway, and this view was reinforced by the 1958 High Seas Convention. Egypt, however, had never accepted this, and had not been a party to the High Seas Convention. In any case Nasser was not particularly concerned about the international view about the legality of rights of passage. Closing the Straits was a move calculated to send his stock rocketing throughout the Arab world and Egyptians, demonstrating in Cairo and Alexandria, roared their approval. Those who appreciated that their President was playing with fire trusted his judgement and hoped that he had got away with a political coup without the need for any fighting. Tunisia and Saudi-Arabia, the least militant of the so-called Arab world, expressed their support and acclaim; Algeria proclaimed a state of alert, and former FLN fighters were asked to volunteer for service in the struggle against 'Zionism'. Only Jordan, whose quarrel with Syria had intensified when a terrorist's bomb exploded in a bus at a Jordanian border post, abstained from the rush to demonstrate Arab unity and approval of Nasser's action.

The Israeli's reaction to Nasser's announcment was one of alarm and despondency. One Israeli doctor was approached by a middle-aged woman who wanted suicide pills to take if necessary — she had lived through one of Hitler's concentration camps and felt she could not live through anything similar. A father told of his 10-year old son returning from school saying that if the Israeli Government would not fight he did not wish to be an Israeli any more — he would go to America and become and American. The Israeli press clamoured for action and Eshkol took the unusual step of consulting the leaders of the opposition parties. Lack of confidence in his government was growing and anxiety was rising even in the Israeli forces. People were calling for changes in the government — for a new Defence Minister and a new Prime Minister in particular. Meanwhile provocative propaganda, broadcast from Cairo and other Arab radio stations was preparing public opinion for war and promising death and extermination to Israel. 'All Egypt is now prepared to plunge into total war which will put an end to Israel' declared the *Saut-al Arab* commentator on 17 May. 'Our basic objective will be the destruction of Israel. The Arab people want to fight', said President Nasser on 27 May. And Ahmed Shukairy is reported to have said that any Jews who managed to survive the war which was imminent would be allowed to stay in Palestine — but he did not expect many to survive.

Against this background the Israeli military leaders, headed by General Rabin, began to urge their government to authorise immediate military action. But the Knesset was divided about the risks of resorting to arms immediately. Influenced by a message from President Lyndon Johnson advising restraint, and asking the Israelis to refrain from any attempt to force the Egyptian blockade of the Straits of Tiran for 48 hours, the Israeli Government decided to try diplomacy first. So it was decided that their Foreign Minister, Abba Eban, should go to Washington to see President Johnson, travelling by way of Paris and London. Meanwhile, in Washington, the American president had issued a vague statement to the effect that the US regarded the closing of the Gulf of Aqaba and a blockade of Israeli shipping as 'illegal and potentially dangerous to peace'. The Soviet Union, who took longer to appreciate the inherent dangers in the worsening situation, issued a statement attributing the crisis to Israeli designs on Syria. But the Russians made no reference to the Gulf of Aqaba and according to French sources, the Egyptian and Syrian ambassadors in Moscow were told that the Soviet Union was not prepared to risk confrontation with the United States by giving military support to the UAR if a war with Israel came about. On 26 May, when reports reached Moscow to the effect that both Egypt and Israel believed an attack on the other was imminent, the Soviet Union sent an urgent warning to both Nasser and Eshkol against taking military action.

In the three days which had elapsed since Nasser announced his blockade of the Aqaba Gulf the situation had certainly deteriorated. On 24 May an Egyptian spokesman declared that Nasser's announcement had been implemented: the Straits of Tiran had been closed the previous day by mines and guns, and that the Egyptian Navy and aircraft of the Egyptian Air Force were patrolling the area. Israeli ships approaching the Straits would be fired on; all others would be stopped and searched. Another announcement reported the arrival in Egypt of an advance party of Kuwaiti troops, some Sudanese personnel and an Algerian military mission. U Thant, now in Cairo, was told by Nasser that the UAR would not strike the first blow, but if Israel wanted peace she would have to give up certain territory, including Elat, and recognise that the Gulf of Aqaba was Egyptian water. Meanwhile, Jordan, believing that her future depended on cooperation with the rest of the Arab world in the crisis, was still intent on getting into the picture, and Jordanian

Above: General Yitzhak Rabin, the Israeli Chief of Staff during the Six-Day War, with Dayan, the Minister of Defence. Rabin was the architect of Israel's mechanised army of the 1960s.

troops, tanks and guns were moved to the Israeli frontier with the same flurry of publicity as was given to the moves of Egyptian formations. A Government spokesman in Amman also announced that Saudi Arabian troops had arrived in Jordan, that more were expected, and that permission had also been given for Iraqi troops to enter the country. In the event no Saudi Arabian troops had arrived, and the Iraqis had no intention of sending troops to support Jordan while King Hussein remained in power. Nor did Nasser seem keen to admit Jordan to the UAR fold, since fresh gestures by Jordan promising cooperation with Egypt were ignored.

From the Israelis' viewpoint the situation was terrifying. If 80 million Arabs really had united for war, and if they struck simultaneously on all fronts before Israel was fully mobilised, they might well achieve the objective which Nasser had proclaimed on 27 May was '.... the destruction of Israel'. Clearly neither the US, Britain nor France had any real intention of honouring the pledges they had made to keep the Straits of Tiran open, and if and when it came to the crunch it seemed unlikely that they would give any other help. The United States was canvassing support for an international naval force, irreverently known as 'The Red Sea Regatta', to escort ships through the Straits of Tiran and the Aqaba Gulf, but there was little real enthusiasm for the idea. The truth was that none of the Great Powers wanted to get involved: Israel was on her own. France, the United States and the Soviet Union all warned both Israel and Egypt against shooting first, and it was the increasing fears of either side that the other might strike the first blow which escalated the crisis to its final stage. The Chiefs of Staff of the Israeli Forces were now pressing for quick action, arguing that every day's delay would mean more Israeli casualties in a war which had become inevitable. When the Israeli Cabinet met on 28 May after hearing Abba Eban's report on his visit to Paris, London and Washington, they deferred a decision on going to war. But Israeli criticism of the Government's inactivity was growing and public opinion was clamouring for a more militant policy and for a more vigorous leadership. This eventually crystallised round General

Moshe Dayan, the 1956 'Hero of Sinai'. Despite Eshkol's opposition, Dayan was appointed Minister of Defence with General Zvi Sur as his deputy.

Perhaps the most spectacular development at this time was King Hussein's sudden decision to fly to Cairo and sign a joint defence agreement with his old enemy, Nasser. The journey was made in great secrecy. 'What would happen if we arrested you', Nasser asked him on his arrival in Cairo. 'Such an eventuality never disturbed me'. the King replied. Under the terms of the agreement Jordan's armed forces were placed under command of an Egyptian general, Major-General Abdul Munim Riad, and Iraqi and other Arab troops were permitted to enter Jordan. The immediate outcome was that two battalions of Egyptian paratroops were flown to Jordan and Hussein announced that Jordan had joined Egypt in 'the holy war'. From Iraq it was also announced that an Iraqi division was marching to Jordan to support Jordan's Arab Legion. More surprising, and perhaps more alarming to the Israelis, was that Ahmed Shukairy accompanied Hussein back to Jordan.

The new military link-up between Egypt, Jordan and Syria could not have made any significant difference to the military balance for some time to come. But the threat of encirclement, however ineffective in the short run, was enough to convince the majority of Israelis that the Arabs were preparing to attack. It also undermined the arguments of those among the Israeli political leaders who were still advocating waiting while continuing diplomatic efforts to deal with the blockade of the Straits of Tiran. On both sides, diplomacy was now fighting a losing battle with public passions and military fears, and the original cause of the dispute, the closure of the Straits, became overshadowed by military considerations. Arabs and Israelis alike both felt that they might lose the advantage by delay, or that the other side might gain advantage by striking first. This was especially so among the Israelis, since Israel's strategy was based on a swift offensive. Most Israelis wanted to get the ordeal over with rather than wait for an Arab attack or for their country's economy to be slowly strangled. In Cairo the mood was somewhat more fatalistic. The Egyptians were crossing their fingers as much as anyone else, and hoping that Nasser had got away with a political coup without the need for war. But they knew that Israel might attack at any time and many were uneasy about the outcome if it did come to war.

Nasser himself was undecided about the next move. He had promised both Moscow and Washington that he would not fire the first shot, and he did not know how the US 6th Fleet would react if he did. Nor did he know how much support if any, he would get from the Soviet Union if he struck first. Neither did he appreciate the readiness and ability of the Israelis to go it alone. This, and his over-optimistic picture of Egyptian military power, were the most serious miscalculations he made.

While Nasser dithered, the Israelis were making rapid preparations for war. On Saturday, 3 June, Moshe Dayan gave the first press conference since the announcement of his appointment as Defence Minister, and made a conciliatory and disarming statement. The Government was trying to bring about a diplomatic settlement, he said, and their efforts must be given a chance. Asked if Israel had lost the military initiative, he replied: 'If you mean to say we stand no chance then I cannot agree with you'. Elsewhere publicity was deliberately being given to Israeli troops on weekend leave, sporting on the beaches. Finally, that evening, the Israeli Cabinet met to decide whether to continue to wait in hope that diplomacy and good sense might still yield a peaceful solution — delay which might mean annihilation; or let the army decide time, place, and method of response to an Arab attack. Seventeeen men met that afternoon and 15 voted in favour of an immediate war against Egypt.

Israel's secret preparations were in vivid contrast with the blare of publicity which attended those of the Arabs. In Cairo the Libyan Foreign Minister declared on 4 June that Libyan troops would be coming to hght alongside the Egyptians, and that the Americans would not be permitted to use their air base in Libya if they tried to help the 'Zionists'. Meantime General Riad had assumed command of Hussein's army, and a brigade of the division which Iraq had said was marching to Jordan arrived on the northern border of that country. A Saudi Arabian brigade had also crossed the Jordan and two others, encamped near Aqaba, were expected to move into Hussein's territory the following day. Some of the Western Powers were still trying to find a solution, but the diplomatic battle had been lost; this was the eve of war.

5 Strategy and Relative Strengths in 1967

A parallel has often been drawn between the war in Israel and the conflict of David against Goliath: two million Jews against 80 million Arabs. In 1967 Goliath was equipped with the most modern weapons but was still living in the Middle Ages, whereas David — for all his fragile appearance and sometimes out of date armament — had already reached the electronic age. In the two decades which had elapsed since the State of Israel was born, the Israeli Defence Forces (IDF) had come a long way. The army had been expanded and organised on conventional lines; conscription meant that practically every Israeli citizen, including women, could serve in its ranks. From a motley collection of obsolescent planes of World War II the Israeli Air Force had been built up into a formidable fighting machine. Without the cooperation and friendship of France during the 1950s this might not have been possible. Well over half of the planes of the Israeli Air Force were French by 1967 — and most of the remainder were French designed Fouga Magisters which had been assembled in a factory set up in Israel by the French firm of Fouga. Because it was allocated almost half the Israeli defence budget of over 350 million dollars and its dedicated professional pilots were the cream of Israeli manpower, the air force was the elite of the IDF. The navy, on the other hand, was the poor relation. Based on Haifa, Ashdod and Elat, it had only about 24 ships and its total manpower was no more than 3,000. Of the three services it was the army which the Israelis regarded as the main bulwark against Arab aggression, and in the event of war the role of the air force — and to a lesser extent the navy — was to support the army's operations. Control, direction and coordination of military policy and operations was the responsibility of the Israeli General Staff, the Chief of Staff being directly responsible for all three Services to the Minister of Defence. In principle the military was subordinate to the civilian authority of the Israeli Government. From the earliest days of the founding of the State, however, the IDF had enjoyed special relationship with its civilian masters. This permitted the Chief of Staff a freedom of action not enjoyed by his contemporaries in any Western democracy. Living in an atmosphere of uncertainty and terrorism, surrounded by hostile people who were continually promising 'the final liquidation of Zionist existence', the need to be able to act rapidly and decisively can be seen as ample justification for this special privilege accorded to the military.

Israel, being a small country with no depth, was unsuitable for fighting defensive battles, and the strategy evolved by the General Staff depended wholly on offensive action outside its borders. In 1967 the main threat was seen to be Egypt whose armed forces had been reinforced and strengthened to an unprecedented degree by huge shipments of arms from the Soviet Union. The regimes in Jordan and Syria were scarcely stable, and Lebanon had

Below: Israeli territory within range of Arab artillery, 1949-1967.

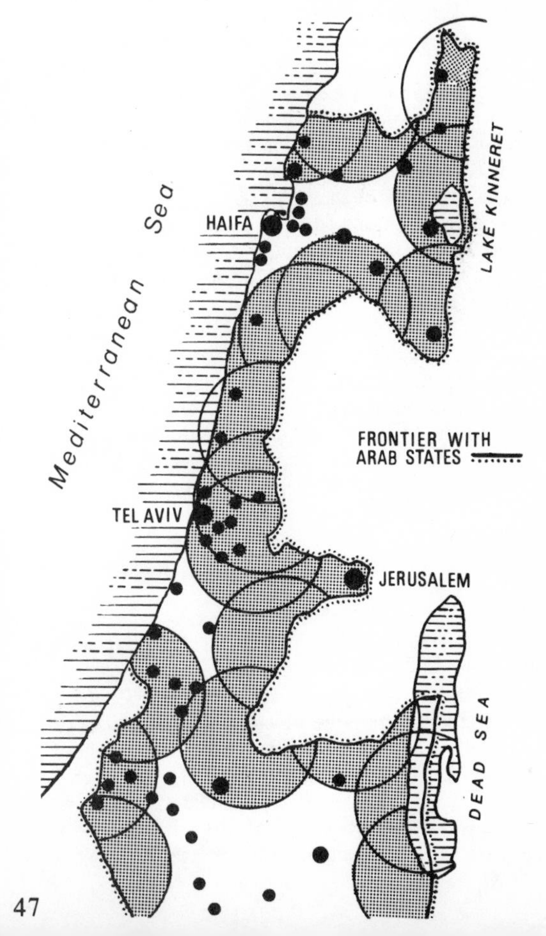

Left: Centurion tank crew.

Below: Israeli subaltern checking her Uzi sub-machine gun.

Right: M-50 Super-Shermans on the Golan Heights. The Israelis had 200 of these vehicles. On the right of the photograph is an AMX-13, of which the Israelis had 150 in 1967. They did not prove particularly suitable for desert operations.

no military strength worth reckoning with. King Hussein's Arab Legion had fought well on the two previous occasions but it was unlikely that Hussein would order them to attack Israel, and it seemed equally unlikely that the Syrians would leave the security of their strongly entrenched positions on the Golan. When war came, the Israeli policy was to parry any move by Jordan and Syria — and Lebanon if need be — while concentrating on the defeat of Egypt. Then, when Egypt had been dealt with, the IDF troops could turn on Jordan and Syria; the object being not to fight on more than one front at a time. If this strategy brought success, an outcry from the Arab world and those who sympathised with it would undoubtedly result in pressure for a cease-fire by the United Nations collectively, or some of its powerful members individually. The Israelis could therefore reckon on no more than a few days to attain their objectives, and the IDF General Staff plans were based on a three-day campaign. After that economic sanctions and shortages of food, fuel and the materiel with which to continue would compel the operations to be halted. On this premise the training of Israeli troops focussed on a three-day period of continuous campaigning, fighting night and day; and Israeli brigades were organised as self-contained formations equipped with three days' fuel and supplies.

From the current population of about two million Israel was able to mobilise a total force of 264,000 within 72 hours. The mobilisation procedure was flexible, and its extent depended on the degree of an emergency. Economic difficulties resulting from the closure of factories or the shortage of labour on the kibbutzim would clearly follow if complete mobilisation was to last more than a few days. So once the Israeli Government had decided that war was inevitable, any doubts about its inevitability had to be discarded. When conscription was ordered, war must

follow, because Israel could not afford to stand-to indefinitely, while demobilisation would probably be interpreted by the Arabs as a sign of weakness.

Each reservist kept his uniform at home, and mobilisation orders summoning him to report at a collection centre were issued in the form of a code message over the radio. Special arrangements were made to collect key men such as unit commanders and staff officers; the remainder reported to a nearby collection centre from where they were taken to the base camp at which their unit was assembling and where arms and equipment were issued. The mobilisation routine had been practised so many times that it was almost perfect. When the Six-Day War began three-quarters of Israel's reserves had been mobilised, and on the morning of the first day the code names of the remaining units were read out over the radio: Love of Zion, Close Shave, Men of Work, Alternating Current, Open Window, Good Fields. Throughout Israel the youths and middle-aged men comprising these units scrambled into the streets with their bundles and knapsacks, heading for their pre-arranged rendezvous with the buses which would take them to the base camps.

In normal times Israel's standing army comprised 2,000 regulars and up to 72,000 conscripts and reservists undergoing training. Some of these men were at basic training centres, but the majority were organised into seven brigades, each roughly equivalent in size and organisation to an American regiment. Of these seven, four were 'conventional' infantry, one other infantry brigade was trained in the paratroop role, and the other two were armoured formations. When the army was fully mobilised there were 31 brigades — 22 of which were infantry, eight armoured, and one elite paratroop formation. Each infantry brigade had about 4,500 men, and the armoured brigades were about 3,500 strong; two of the reserve infantry brigades had also been trained as paratroopers. The percentage rates of 'teeth' to 'tail' was thus in the order of 50:60, which compares very favourably with the ratio of 20:80 (or more) in the armies of the United States and Britain.

The brigades were the basic formations in the Israeli army, and they were not constituted into divisions. For a special operation, however, several brigades could be grouped into a task force known as an *Ugda.* A number of Ugdas were formed during the Six-Day War, and command of these was given to officers whose peaceful appointments had lapsed with the onset of hostilities. These included Brigadier Elad Peled, Commandant of the National Defence College, Brigadier Ariel Sharon, Director of Military Training, and such officers as Brigadier Uzi Narkiss, commander of Israel's Northern Command, Brigadier Yeshayahu Gavish, commander of Southern Command and Brigadier Israel Tal, the Armoured Corps Commander; Brigadier Avraham Yoffe was called out of reserve to command an Ugda in Sinai, where he had distinguished himself in 1956.

With the accent on offensive action and mobility, the infantry battalions — three of which were organic to each infantry brigade — were all motorised. The armoured brigades, usually comprising two tank battalions and one infantry battalion carried in armoured half-tracks, were equipped with a variety of tanks of British, American and French origin. In round figures the total number of tanks available was about 250 Centurions, 200 M-48 Pattons, 150 AMX-13s and 200 'Super'-Shermans, all of which had been adapted for war in the desert. The Super-Sherman was basically the old American 30-ton M-4 Sherman of World War II, modified and rebuilt, with a more powerful engine, a 76mm gun and broader tracks. The 14.5-ton French AMX-13, a fast and manoeuvrable light tank, had a 75mm

Above: Fouga Magisters at Lod Airport. / *via Jackson*

Above right: Boeing Stratocruiser converted by the Israelis for use as a military transport. / *via Jackson*

or 40mm gun and carried French SS.10 or SS.11 guided anti-tank missiles. The powerful 45-ton Pattons, with maximum speed of 35mph and high-velocity 90mm guns, were the same tanks as those which until comparatively recently had been the main battle tank of the US Army. As such they were one of the most powerful tanks in the Middle East; only the 50-ton British Centurions were superior in armament and armour, and they were much slower. These were Mark V and Mark VI models, fitted with 105mm guns in place of their original 20-pounders.

In addition to the 800 tanks of the types described Israel also had about 250 self-propelled guns — 155mm howitzers mounted on Sherman chassis, and 105mm howitzers mounted on AMX-13s. Infantry weapons were of conventional types — many of them being of World War II vintage. But there were plenty of 120mm and smaller calibre mortars, and locally manufactured Uzi sub-machine guns.

The Israeli Air Force, when finally mobilised, amounted to about 20,000 men. Before the war started Israel possessed about 450 aircraft of which 350 could be classed as first-line and operational machines. These were divided into 13 squadrons — four of interceptors, five of fighter-bombers, two of transport aircraft, and two of helicopters. Having no long-range bombers, there was no strategic bomber force, and as the range of most of the Israeli planes was limited to about 400 miles or less, large areas of Egypt, Iraq and Saudi Arabia were beyond their reach. Of the 350 operational planes there were 20 French Super Mystère fighter-bombers, between 40 and 60 of the earlier Mystère Mark IVA ground-attack fighters which were about 10 years old, 73 Mirage Mark III supersonic interceptor/ground-attack fighters, 48 obsolescent Ouragan fighter-bombers, 60 of the locally assembled Fouga Magisters, modified for use as ground-attack fighter-bombers, 25 Vautour ground-attack bombers, 20 Noratlas and Stratocruiser transports — each capable of carrying some 45 combat soldiers or 18 stretcher cases — and approximately 25 assorted helicopters. Of these planes only the Mirage interceptors and the Super-Mysteres were considered capable of challenging the Egyptian MiG-21s supplied by the Soviet Union. Technically all these types of planes were an approximate match. All were supersonic; all were fitted with 30mm cannon and carried air-to-air missiles. Schooled by their Russian instructors, however, the Egyptian pilots firmly believed that their MiG-21s were superior to anything the Israelis could put into the air; time was to show that the training and skills of the Israeli pilots would compensate for any technical differences between the Soviet and French designed aircraft.

On 'the other side of the hill', the four Arab nations under Egyptian military command had recently been equipped with large quantities of some of the most modern weapons in the world. Egypt itself had an army which in terms of armoured might and destructive capacity rivalled that of the German Wehrmacht which crushed France in 1940. Supporting this army was a large up-to-date air force, and a navy possessing the most powerful fleet of any Mediterranean country except France. Jordan, Syria and Iraq were less powerful adversaries; oil rich Kuwait which sent a brigade to the Canal zone when the war started, Algeria which sent another brigade and three squadrons of MiGs, Saudi Arabia which also contributed a brigade and the Sudan which pledged troops but never sent them, could be judged even less of a menace on their own. But the combined order of battle of Egypt, Jordan, Syria and Iraq consisted of over 400,000 men, 2,700 tanks and more than 700 aircraft — backed up by a comprehensive logistic organisation, and training in Soviet military methods.

Following the Egyptian army's shattering defeat by the Israelis in the Sinai campaign of 1956 the Soviet Union started to rearm the Arabs. Between 1957 and 1967 some $1,000million of arms and equipment were sent to Egypt — many of the latest types of weapons being sent to Egypt before the demands of Soviet Eastern Bloc allies had been

satisfied. All this materiel was supplied to the Arab countries for a fraction of the cost of its Western equivalent, and on generous long term payments in local currency. Along with the equipment came hundreds of Russian instructors to provide technical advice and to teach Soviet strategy and tactics. By 1960 the Egyptian army had become, on paper anyway, the most powerful in the Middle East, and it was still growing. By 1967 Egypt possessed about 1,200 tanks, 200 self-propelled guns, 1,200 armoured personnel carriers and over 1,000 conventional guns. Most of the armour was Russian — nearly a thousand of the tanks being versions of the famous 32-ton T-34 of World War II. The original T-34, of which the Egyptians had received about 450, was equipped with an 85mm gun capable of a high rate of fire but lacking adequate means of fire-control. The T-54, of which there were about 300, was an upgunned version of the T-34; and the T-55, of which the Egyptians possessed some 200, was an improved and modified T-54. Like its predecessor, which was the standard tank of the Soviet army, the T-55 carried a gyro-stabilised 100mm gun, but it had thicker armour and was provided with sophisticated direction-finding and fire-control devices.

Of the remaining tanks the 46-ton Joseph Stalin, JS-3, with its heavy armour and powerful 122mm gun, was the most formidable. 90 American Shermans, 30 British Centurions, 20 French AMX-13s and about 30 others of various age, origin and rôle completed the Egyptian tank armoury. To support this armour the Russians had thoughtfully provided a range of self-propelled guns, including SU-100 'tank destroyers', JSU-152s — which as the name implies mounted a 152mm gun — ASU-57 light anti-tank guns which were capable of being air-transported, and S-57 anti-aircraft tanks mounting twin radar-controlled 57mm AA guns. A wide range of Soviet artillery field pieces was supplied to give additional artillery support; these included 130mm field guns, 122mm howitzers and 122mm guns. To thicken up their fire the Egyptians were also issued with a few of the old Katyusha truck-mounted rocket-firing vehicles. 57mm, 85mm and 100mm anti-tank guns, supplemented by anti-tank guided missiles mounted on trucks and known as *Schmel*, were provided to counter the Israeli armour. And for the infantry and the supply columns there was the BTR-152 six-wheeled armoured personnel carrier, as well as a host of the same types of trucks and vehicles as were in current service with the Soviet Army. Infantry weapons such as the mortars, small arms, anti-tank bazookas and grenades included in the Arab hand-out were also the same as those in use in the Russian army.

With a population of 30 million, expanding at the rate of three-quarters of a million every year, and a three-year conscription period, manpower was no problem for those intent on expanding Egypt's armed forces. But the calibre of the individuals was a drawback. The hardships imposed by his background have given the Egyptian *fellah* a certain tough endurance, and with patience and good training he can be turned into a good soldier. But he lacks education, imagination and initiative and these shortcomings, superimposed on language difficulties, did not make the task of the Russian instructors any easier. A shortage of competent regimental officers was another problem. Soviet arms and equipment in Arab hands might well be superior to that of the Israelis, and available in greater abundance, but the exploitation of these advantages necessitated a proper understanding and familiarisation with the weapons. In the time available this was not possible. Lack of Soviet experience in desert warfare, exacerbated perhaps by the instructor's own training in tactics more suited to warfare in Eastern Europe, and an inflexible outlook, did not help either.

The fighting element of the Egyptian Army comprised three armoured divisions and four infantry divisions, all organised on the same basis as divisions in the Soviet Army. Each division had the support of two artillery regiments. Additionally there was an independent paratroop brigade and 15 commando battalions with a relatively high level of training performance. Two Egyptian commando battalions were flown to Jordan on the eve of the war and these attempted to organise a campaign of terror in Israel's Ramle-Sha'ar Haggai area on the vital road connecting Jerusalem with Tel Aviv.

The Egyptian Air Force was about the same size as the Israeli Air Force, but its aircraft were more modern and almost all of Soviet origin. By types these consisted of about 130 of the latest MiG-21 fighters, 80 MiG-19s, 180 of the earlier MiG-17s and original MiG-15s, 20 Sukhoi Su-7 fighter bombers, 30 Tupolev Tu-16 reconnaissance bombers and 40 Ilyushin Il-28s. There were also about 90 transport planes — Ilyushin Il-14s and Antonov An-12s — as well as about 60 helicopters. Some of these were in the Yemen, supporting the Egyptian troops fighting there. By the end of May 1967, however, most of them had returned to Egypt.

The combination of Tupolev bombers with a large MiG aerial umbrella represented a formidable offensive weapon for a first-strike knock-out blow. Acting alone it could deliver 300 tons of high explosive in a single raid on Israeli cities; and if the air forces of Jordan, Syria and Iraq struck with it the overall capacity was 500 tons. The threat represented by the transport aircraft was no less awesome. Under Soviet guidance the Egyptians had made significant advances in air-landing and air-dropping techniques. Using all their Ilyushins, Antonovs, MI-4 and MI-6 helicopters, they were capable of dropping 3,000 men in one flight and landing another 4,000 together with 600 tons of equipment and supplies. Shielded by a comprehensive radar warning system, as some of whose installations were well forward in the Sinai, and their airfields spread over a wide area, the Egyptians were also much less vulnerable to bombing than the Israelis. Israel's cities and industries were concentrated in a tiny restricted zone, while those of Egypt — with the exception of Cairo — were widely dispersed. In any bombing and counter-bombing contest, therefore, the Israelis would undoubtedly suffer most.

By comparison with that of Israel, superiority of the Egyptian Navy was overwhelming. Israel possessed only four destroyers (all ex-British and of World War II vintage including the *Haifa*, captured from the Egyptians in October 1956), two old submarines, an ex-German coastguard cutter, three old American landing craft and 12 motor torpedo boats. Egypt, on the other hand, had a fleet of more than 100 vessels, including eight destroyers — six of which were of the Soviet Skory class; 18 fast Soviet missile boats equipped with Soviet surface-to-surface Styx missiles; and 12 submarines of the Soviet V and R classes. Three-quarters of this fleet was based on Port Said and Alexandria, and as soon as hostilities commenced Nasser warned all international shipping to keep clear of the Israeli coast.

Like those of Egypt, the forces of the other Arab states had been built up in the decade prior to 1967. The Jordanian Army, smaller than that of Egypt but the most professional and best-trained of all the Arab armies, was very well equipped with modern British and American weapons. Its total strength amounted to about 55,000 organised on the British pattern into seven infantry and two armoured brigades. Each of the latter had two armoured regiments equipped with 40 Patton tanks (M-47s and M-48s) or Centurions; and the infantry element of these brigades was carried in US M-113 armoured personnel carriers, of which America had supplied over 250 as part of five million dollars of military aid to Jordan. Over and above the tanks with the regular armoured regiment there were at least 50 in reserve, and the Israelis claim that Jordan deployed 270 tanks and 150 field guns during the course of the Six-Day War. (Some of these 'tanks' were probably other types of armoured vehicles of British origin, perhaps.) Artillery consisted mainly of British 25-pounder field guns and 17-pounder anti-tank guns, but there were also some 155mm 'Long Toms'.

The Jordanian Air Force was small; it was also very short of pilots, and according to King Hussein there were only 16 pilots for his two squadrons of Hawker Hunter ground-attack fighters. Six months before the war broke out America had provided Jordan with 36 F-104 Starfighters, and six of these had actually been delivered. In the event, with no Jordanian pilots to fly them, however, Hussein asked the American instructors who had flown the Starfighters to Amman, to take them out of his country. Thus the Jordanian air war effort was restricted to 22 Hunters, three Doves, three old Dakotas and three helicopters.

Syria's army in 1967 consisted of two armoured brigades, two mechanised brigades and five infantry brigades with a total manpower of about 65,000. Like Egypt's army it had been organised on quasi-Soviet lines and lavishly equipped with Soviet weapons. More than 500 Soviet tanks had been delivered to Syria, most of them T-34s and T-54s; and Syrian artillery was especially well provided with a large variety of Soviet field guns, howitzers, anti-tank guns and mortars. There was also a large number of anti-aircraft guns. The Syrian Air Force, with a strength of approximately 9,000 men, possessed about 120 Soviet aircraft. These were organised into two operational fighter squadrons of MiG-21s and MiG-19s, and two squadrons of MiG-17s. Like Jordan, Iraq and to a lesser extent Egypt, Syria was short of trained pilots and although Soviet instructors had made good progress, the Syrian pilots and ground crews were far from attaining a standard of efficiency approaching that of the Israelis.

The Iraqi Army, which contributed a force of divisional strength to Jordan, numbered about 75,000 regular troops organised on the Soviet pattern into four infantry divisions and one armoured division. As in the other Arab armies their equipment was modern Soviet material, and the Iraqi Air Force of some 200 aircraft boasted two MiG-21 fighter squadrons, three MiG-15 or MiG-17 squadrons and one squadron each of Tu-16 and Il-18 bombers as well as transport and helicopter squadrons. Again like the other Arab States, the Iraqis had barely enough trained pilots to fly all the planes which they possessed.

From this brief review of the Israeli and Arab military machines it is clear that the Arabs had the advantage over the Israelis in manpower and equipment. Coupled with the strategic position of Israel vis-a-vis the Arab countries this put the latter in a very strong position. Furthermore the Arabs had declared their aim of seeking a 'Final Solution' to the Palestine problem and the combined military might of Egypt, Syria, Jordan and Iraq was arrayed on the borders of Israel and ready to move. Reinforcements were moving up from Algeria, Kuwait, and Saudi Arabia and General Mortaji, the commander of the Egyptian troops in Sinai, issued an Order of the Day declaring 'The eyes of the whole world are upon us in the expectation of seeing the results of our Holy War. With the force of our arms and the unity of our brotherhood, we will conquer the plundered soil of Palestine.'

6 Israel's Pre-emptive Attack

What has gone down in history as the 'Six-Day' War began early in the morning of Monday, 5 June 1967. It was virtually won by Israel before noon that day, but before it ended, six days later, there was much hard fighting and thousands of lives were lost.

Perhaps nobody will ever really know who fired the first shot. Nasser, in welcoming Iraq to the UAR and Jordanian alliance the night before, had proclaimed: 'We are eager for battle in order to force the enemy to awake from his dreams and meet Arab reality face to face'. In the event air raid sirens screamed in Tel Aviv and at 0745hrs the Israeli radio announced that an Egyptian column was rolling towards the Negev and Egyptian planes heading for Israel had been picked up on Israel's early warning radar. Few people regarded this information as other than a rationalisation. A tiny country like Israel could not possibly fight a defensive war; only pre-emptive action could make sense to those responsible for preventing disaster overtaking their country. Defence against an attack from the air was difficult, because the country was too small for any early warning system to give sufficient time for Israeli fighters to scramble. Cairo was 25 minutes' flying time from Tel Aviv, but Tel Aviv was only four-and-a-half minutes' flying distance from the forward Egyptian air base at El Arish. Anti-aircraft guns were not effective against

Below: Generals Bar-Lev and Rabin with the flamboyant Israeli Air Force commander Ezer Weizman. During his long tenure as commander of the IAF, Weizman shaped the air force that decided the outcome of the Six-Day War.

Israeli Air Force strikes, 5 June 1967.

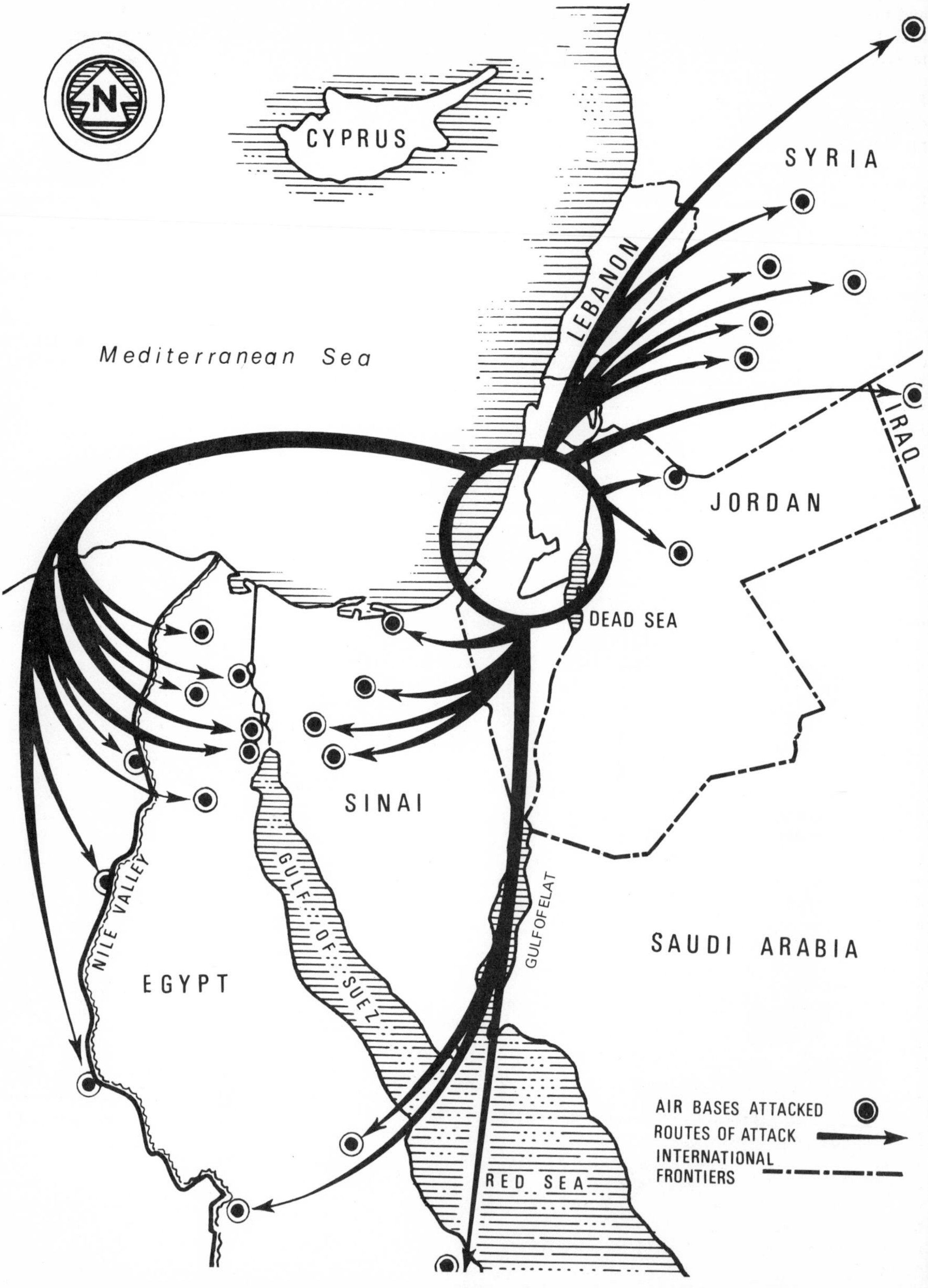

CYPRUS

SYRIA

LEBANON

Mediterranean Sea

IRAQ

JORDAN

DEAD SEA

SINAI

GULF OF SUEZ

GULF OF ELAT

NILE VALLEY

EGYPT

SAUDI ARABIA

RED SEA

AIR BASES ATTACKED

ROUTES OF ATTACK

INTERNATIONAL FRONTIERS

fast, high-flying jet bombers targeting on populated areas, and the few ground-to-air missiles which Israel had been able to afford were sufficient only to give a limited protection to Tel Aviv, and the Israeli nuclear installation in the Negev. For this reason, therefore, the Israeli Air Force had prepared and trained for an offensive role designed to obliterate the enemy's air forces. In uninhabited parts of the Negev the Israeli pilots had been practising low flying, precision bombing and the shooting up of model ground targets which bore a distinct resemblance to the Egyptian airfields. At the same time the ground crews had been training in the rapid refuelling, servicing, and turn-round of the aircraft. Thus, when the day came, every pilot was supremely confident in his ability to destroy his target, and all the ground crews were equally confident in their ability to keep the aircraft flying.

The Israeli Air Force went into action at 0745hrs (0845hrs Cairo time). The target was 10 Egyptian airfields, and the plan was to strike them all simultaneously. The time had been shrewdly chosen as the moment when the Egyptians would be least expecting an attack. Visibility would be good, the customary dawn stand-to, during which airborne MiGs would be waiting to pounce on intruders was over. Most of the Egyptian pilots would be having their breakfast and their commanders would not yet have reached their offices. Furthermore the Israeli pilots, who had a long day ahead, would be able to get a good night's rest.

One additional advantage which came as a welcome bonus was unplanned, unanticipated and unexpected. Two of the key Egyptian commanders were caught literally up in the air. Field Marshal Ali Amer, the UAR commander-in-chief, and his air force commander, General Mamoud Sidky, were in an aircraft flying from Cairo to inspect Egyptian troops in Sinai when the Israeli fighter-bombers screamed in to their targets. As a safety measure the Egyptian anti-aircraft batteries had been given orders not to fire on any aircraft over Sinai while Amer's Ilyushin was airborne. The latter could not land in Sinai because all the airfields were under attack, and ultimately had to return to Cairo. For 90 vital minutes the two key UAR commanders were out of touch with their forces and unable to give orders. To make matters worse the senior Egyptian field commanders in Sinai had left their posts to go to Thamed to greet Amer.

As the Israeli planners had hoped, the attack came as a complete surprise to the Egyptians — 'an hour earlier than anticipated' — as Radio Cairo ruefully put it. The Israeli pilots had nine objectives in all: the airfields at El Arish, Jebel Libni, Bir Gifgafa and Bir Thamada in the Sinai; Fayid and Kabrit on the Suez Canal; Abu Sueir and Cairo West in the Delta area; and Beni Sueif about sixty miles south of Cairo. With the exception of Fayid, which the Israeli pilots took some time to find because it was shrouded in mist, all these airfields were hit within 15 minutes of the scheduled time. The attacking planes flew in low to avoid detection and only as they approached their targets did they climb and suddenly become visible on the Egyptian radar screens. The final climb was a deliberate ruse to give the Egyptians a belated warning and so induce their pilots to attempt to scramble. Caught on the runways or in the cockpits of their machines they would then be destroyed with their aircraft.

Approaching their targets under cover of an air umbrella of about 40 Mirage fighters, the first waves of Israeli Mysteres met virtually no opposition. Because of their orders about Amer the Egyptian anti-aircraft gunners held their fire, and the only Egyptian aircraft airborne at the time of the initial strike were four unarmed training planes which were promptly shot down. Subsequent waves of attackers, which arrived over the targets as previous flights flew back to refuel and rearm, prior to another attack, ran into slightly more opposition — mostly from the AA guns which came into action when their crews realised what was happening. Only eight MiGs managed to take-off during the action and at the cost of two Israeli Mirages these were all brought down. The Israeli aircraft spent no more than ten minutes over their targets; this allowed them to make three or four attacks before their ammunition and bombs were expended, and fuel limitations compelled the pilots to turn back. During the initial sorties the runways and aircraft parking areas were strafed with cannon fire, and the Mirages' bombs were dropped on the runways during the final attack. Attack followed attack in successive waves — each consisting of about 40 planes — as the Israeli flights followed one another at ten-minute intervals. As one assault lifted, the planes of the following wave flew in to the target, the next was on its way, the fourth was preparing to take-off, and the ground crews were waiting to refuel, rearm and turn the returning aircraft of the first wave. Within 50 minutes the first wave was back over the same targets, and a pattern of successive and continuous attacks on the Egyptian airfields was maintained until noon — by which time Nasser's air force had been practically wiped out. Then, after a short interval, the same Israeli planes took-off again to attack the Egyptian airports further afield. The Ilyushin carrying Field Marshal Amer and General Sidky had to stay in the air for an hour-and-a-half until it eventually managed to land at Cairo International Airport. Seventeen major airfields were attacked and in just under three hours nearly 300 planes of the Egyptian Air Force were destroyed. These included 30 Tupolev Tu-16 heavy bombers, 27 Ilyushin medium bombers, 70 MiG-19 fighters, 12 Sukhoi Su-7 fighter bombers, 90 MiG-21 fighters and 32 transport planes and helicopters.

The surprise on which the Israelis had gambled was utterly complete. At nearly every UAR airfield the Egyptian aircraft were trapped on their parking aprons — wingtip to wingtip — and no attempt had been made at dispersion or camouflage. This, said the Arabs later — and Soviet spokesmen in Moscow angrily concurred — was a clear indication that Israel had struck the first blow. In Cairo the saddest remark that was heard during the war was: 'Trust those Jews to attack when they knew all our pilots would be having breakfast.'

To the Arabs the devastating power of the Israeli attack was as stunning as the surprise with which it took place. The majority of the Egyptian aircraft were destroyed by incredibly accurate cannon fire, and the airfields were put out of action by bombing which disrupted the runways. Most of these bombs were conventional 250lb, 500lb and 1,000lb types, but some of those dropped on the airfields

west of the Suez Canal had been developed for the express purpose of cracking the hard surface of concrete runways. (None was dropped on the Sinai airfields, which the Israelis hoped to capture for use by their own planes.) When one of these bombs struck the ground, booster rockets drove its 365lb warhead down into the hard surface, while delayed-action fuses made the moment of detonation uncertain. Known as concrete 'dibber' bombs, they were new to the Egyptians, and the Israeli success was partially attributed to the use of this 'secret' weapon. In the first few minutes of the early attacks the ground crews and Egyptian soldiers gallantly tried to repair the damaged runways and put out fires and salvage aircraft which had not been hit. But continual explosions of delayed action 'dibbers' and Israeli cannon fire eventually compelled them to give up. Once they had recovered from their initial surprise, the Egyptian anti-aircraft gunners fought back hard, and it was they who accounted for most of the planes which the Israelis lost. A number of the much-vaunted Soviet SAM-2 air defence missiles were released against the attacking Israeli aircraft during the course of the day. But the Israelis flew too low and too fast for them, and none of the missiles scored a hit. Slow to get off their launching pads and slow to accelerate, the performance of the SAM-2s was demonstrably less effective than that of the AA guns.

By noon on the first day of the war rumours that their air force had destroyed about 200 Egyptian aircraft were circulating among the Israelis. But no confirmation was forthcoming from official quarters, and on General Dayan's orders the rumours were deliberately played down. 'Let the Arabs do all the talking', Dayan told the Israeli spokesman. He had guessed that Nasser's generals would be reluctant to tell their chief of the Egyptian losses, and that when Nasser did learn their magnitude there would be a demand for UN intervention or a cease-fire to stave off further disaster and prevent the Israelis from exploiting their success. Dayan was also apprehensive of Soviet reaction when Moscow learned that many of the aircraft and other war materiel supplied to Egypt had been destroyed. Thus, until the facts were revealed at an Israeli press conference on the morning of the second day (6 June), Arab bulletins teeming with false claims of Israeli planes shot down, were retransmitted without comment by the Israeli Broadcasting Service. In Cairo each fresh bit of wishful reporting was jubilantly received by people gathered round transistor radios at street corners, and mobs of students chanted 'We shall fight, we shall fight. Our beloved Nasser, we are behind you to Tel Aviv!' One report from Radio Cairo told of an Israeli pilot whose plane had been shot down near Zagazig in the Nile delta. Landing by parachute, he had been seized by the local fellahin who had chopped him to pieces with the axes they used in the fields.

Whilst such news kept the Arabs in optimistic darkness, the Israelis — who could also listen in to Radio Cairo, and many of whom could understand Arabic — were naturally anxious. To some extent their fears were soothed by a statement put out by General Chaim Hertzog, the chief

Left: Napalm canisters shower down from a flight of Mystère IVAs. */ via Jackson*

Right and below: Egyptian airfields under attack 5 June 1967.

military commentator, who condemned the Egyptian claims as 'premature, unclear and utterly unauthorised.' and there can be little doubt that the Israeli policy of refusing to lift the fog of war for the benefit of their enemies paid off. Nasser himself did not learn of the full extent of the Israeli blow until some six or seven hours later, and the Egyptian High Command was slow to appreciate its significance for the air battle. When Nasser welcomed Jordan's entry into the war that morning he thought he still had an air force. When he learned the truth he tried to explain it away by accusing the US and Britain of having shared in the attack.

In Tel Aviv the unfamiliar wail of air raid sirens shortly before 8am was the first indication that the war had started. But no amount of warning, however shrill, ever quite prepares a people for an event of this nature; people were reluctant to take shelter and the morning bustle of Tel Aviv was scarcely disturbed. The same sort of attitude was prevalent in Jerusalem and other places, and it was not until about 0900hrs when both Israeli and Arab radios announced the opening of hostilities that the mood changed. Many inhabitants then scrambled for places in the air raid shelters, where many of them slept for the next three or four nights. In Tel Aviv the warning siren screamed 12 times during the first day — the longest alert being at noon when Jordan started to shell the city.

Above: After destroying the Arab airfields in a few hours, the Israeli Air Force attacked ground forces. This photograph shows the devastation caused around the Mitla Pass.

Throughout the crisis the Israelis had been hoping that Jordan would stay out of the war, and frantic messages had been sent to King Hussein through local agencies of the United Nations asking him to hold his fire. If he would keep his peace, so too would they, the Israelis said. But Hussein, the most moderate of the Arab rulers, had gone too far to be able to back down now; he was trapped by his commitments to the rest of the Arab world. At 0900hrs a message was received from Field Marshal Amer informing Hussein that the war with Israel had begun and urging Jordan to commence hostilities immediately in accordance with the pact signed in Cairo. In attacks against the UAR airfields 75% of the Israeli air force had been destroyed, the message continued. This, of course, was complete fabrication, as was the claim that Egyptian aircraft were now attacking Israel. But any doubts which Hussein might have had at this time were quickly dispelled by what appeared to be confirmation of Amer's statement from a Jordanian source, when what were identified as a large number of aircraft flying from Egypt towards Israel were picked up by Jordan's radar stations. (These were Israeli planes, in fact, returning to base after their first sorties.) So Hussein decided to act, and at 09.30hrs Israeli hopes that Jordan would stay out of the fray were shattered. Broadcasting over Radio Amman, the king called on his people to join in the *jihad*; Jordan had been attacked, he said, the Jordanian army and air force had been placed under the command of General Riad, and the 'hour of revenge' had come. The Israelis were surprised, but many were not dismayed — for if the war with Egypt was long prepared, action against Jordan was opportunity itself. The fight for the holy city of Jerusalem was the chance to fulfil Jewish prophecy.

Following King Hussein's broadcast, the Jordanians were expected to attack in conjunction with Syria and Iraq. Confusion attributable to a spurious message — purporting to come from Field Marshal Amer, but originated by Israeli Intelligence — and a message from the Syrians which said that they had been caught unawares by the suddenness of the outbreak of hostilities, inevitably caused delay. The Syrians said that their force was not yet ready to strike Israel. No doubt they were hoping that Hussein's planes would be destroyed by the Israelis before they committed their own to battle. To the Syrians Hussein was still the 'Tom Thumb Tyrant', and they had a sharp eye to a settlement of differences with Jordan when the war with Israel was over. The Iraqis were also slow to respond to the holy war call. But at 1100hrs a signal to Hussein stated that Iraqi aircraft had already taken off to bomb targets in Israel. Subsequently the Iraqis claimed to have raided Tel Aviv and to have destroyed 'seven aircraft on an Israeli airfield'. Neither the initial statement nor the claim which followed were true. Throughout the war Iraqi air activity was confined to a single sneak raid by a solitary Tu-16 which dropped a few bombs on Nathanya. So far as Hussein was concerned, however, there was no reason to suppose that the Syrian and Iraqi messages were not authentic and he ordered his aircraft to attack Israel. Sixteen of Jordan's 22 Hawker Hunters took off to bomb the airfields at Nathanya, Kfar Sirkin, Kfar Sava and other targets. By about 1130hrs all 16 Hunters were back at the airfields, and their pilots reported they had destroyed four Israeli planes on the ground.

The Israelis' reaction was both prompt and devastating. Having dealt with the Egyptian air force, they turned their efforts to the elimination of that of Jordan. Shortly after noon two flights, each of four Mirages, took off to attack the Jordanian air bases at Mafraq and Amman. There they caught the Hunters refuelling and rearming after their bombing mission over Israel. When the Mirages turned for home 18 Hunters were left blazing, destroyed beyond repair; and bombs had disrupted the runways. To round off their mission the Mirages then attacked and shot up what appeared to be suitable targets encountered on the return journey. Such targets ranged from moving vehicles to — according to the Jordanians — King Hussein's palace. In the course of the raid one Mirage was hit by Jordanian anti-aircraft gunners, but the pilot managed to bail out over the Sea of Galilee, where he was picked up by an Israeli patrol boat.

In one short raid the Israelis had crippled the Jordanian air force which was left literally without planes. Most of the pilots escaped death, and Hussein packed them off the Iraq where they spent the rest of the war flying Iraqi Hunters. Worse was to come, and Hussein claimed later that if the Syrians had carried out their part of the Arab pact and struck at Israel when they were called upon to do so his planes would have been airborne sooner. Then they might well have caught the Israeli aircraft returning from their raids against Egypt — airborne but short of ammunition and fuel, or on the ground refuelling — and, by destroying them, blunted the weapon which gave the Israelis ultimate victory. Maybe this could have been so; since the Hawker Hunter is reputedly more manoeuvrable than the Mystère and Mirage. But history abounds with ifs and might-have-beens, and it seems unlikely that anything the Jordanians could have done would have affected the ultimate result.

The Syrian air force was struck and paralysed about the same time as that of Jordan. At 1215hrs 16 Mystères attacked the four main airfields south of Damascus. After 20 minutes' of bombing and strafing, a blazing mess of wrecked Syrian aircraft and cratered runways testified to the swift vengeance of the Israelis which Radio Damascus had that morning rashly promised would be 'destroyed within four days'. Schools in Damascus had been closed, more in celebration than precaution against air raids, and school children were now put to work filling sandbags to stack round public buildings. No air raid shelters had been prepared in the Syrian capital, and after this brief demonstration of Israeli air power the Syrians hastily converted a couple of discothèques. West of Damascus, the population of Beirut was also frantically taking some half-hearted precautions against air raids. Like other Arab states the Lebanon had also declared war on Israel, but apart from broadcasts containing the same mixture of exhilaration and invective as that from the other Arab radio networks, the Lebanese Government made no hostile move. The Lebanese Prime Minister, Rashid Karame, was keen to get in at the kill, but the army's chief of staff, General Bustani, knew that his country's armed forces were no match for those of Israel, and when on the Tuesday (the second day of the war) Rashid Karame ordered him to take the field, Bustani refused. The Prime Minister then ordered Bustani's arrest, but as no one would comply with this order either, nothing happened. Fortunately for the Lebanese this stalemate lasted long enough for the truth to overtake the wishful reporting that had set the tone of the first day's battle bulletin from Cairo. Karame, realising his mistake toned down his bellicosity and tried to forget that he had ever wanted to wage war against Israel. Apart from one clash between Israeli aircraft and two Lebanese Hunters over the Sea of Galilee the Lebanese stayed out of the war and the Israelis were content to leave them alone.

In the event neither the Syrians nor the Lebanese were disturbed by further air raids on the first day of the war. Except for one raid against the main Iraqi airfield, once the wings of the Syrian Air Force had been clipped and

Hussein's air power pulverised, the Israelis turned their attention back to the major enemy, Egypt. The airfields which had been hit in the early raids were struck again, while a series of other attacks were concentrated on the Egyptian radar stations. By nightfall all the radar installations in Sinai as well as most of those in the Delta and Canal zones had been knocked out, and the Israeli air force could claim almost complete freedom of the skies. Apart from three or four isolated attacks by Egyptian MiGs on Israeli troops in the Sinai no Arab aircraft ventured anywhere over Israel or attempted to intervene in the land battles after this. In contrast the Israelis gave massive aerial support to their ground forces, and flew at will whenever and wherever they wished — making frequent flights over Cairo and the Delta area, parts of Iraq, Syria and Jordan, as well as all over Sinai before it was overrun. On occasions the Arabs attempted to resist the incursions into their air space. But SAM missiles fired at the intruders proved to be as ineffective as they had been on the first day of the war, and the Israelis quickly got the measure of the anti-aircraft gunners. On a number of occasions dog fights developed when Egyptian MiGs and Iraqi Hunters intercepted Israeli aircraft. After the war the Israelis claimed to have downed 61 Egyptian aircraft and 16 other Arab planes in aerial combat. The cost in terms of Israeli planes is believed to have been about 40, although the Israelis have never confirmed or denied this figure. Thirteen Israeli pilots were taken prisoner — nine by the Egyptians, two by the Jordanians, and two by the Syrians; and five other Israeli pilots who had to bail out over enemy territory were killed on landing.

It was the pre-emptive attack by the Israeli air force which formed the key to their success in the land battles which were to follow. Possibly they would still have won the war without this massive air assault, but victory could have entailed many more Israeli casualties and it would have taken longer. Some of the Arab troops fought stubbornly — the Jordanians in particular. But absolute mastery of the air by the Israelis meant ultimate Arab defeat. Hussein, unaware of the extent of Egypt's losses, could not believe that the Israeli air force was capable of the sustained effort deployed against his Arab Legionnaires. Thus it was partially understandable that for a while, at least, he should support Nasser's claim that American and British aircraft had joined in Israel's attack.

How this canard originated is still shrouded in mystery. But it seems that when the truth about the destruction of the Egyptian air force could no longer be hidden from Nasser, the UAR High Command tried to explain it away by laying the blame on the United States and Britain. The accusation was fed by the prevailing bewilderment and confusion, and Nasser was desperate to find an excuse for the Arab debacle. By implicating the United States and Britain he probably hoped to persuade Moscow to come to his rescue. In effect there was never a chance of this ploy working. Russian ships monitoring air movement in the Mediterranean knew from their own radar that no American or British planes were involved and the Soviet ambassador in Cairo went to Nasser and bluntly told him so. Nevertheless Nasser stuck to his claim and just before dawn on the morning of the second day the Israelis monitored and tape-recorded a radio-telephone conversation in which Hussein telephoned Nasser to say that 400 aircraft were attacking Jordan, and after some discussion both Arab leaders agreed, according to the taped dialogue released by the Israelis, to say that the United States and Britain were participating in the war. The vital passages were spoken by Nasser:

Nasser: Hello — will we say the US and England or just the US?
Hussein: The US and England.
Nasser: Does England have aircraft carriers?
Hussein (answer unintelligible)
Nasser: By God, I say that I will make an announcement and you will make an announcement, and we will see to it that the Syrians make an announcement that American and British planes are taking part against us from aircraft carriers. We will stress the matter and we will drive the point home...

The United States and British governments promptly denied this allegation, and both countries asked the UN to send observers to the airfields and carriers from which air support for the Israelis was supposed to have been flown. None was sent and Hussein admitted later that the 'vast umbrella' over Jordan had been entirely Israeli. Nasser, however, stuck to his story, insisting that 'three times as many' planes as Israel possessed had attacked the Arab force. This, combined with the fact that it was inconceivable to ordinary Egyptian opinion that little Israel could beat them without outside assistance, meant that the Arabs believed, and probably still continue to believe, that American and British aircraft were instrumental in forcing an Israeli victory.

The truth of course is different. That the pre-emptive strike on Egypt and consequent destruction of Arab airpower played the decisive part in deciding the outcome of the war, there is no denying. But the credit must go entirely to the Israelis, for their professionalism, careful planning, hard training and meticulous preparations.

7 The Land Battles

THE EGYPTIAN FRONT

At the end of May there were nearly 100,000 Egyptian soldiers and 1,000 tanks in Sinai: seven divisions, two of them armoured. Of these divisions, only the 20th Palestine Division stationed in the Gaza Strip, and the 7th Infantry Division deployed along the Israeli border, had been there before the crisis. The other five divisions had been rushed across the Suez Canal when Nasser began his brinkmanship, and when hostilities commenced they were not ready. Most of the Egyptian officers did not really expect to have to fight; other crises had stopped short of war, and they were confident that Nasser's victory would be diplomatic and non-military. Consequently few of them were concerned about instant readiness. Communications and administrative facilities had not been properly organised, and although there were ample stocks of rations, fuel and ammunition in the Sinai supply dumps they had not been distributed. One of the causes of this operational and administrative confusion lay with the way in which the much publicised build-up was conducted. Division followed division into the forward area, units were shuffled pointlessly from one location to another. Thus on the morning of 5 June it was estimated that about a quarter of the Egyptian vehicles were non-runners because they had broken down or had no fuel.

The Egyptian High Command deployed their seven divisions both for offensive action and for defence. The 20th Palestine Division in the Gaza Strip had an almost rigid defensive role in that region, while the 7th Division sat in strongly fortified positions from Rafa to El Arish covering the coastal road across Sinai to Kantara. In the Abu Ageila area further south the 2nd Infantry Division blocked the central Sinai road to Ismailia. Behind the 2nd Division the 3rd Infantry Division was dug in across the central Ismailian road and the main road to Suez between Jebel Libni and Bir Hassana. In the south the 6th Infantry Division, based on Kuntilla and Nakhl, covered the Pilgrim's Way which ran from Kuntilla and Ras-el-Nagb near the Israeli border to Suez. All five infantry divisions had three infantry brigades, each of which was supported with a battalion of T-34 tanks or SU-100 self-propelled guns and a battalion of Schmel anti-tank missiles. The 4th Division, equipped with the newest and best of the Soviet tanks, was held in reserve in the Bir Gifgafa area while the second and smaller of the two armoured divisions covered the Nakhl and Thamad areas on the routes into Sinai from Kuntilla and Ras-el-Nagb. (This division was not officially constituted as the 2nd Armoured Division, although it is often referred to as such. It was, in fact, known as Shazli Force after the name of its commander, and consisted of four tank battalions, a motorised infantry brigade, a commando battalion and three artillery regiments.)

This deployment presented a strong defence; it also provided an excellent springboard for offensive action. By thrusting eastwards across the southern Negev, Shazli Force and the 6th Infantry Division could join hands with Jordan and cut off Elat. Israel would thus be deprived of her port on the Gulf of Aqaba, the proposed British and American-backed Red Sea Regatta would have no future, and Nasser would have gained a valuable bargaining counter if and when the UN intervened to impose a cease-fire.

In the 1956 campaign the Israelis had begun their assault up the central route and along the roads into Sinai from Elat and the frontier post of Kuntilla. They had been able to do so and to make a dash down the coast to Sharm-El-Sheikh because the Egyptian forces in the north of Sinai were weak, owing to the greater part of the Egyptian Army being deployed on the west side of the Suez Canal to resist the Anglo-French invasion. Because the circumstances were very different the Israelis could not repeat the same strategy. But they could try to make the Egyptians believe that they would. And just as the Israeli Air Force succeeded in persuading the Egyptians to move aircraft from the north, which was to be the theatre of operations, to the vicinity of the Red Sea an Israeli army deception plan also succeeded. From aerial photographs taken by an Egyptian reconnaissance aircraft during the week before the outbreak of war the Egyptians concluded that an Israeli force of two or three armoured brigades had concentrated between Mizpe Ramon and Suiwila opposite Kuntilla. In fact there was only one brigade; the rest of the tanks and vehicles appearing on the photographs were carefully camouflaged dummies.

In the land battle, as in the air, the Israeli tactics were based on surprise and speed. They were the same tactics as had been employed in the 1956 campaign. In the Sinai the main objectives were much the same as they had been in 1956; to break the back of the Egyptian army on its borders, then to sprint forward to seize the range of mountains just east of the Suez Canal, to cut off the

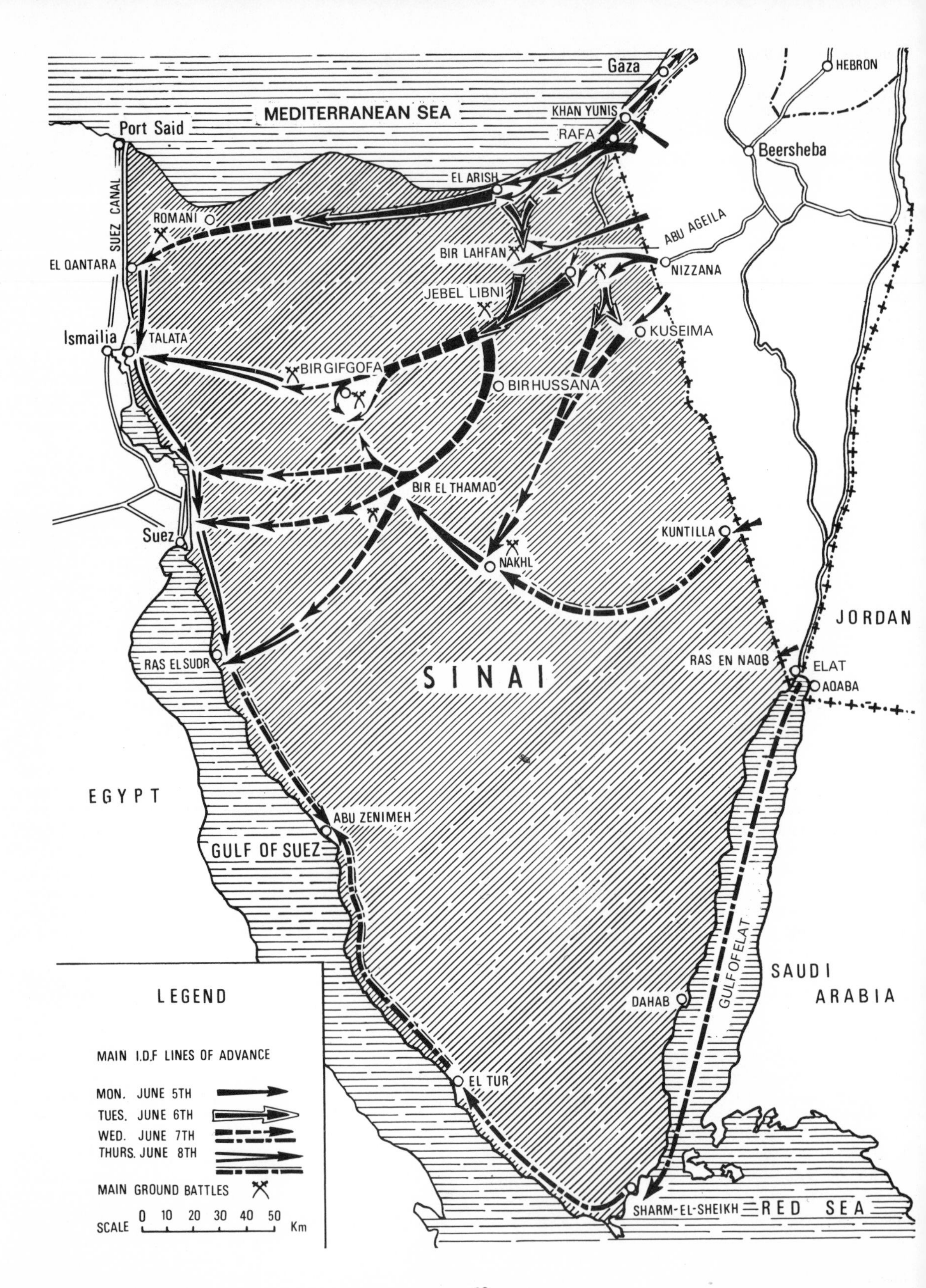
Gaza
MEDITERRANEAN SEA
Port Said
KHAN YUNIS
RAFA
HEBRON
Beersheba
EL ARISH
ROMANI
SUEZ CANAL
EL QANTARA
ABU AGEILA
BIR LAHFAN
NIZZANA
JEBEL LIBNI
Ismailia
TALATA
KUSEIMA
BIR GIFGOFA
BIR HUSSANA
BIR EL THAMAD
Suez
KUNTILLA
NAKHL
JORDAN
RAS EL SUDR
SINAI
RAS EN NAQB
ELAT
AQABA
EGYPT
ABU ZENIMEH
GULF OF SUEZ
SAUDI ARABIA
GULF OF ELAT
DAHAB
LEGEND
MAIN I.D.F LINES OF ADVANCE
MON. JUNE 5TH
TUES. JUNE 6TH
WED. JUNE 7TH
THURS. JUNE 8TH
MAIN GROUND BATTLES
SCALE 0 10 20 30 40 50 Km
EL TUR
SHARM-EL-SHEIKH
RED SEA

Left: **Operations in Sinai and the Gaza Strip, 5-8 June 1967.**

Right: Generals Haim Bar-Lev (Israeli Chief of Staff 1968-71), the controversial Arik Sharon and Gavish, GOC Israel's Southern Command during the Six-Day War.

Egyptian escape routes. Once the Egyptian army was defeated the opening of the Straits of Tiran would follow automatically. The Israelis were confident in their ability to defeat the Egyptians; their difficulties centred on the terrain. The few roads which then existed in Sinai were rough and separated from each other by rocky ridges or by shifting sandseas. Movement from east to west was not easy, and laterally from north to south was barely possible at all. Yet the war would have to be fought and won in Sinai, for the Israelis could not afford to let their country become the battlefield. They would have to move forward to meet the enemy which, in effect, meant an invasion.

For this invasion the Israeli forces were grouped into three highly mobile Ugdas commanded by Brigadiers Tal, Yoffe and Sharon respectively. Brigadier Gavish, GOC of Israel's Southern Command, was in overall command of the operations in this area; as such his authority was analogous to that of a corps commander. The exercise of this authority was, however, largely restricted to broad directives to the separate Ugda commanders rather than the issue of precise orders. Tal's Ugda of two armoured brigades, to which was attached the regular paratroop brigade (less one battalion which fought with the Sharon Ugda) had the elite of the Israeli Armoured Corps — 300 tanks, 100 half-tracks and about 50 guns many of which were self-propelled. The Sharon Ugda consisted of one armoured brigade, an infantry brigade, a paratroop battalion and six regiments of artillery — totalling about 200 tanks, 100 half-tracks and about 100 guns. Yoffe, whose Ugda was composed entirely of reservists, had two armoured brigades and a battalion of mechanised infantry — 200 tanks, 100 half-tracks, but no guns. Like American or British divisions, each Ugda was completely self-contained, with its own engineers, signals and medical units; it also had its own supply vehicles carrying fuel, ammunition and rations for three days' of war. Many of these vehicles were 'reserves' too: civilian laundry lorries, ice-cream trucks and similar vehicles which had been commandeered for the duration.

Gavish's three Ugdas constituted the striking force. Three other brigades deployed along the Sinai front were regarded as reserves which could be thrust into the fighting later. One infantry brigade faced the Gaza Strip, one armoured brigade was positioned opposite Kuseima, and the third brigade — also armoured — faced Kuntilla. The defence of Elat was in the hands of a single infantry battalion.

Mention has already been made of the deception measures taken in an effort to persuade the Egyptians that the Israelis were planning a dash down the coast road to seize Sharm-El-Sheikh and open the Straits of Tiran. The real plan envisaged a three-pronged thrust, directed towards the Gaza strip, El Arish and Kuseima. Tal was charged with the difficult task of breaking into the Gaza Strip. His troops would storm the defences of Rafa, the hinge between the Strip and Egypt proper, and then move down towards El Arish. Meanwhile Yoffe's troops would battle their way across the desert to block the flow of Egyptian reinforcements to the Gaza region, and ultimately join Tal's men in a combined assault on El Arish. Sharon's task was to seize Abu Ageila, where the junction of roads from El Arish, Jebel Libni and Kuseima effectively blocked the main line of advance of Israeli forces into Sinai's central region.

Tal decided to break into the Gaza Strip by way of Khan Yunis, a town east of Rafa. This meant crossing a formidable minefield, and tackling part of the 20th Palestinian Division as well as troops of the Egyptian 7th Division — all of whom were well dug-in and supported by well-sited anti-tank guns. As the Egyptians had laid a continuous belt of mines along the entire border of the Strip there was little to commend any one particular crossing place over any other. Once his armour had smashed or cleared a passage through the minefield it could fan out and use the roads inside the Strip, as the latter were unlikely to have been mined. The chief advantage in Khan Yunis as the nodal point for the Israeli assault derived however from the fact that it would be almost out of range of the guns of the T-54 tanks which the Egyptians were using to cover the town of Gaza. (The Gaza Strip, occupied by more than 750,000 people — many of them Palestinian refugees — is poor tank country, and the Egyptians had dug pits for the T-54s.) Once Tal's tanks had penetrated the Egyptian defences they would turn west to attack Rafa; when Rafa was taken the armour would continue along the coast road to El Arish. Behind them the reserve brigade which had been deployed opposite the Strip would clear the area and round up the remaining Egyptians.

This was to be the first land battle of the war and it was deemed to be the most important. No matter what the cost, the Israelis had to win. 'If we are to win the war', Tal told his men, 'we must win the first battle. The battle must be fought with no retreats, every objective must be taken — no matter what the cost in casualties. We must succeed or die...' This 'regardless of cost' policy was pursued until it became obvious that the war was won. Counted in blood the bill was high: official Israeli casualties for the fighting in Sinai were given as 275 killed and 800 wounded, which — expressed in American Vietnam terms (taking into account America's hundredfold larger population) — would be around 27,500 dead and 80,000 wounded. But the Israeli commanders knew that failure would have been disastrous and in the long run would have resulted in even more casualties. Israeli morale would have suffered and Egyptian morale would have received a corresponding boost.

Shortly after 0800hrs on the first morning of the war Tal received the green light for the Sinai offensive in the form of code-words Beni Or (Sons of Light, after the theme of the Dead Sea Scrolls), and Sadin Adom (Red Sheet). The first wave of Israeli planes was already on its way to the Egyptian airfields, and by the time Tal's tanks crossed the Sinai border half the Egyptian Air Force had been reduced to a charred mess of twisted metal. But neither the Israeli crews nor the Egyptian soldiers in Gaza knew anything of this.

As a battalion of Pattons, closely followed by another battalion of Centurions, raced across the desert towards the minefield, Israeli Fouga Magisters flew in to attack Egyptian artillery near Rafa. The assault was made on a front of just over half-a-mile wide and, as expected, mines accounted for the first Israeli casualties. Many of these mines were plastic, and as they could not be found with mine detectors, the Israelis made no attempt to clear them. The mines, other anti-tank obstacles, and surprisingly stiff Egyptian resistance slowed the Israelis' progress considerably. Casualties, both in men and vehicles, were heavy — although some of the tanks were quickly repaired and were soon back in action. Because the Israeli tank commanders habitually advanced with open turrets and signalled manually from them in action their casualty rate was high. The Israelis defended the practice on the grounds that the tank commanders had a better view and could react more quickly than their battened-down enemies. In a battle where the cost is secondary to the achievement of the objective it may be justified, in other circumstances the loss of trained tank commanders may well hazard future operations.

Once his two battalions of tanks had crossed the minefield and broken through the outer crust of defences, Tal's original plan was for the leading battalion of Pattons

to crash through Khan Yunis while the second battalion of Centurions veered west, bypassing the town and then down the main road to Rafa. Approaching Khan Yunis, however, the Pattons came under heavy fire from the Beni Souhila ridge to the east, and it was clear that the town was held in far greater strength than had been supposed. A quick change of plan followed. Bypassing the ridge, the Pattons attacked Khan Yunis from the north-west while the Centurions charged forward into the town instead of circling round it. As the converging columns of tanks pounded through the streets, white flags began to flutter from the shuttered windows and the firing died down. Pattons met Centurions in the market square where posters advertised the current film showing at the main cinema. By some ironic quirk of fate this was entitled *Help*. Sniping was to break out again later when the tanks resumed their advance and remnants of the Palestinian garrison ventured out of their hiding places. But the Israelis had attained their first objective. Leaving a company of infantry to mop up the town the Pattons and Centurions moved westwards towards Rafa.

Here again the Israelis were surprised by the strength and resistance of the defenders. A brigade of the 7th Egyptian Infantry Division and a battalion of the Palestinians supported by about 150 JS-3 tanks and 90 guns were holding four localities north and south of the town, and when the Israeli tanks appeared heavy fire was brought down on them. Tank after tank went up in flames as groups of anti-tank guns fired 10-round salvoes. 'We left there at Rafa many of our dead soldiers and burnt-out tanks' the Israeli brigade commander told a press conference later. To continue with the frontal attack would

Left: Casualty Clearing Station at Rafa.

Below: Colonel Rafael Eytan, a fighting commando soldier. In the 1967 Rafa battle he led the Isareli paratroop force; subsequently in 1973 he commanded the Golan theatre of operations.

Right: 'Winkling out' isolated Egyptians in the Rafa area.

clearly be suicidal, so another bypass was ordered. Swinging round the Egyptian positions, the tanks headed west to crash through the main street of Sheikh Zuweid, surprise its Egyptian garrison, and destroy an unsuspecting convoy of Egyptian vehicles on its way to a supply centre nearby. From there Tal's armour clattered on to the mouth of the Jiradi Pass about 10 miles beyond Sheikh Zuweid. Seven miles long, the narrow pass was held by one of the brigades of the 7th Egyptian Infantry Division, supported by T-34 tanks and artillery, and its approaches were heavily mined. The Egyptians were not expecting to be attacked. But without pausing, the Centurions roared straight into the pass and were almost through the defences before the defenders reacted. Only the last two of the Centurions were hit, but the Israeli convoy of lightly-armoured and thin-skinned supporting vehicles which was following was stopped by a devastating hail of fire. Meantime the Centurions had rattled on through the pass to the outskirts of El Arish unaware that they were on their own. There they stopped, to await the rest of the brigade which they assumed would be coming up behind them and for dusk when El Arish was scheduled to be hit by an Israeli air strike.

While all this was happening two battalions of Tal's attached parachute brigade had been driving across country further to the south. This force was heading for an old disused road running south from Rafa which the Israelis believed would provide an unopposed route into the Strip and enable them to get behind the Egyptian defences at Rafa. Good progress was made to the road and when it was reached the advance guard turned north — only to be stopped when the leading Patton tanks came under intense

Right: Israeli armour moving into the Rafa Junction area through the sand dunes south of the Gaza Strip, 5 June 1967.

Below: The tank battle at Rafa Junction.

fire. A brigade of the 7th Egyptian Infantry Division, supported by about 100 guns, 35 JS-35s and some T-34s, was deployed across this southern approach to Rafa, and from their well prepared defences the Egyptians were prepared to offer stout resistance. The Israeli Pattons charged the defensive perimeter head-on, and although their company commander — leaning out of the turret of his tank — was killed, the tanks crashed through the first line of Egyptian defences. But their troubles were only just beginning. At a second line of trenches the tanks were stopped by more anti-tank fire and the guns of some IS-3s. In the circumstances all they could do was to sheer away and these Pattons with a company of paratroops eventually carried on to the Rafa-El Arish road. There they had a successful little engagement in which they knocked out 22 Egyptian tanks. Meanwhile the main force of paratroops, following in half-tracks, had run straight into the trouble which had forced the Pattons off course. Halted and pinned down by fire, the commander quickly realised that he was not going to be able to fight his own way out of the situation, and he signalled Tal asking for help. Now that there was little danger of interference by Egyptian aircraft, the Israeli Air Force was able to cope with situations like this. Fouga Magisters quickly appeared on the scene to bomb and strafe the Egyptians in front of the paratroops. Tal also despatched a column of tanks to relieve the pressure, but the Egyptians had begun to pull out before they approached the battlefield. Battling their way forward against diminishing resistance, the paratroops cleared the area of pockets of defenders. Exhausted, scattered and urgently in need of fuel, the brigade reached the outskirts of Rafa as night descended.

Judging by the number of burnt out and disabled vehicles littering the Rafa-El Arish road by this time, the Egyptians had already suffered defeat. But the Gaza Strip behind Tal was still holding out. In Khan Yunis, which had been overrun in the morning, groups of Palestinians from the 20th Palestinian Division had formed pockets of resistance when the Israelis moved west. These groups had plenty of anti-tank weapons and the task of rooting them out eventually had to be undertaken by the paratroops who had fought the exhausting battle south of Rafa.

The town of Gaza, capital of the Strip and headquarters of the Egyptian administration, was even more fiercely defended. Both Gaza and Khan Yunis constituted a threat

Below: Israeli morning prayers in Gaza.

Above: **General Abdul Monan Husseini, the Egyptian Military Governor of Gaza.**

Right: The Israeli flag being hoisted at El Arish airfield.

to further Israeli advances while they were unoccupied, and as Gaza had political significance it was decided to capture it first. At dawn on Tuesday, the Second Day, four battalions of infantry and a battalion of Sherman tanks began to close in on the town from several directions. Their advance was covered by a heavy barrage of mortar and artillery fire, followed by a bombing strike by the Israeli Air Force, now jubilant at the victories of the day before. In this attack 14 UNEF soldiers were killed and 25 wounded when the UN building in Gaza where they were awaiting repatriation was hit by mortar fire. In the streets a fierce battle developed as the tanks literally shot their way into the centre of the town; while this was going on the civilian population cowered in hastily dug shelters. By Tuesday night the Israelis had the centre of Gaza and General Abdul Monon Husseini, the Military Governor, formally surrendered the town at 1020hrs on Wednesday morning. Sporadic fighting and sniping continued in Gaza for two more days while the Israelis combed out the Egyptians house by house. But as soon as it was clear that the back of the resistance was broken the Israelis turned their attention to Khan Yunis. Groups of Palestinians resisted stubbornly and there was a good deal of hard fighting before they were winkled out. Many of their positions fought on until they were actually overrun by tanks and it was Wednesday night before the Israelis could claim that resistance had completely collapsed.

While Tal's forces had been battling round Rafa one brigade of Yoffe's Ugda, 20 miles further south, had advanced across a sea of sand dunes towards Bir Lahfan, where it would be in a good position to prevent Egyptian reinforcements being sent to El Arish. Believing that the camel track running from the frontier to Bir Lahfan was impassable to vehicles the Egyptians were content to scatter a few mines and leave it unblocked. Loose sand made the going slow and Yoffe's Centurions took nine hours to cover 30 miles. Apart from a skirmish with the garrison of an Egyptian outpost and a fleeting glimpse of some Egyptian vehicles, however, the tanks reached the Abu Ageila-Bir Lahfan road without incident. But when the leading tanks turned up the road towards Bir Lahfan and El Arish they came under heavy fire. In the fading daylight further progress was not now possible, so the Centurions turned off the road to take up positions from which they could ambush any vehicles approaching the Bir Lahfan road junction from the south. Soon after dark they were joined by the rest of the brigade. Barely had the brigade settled into position when a convoy of vehicles was seen approaching from the direction of Jebel Libni. As expected the Egyptians were trying to reinforce their troops in

El Arish, and these vehicles constituted elements of an armoured brigade and part of a mechanised infantry brigade. The Israelis waited until the Egyptian convoy was almost on them; when they opened fire, the first shots hit three T-55 tanks. For a few moments the convoy was thrown in confusion, and all lights on the Egyptian vehicles were extinguished. Both sides started then to shoot at each other and fighting continued intermittently throughout the night.

Further south Ariel Sharon's Ugda had run into trouble. Sharon, it will be recalled, had been given the task of breaking into Sinai along the so-called Central Route. His objective was the Abu Ageila road junction, and before he could get there he had to smash through a strongly fortified position on the Um Katif plateau about 15 miles west of the Israeli border. Because the roads from El Arish, Jebel Libni and Kuseima all met at Abu Ageila and the key to Abu Ageila was Um Katif, there was no alternative to a direct assault. The Israelis could not afford to advance further into Sinai while leaving such a strongly held position behind them. Nor could Yoffe's second brigade advance until Abu Ageila had been taken. Like Tal's break-in operation this assault was considered to be in the 'regardless of cost' category.

At Um Katif the Egyptians were firmly established in defences ideally suited to the tactics they and their Russian advisers preferred. Their main position centred on a low ridge, wedged between a sandsea to the north and a rocky mountain massif known as Jebel Dalfa on the south. Behind a protective minefield 300 yards deep, three parallel lines of trenches nearly three miles long had been dug — with 300 yards between first and second — and 600 yards between the second and the third lines. Concrete emplacements had been set at intervals along the trenches and each line was held by an infantry battalion of the Egyptian 2nd Infantry Division. To support them, about ninety T-34s and SU-100s had been deployed and dug in behind the forward perimeter; further back, six regiments of artillery equipped with 122mm guns promised further support, and Schmel anti-tank projectors had been liberally distributed among the lines of infantry.

Sharon's original plan of attack was based on the premise that the Um Katif position was held by only one Egyptian battalion — which was in fact true until two days before the war started. As the cost of men and material was secondary to success, he decided that a direct frontal assault offered the best chance of a speedy break-through. Thus, shortly before 0900hrs on the Monday morning, Fouga Magisters struck the Egyptian positions and Sharon's Centurion battalion — followed by a company of mechanised infantry — charged across the undulating ground which lay between the Sinai border and the Um Katif. At the minefield, where seven of the Centurions were disabled, the charge came to a halt, and Sharon saw that he was not going to break into Um Katif by way of the front door. Another air strike was called up, and in this attack one of the planes was shot down — a fact which no doubt provided tremendous encouragement to the Egyptians. Meanwhile, Sharon had ordered the Centurions which had survived the minefield to veer northwards round the Um Katif plateau and follow a camel track which eventually joined the Abu Ageila road. At the same time his battalion of Shermans which had been advancing behind the Centurions were told to take over the front attack and to crash through Um Katif. During the air strike the Shermans were able to make some progress but as soon as the planes turned away the Egyptian guns poured a concentrated volume of fire on the advancing tanks, which compelled them to stop.

The Centurions, struggling up the camel track in single fire, had also been brought to a halt and compelled to shelter among the sand dunes. From their positions both the Centurions and the Shermans were able to shoot into the Egyptian defences. But they were pinned down by Egyptian fire even after dark, and any attempt to make another frontal assault would clearly have been suicidal. Sharon decided that his best means of breaking the impasse lay in an infantry assault on the flank of the Egyptian position. So his infantry was put into civilian buses and motored as far forward as the two-wheeled drive vehicles could get before they were bogged down in the sand. This was not far, and the heavily-laden infantry had to march the rest of the way. With 10 miles still to go it was several hours before they reached the area from which they would be ready to assault and 'roll up' the lines of Egyptian trenches.

While his infantry were tramping through the sand Sharon had been considering how best to silence the Egyptian artillery, and he had decided to give this task to his independent paratroop battalion. Having been promised 12 helicopters to lift the battalion into action he planned to put the paratroops down in the desert about three miles north of the Egyptian gun position. They would then attack at the same time as the main assault went in on Um Katif. In the event only six helicopters arrived, and when they were spotted landing in the desert the Egyptians mortared the landing zone and forced them to move back. This meant that the paratroops had farther to march, and the time of the combined assault to be put back. When Sharon received a signal saying that the air strikes he had asked for to soften up Um Katif had had to be called off (Jordan had entered the war and the Israeli Air Force's resources were being diverted to the fighting for Jerusalem), it seemed as if his Ugda was dogged by misfortune. But Sharon refused to be daunted. Massing his artillery, the biggest concentration of fire ever shot by the Israelis was put down on the Egyptian trench system. It was nearly midnight when this barrage was lifted, and the Israeli infantry, carrying coloured lights to show their positions to their gunner observers behind, launched their attack.

As the Israelis moved systematically along the parapets of the Egyptian trenches, shooting down into the firing bays, the Egyptians scrambled to the shelter of their dug-outs. Two miles west of this battle, the paratroops had also gone into action. They had reached the Egyptian artillery without undue difficulty, although the going through deep soft sand was a fatiguing business, and in one rush they had overrun some of the gun positions. But the Egyptians had rallied and the Israeli paratroops found themselves pinned down by small arms fire. When dawn came up at 0400hrs they had four dead and 13 wounded; and as the Israelis never abandoned their casualties the need for two men to carry each body reduced the effective strength of the original 150-strong paratroop force by a third. By this time, however, the battle for the trenches had reached a stage which enabled Sharon to call off the paratroop operation. With a mile of trenches already cleared, the armour was able to resume its advance on Sharon's real objective, Abu Ageila. So as the Shermans ground forward up and over Um Katif and then westwards along the axis of the road to Abu Ageila, the paratroops were ordered to pull out, and make their way through the sand dunes to the road east of Um Katif. At 0600hrs the battle was by no means over, but the road through Abu Ageila to Jebel Libni and beyond was open. Sharon's infantry brigade spent the rest of the day winkling out the Egyptians who still remained at Um Katif, while Sharon himself collected his armoured brigade and took it off to deal with Kusseima.

Yoffe's second armoured brigade (two battalions of Centurions and a mechanised infantry battalion) had been impatiently waiting for Sharon's troops to open the road through Abu Ageila. As soon as the Shermans fought their way past Um Katif, Yoffe's Centurions trundled up to the Abu Ageila road junction. There they turned north, heading towards Bir Lahfan where Centurions of Yoffe's other brigade, with the backs to the Egyptian defences at Bir Lahfan were having a tough battle with two Egyptian armoured brigades. To enable them to get through to Abu Ageila hundreds of Sharon's support vehicles — buses, milk trucks and almost every other form of civilian transport which had been pressed into service — had to be pushed clear of the track into the sand.

Once past the road junction the Israeli Centurions roared up to the Bir Lahfan tank battle, coming up behind on the flanks of the Egyptian T-55s. For some time the Egyptians fought back but they had been pounded by the Israeli Air Force since first light, and the Israeli Centurions, whose hitting power was greater than that of the T-55s, turned the scales. By 1000hrs the Egyptians had had enough, the survivors broke off the action to turn westwards into the desert. Behind them they left the victorious Israeli Centurions to reassemble amid the broken and smouldering wreckage of many Egyptian vehicles.

Above: The Abu Ageila road. Because of its importance as a major artery several bloody battles have been fought at this spot in the past 25 years.

With the Egyptian armour now in full retreat, Jebel Libni, where the Egyptians had built a large airfield, became the next objective of the Israelis in their advance into Central Sinai. Thus, as soon as his tanks were refuelled, Yoffe set off with one of his armoured brigades south-west towards Jebel Libni. Following close behind came Tal with one of his armoured brigades; some distance behind that the second of Tal's armoured brigades. Back at the Abu Ageila road junction the column turned west along the Central Route, and the leading tanks reached the outskirts of Jebel Libni about 1600hrs. As Yoffe's tanks swung left, Tal's leading brigade swung right to complete a pincer move which snapped tight on the airfield. As the Israeli tanks charged towards each other from opposite sides of the airfield, Israeli planes dived on Egyptian tanks deployed on and around the airfield. Several of these tanks were destroyed and others left their positions to rumble westwards into the desert. Seeing their tanks were leaving Egyptian infantrymen and gunners also left their positions and ran off into the desert. But the airfield was still strongly defended and the two Israeli brigades spent the night (Tuesday/Wednesday) on opposite sides of the airfield, resting, refuelling and planning a dawn attack.

At daybreak all went as the Israelis had planned; the Egyptian opposition suddenly collapsed and the airfield was quickly captured. Yoffe and Tal now parted company, with Yoffe's brigade taking the road south to Bir Hassana while Tal's force headed towards Bir Gifgafa to block the Central Route through the hills leading to Ismailia. Yoffe's advance guard arrived at Bir Hassana about 0900hrs on the morning of the third day (Wednesday). Racing towards their objective the Israeli tanks had overtaken and often intermingled with columns of retreating Egyptian vehicles.

In their haste to get away some of the Egyptian tanks fired at each other as well as at the Israelis; others simply left the road and drove off into the desert. In the event there was little opposition at Bir Hassana, which was lucky for the Israelis because Yoffe's prime concern now was to get ahead to the Mitla and Giddi Passes. Here he would be able to block the Egyptian escape routes and so cut off both the 'Shazli' Armoured Division and the 6th Egyptian Infantry Division whose troops were deployed along the 'Pilgrim's Way' between El Thamed and Nakhl.

Yoffe's Centurions were now beginning to show signs of the hammering to which they had been subjected over the past three days, and when it came to leaving Bir Hassana only 20 'runners' could be mustered. And by the time the eastern end of the Mitla Pass only nine of these were running under their own power, and they were perilously short of fuel. The remainder had either run out of petrol or were suffering from mechanical defects. As the column approached the mouth of the pass other columns of retreating Egyptians coming across the desert converged on them. But as the Egyptians also had Centurions the Israeli tanks were assumed to be theirs and without interference they were allowed to take up positions near the Parker Memorial, the stone monument to a former British administrator set on a hummock near the mouth of the pass. Once in position, the Israeli tanks were not long in showing which side they were on. Egyptian vehicles approaching the pass were either destroyed, damaged or dispersed; and the mouth of the pass soon became a graveyard cluttered with wrecked trucks and tanks. In the fading light a few vehicles did manage to weave their way through this litter, but they were bombed and strafed by the Israeli Air Force as they moved through the pass.

Further north a similar scenario was being enacted at the Ismailia Pass, a few miles west of Bir Gifgafa. But here the Israelis did not fare so well. After leaving Jebel Libni, Tal's force had run into trouble at Bir Hamma, where a brigade of the 3rd Egyptian Infantry Division supported by a battalion of T-34s and some SU-100 guns was defending the airfield. Under the cover of an Israeli air strike, Tal's Centurions charged the Egyptian positions. Within half an hour the battle was over, and the Egyptians had fled into the desert. With his reserve brigade now taking the lead, Tal's force sped westward again along the road to Bir Gifgafa. En route there was a brief exchange of fire between Tal's Pattons and some Egyptian T-55s, and when the Egyptians broke off and fled their supply vehicles fell into Israeli hands. For Tal, whose vehicles — like those of Yoffe — were now running desperately short of petrol, this was welcome booty indeed.

Bir Gifgafa was surrounded by a sprawling complex of military installations. But it was the fact that the lateral road from Bir Thamada terminated here which was the important issue for Tal at this time. Yoffe had been ordered to block the Mitla and Giddi Passes in the south, and if the retreating Egyptians could not get past him only the Ismailia Pass remained open to them. As the Israeli tanks left Bir Gifgafa to attack the defensive positions at the mouth of the pass there was a clear indication that the Egyptians were already being forced to use this escape route. A cloud of dust disclosed the approach of a long column of vehicles; it was part of the Egyptian 4th Armoured Division which had been ordered to fall back to take up positions on the Central Ridge behind the Ismailia Pass. Tal promptly ordered every tank he had in the area to attack the Egyptians in the flank. So began a

Left: **The Israeli Air Force destroyed Egyptian air power in three hours. After that its planes dominated the skies completely and inflicted devastating damage on the Arab armies. (Aerial photograph of the Mitla Pass.)**

Right: The first Israelis reached the Suez Canal on the morning of 8 June 1967.

bloody battle which continued until night descended — by which time the Israelis had exhausted most of their ammunition and fuel. About a dozen T-55 tanks and 50 Egyptian armoured personnel carriers were destroyed and hundreds of Egyptian soldiers were killed in the course of the fighting. The Israelis also suffered heavy casualties, however, and — for the first time since the beginning of the war — Egyptian planes appeared over the battlefield. Israeli aircraft were quickly on the scene, but in the ensuing dogfights one Israeli plane returning from a raid in the Canal area was shot down.

Although Tal's forces had inflicted heavy punishment, the fact remained that it had failed to close the vital Ismailia Pass. All that night vehicles of the 4th Egyptian Armoured Division streamed through it, and the Israelis had to stand up to a strong counter-attack which drove them back from the positions they had taken to harass the traffic approaching the pass. But when dawn broke on the morning of the fourth day, Thursday, Tal's tanks returned to the battle — reinforced, reorganised and refuelled. When they began their advance, slowly and methodically clearing the series of defensive positions which obstructed them, the Egyptians steadily gave ground. Yet again the Centurions demonstrated their superiority over the T-54s and T-55s which the Egyptians had deployed along the five mile stretch of road leading to the mouth of the pass. The Israeli planes, which signalled the exact location of the Egyptian tanks and then dropped napalm on them, can also be credited with making a major contribution to the success of the operation. By 1600hrs some 40 Egyptian tanks had been destroyed for the loss of only two Israeli tanks, and shortly after that the Egyptians broke off the battle, withdrew their tanks and tried to get them back through the pass. Crammed with vehicles frantically trying to force their way back towards the Canal, the Ismailia road became a bomber's dream, which the Israeli Air Force was not slow to take advantage of. Blazing napalm and bombs created an inferno from which the only escape was on foot.

Behind the fleeing Egyptians the Israeli Centurions crashed through the pass, dragging or pushing wrecked and disabled vehicles aside to clear the way for Tal's Patton battalion to race through to the Suez Canal. The Egyptians had had neither time nor opportunity to organise any defensive line between the Ismailia Pass and there was virtually no opposition between there and the Canal crossings. Everything had happened so quickly and the confusion, consequent on the false information fed to them by the Arab radio had been so complete, many Egyptians could not comprehend the extent of the military disaster which had overtaken them. When Tal's leading Pattons approached the Canal in the early hours of the morning of Friday, 9 June, Egyptians on the Canal bank flagged them down with flashing torches, thinking that the Pattons were Egyptian tanks making for the bridge across the Canal.

Tanks from Yoffe's Ugda reached the Canal bank farther south about two hours after Tal arrived opposite Ismailia. Setting out from the Eastern end of the Mitla Pass at dawn on the Thursday (the fourth day) it was noon before Yoffe's vehicles emerged at the Egyptian end, 15 miles away. As at the Ismailia Pass the narrow road through Mitla was choked with the debris of war, and many burnt-out and wrecked vehicles had to be pushed aside before the Israeli tanks could get through. When they did arrive at the western end of the pass they were met by Israeli paratroops who had been put down by helicopter to seal off the pass. Meantime Yoffe's other armoured brigade had raced 20 miles north from Mitla to block the sole remaining avenue of Egyptian escape: the Giddi Pass. Under cover of darkness many Egyptian vehicles had already slipped through this pass and a battalion of T-55s and T-54s remained in its defence when the Israelis arrived on the scene. The same tactics as Tal had employed at the Ismailia Pass were repeated here, and by 1900hrs Yoffe's tanks and Israeli aircraft had shot, bombed, strafed and napalmed a clear route through the pass. From its western mouth the Canal was less than 30 miles distant and Centurions raced forward to take up positions opposite Port Suez.

Troops of a composite Israeli force which had motored along the coast road from El Arish were, in fact, the first to reach the Canal. Starting out in the early hours of Wednesday morning, after mopping up operations in Khan Yunis were considered as good as over, a scratch force had charged along the road with headlights blazing. Israeli aircraft had reported that the Egyptians appeared to have no set defences between El Arish and the Canal, so it was possible to throw caution to the winds. Apart from a few shots fired by the bewildered occupants of supply dumps and staging camps as the Israeli vehicles roared past, there was, in fact, no opposition until the Israelis passed Romani, a small coastal town about 40 miles from Port Said. Shortage of fuel compelled a halt here, and the Israelis snatched a few hours' rest before setting off again at dawn on Thursday morning. By now the Egyptians had been alerted to their presence and the Israelis' progress was slowed down by increasing opposition. Blocks held by Egyptian commando troops supported by T-55s brought delays; so too did a number of attacks by the Egyptian Air Force. A fierce battle developed a few miles from Kantara, a fair-sized town on the Canal bank — close to the El Firdan railway bridge, which the Egyptians were intent on holding to get some of their own tanks back across the Canal. When the Israeli Air Force was called in, however, the way was opened. At 2000hrs the first Israeli troops entered the now deserted town of Kantara and began to close in on the bridge. By dawn they had cleared the area of Egyptians, and had seized the Sinai end of the bridge. Soon after that a patrol from Tal's force opposite Ismailia contacted them on the Canal bank.

This virtually spelt the end of the war in the Sinai. But the account would not be complete without mention of the vicissitudes of Sharon's Ugda after the battle at Um Katif, and of the seizure of Sharm-El-Sheikh.

Sharon, with one armoured brigade had set off from Um Katif about 0800hrs on the Wednesday morning (the third day); his men, dog tired after the battle, had rested, and his vehicles had been replenished. Sharon's task now was to seek out and destroy the 'Shazli' Armoured Division; but he was ordered to hold off until Kuseima had been secured by the independent brigade which had been sitting opposite Kuseima and which so far had seen no action. As the 2nd Egyptian Infantry Division had been deployed in and around Kuseima this was the logical course to take. In the event, however, the 2nd Egyptian Infantry had crept away while Sharon's men were sleeping and when the Israeli tanks probed cautiously forward the Egyptian positions were found to be deserted.

With Kuseima empty, Sharon's Ugda drove south towards Nakhl. Not until they were about 20 miles from Nakhl was there any opposition. Then, near a long ridge known as Jebel Karim, the leading vehicles ran into a minefield and a jeep was blown up. When the bullets began to fly, it seemed that the Israelis had arrived at the outposts of the 6th Egyptian Infantry Division and that Egyptians were still occupying their defences. As it was now dark, Sharon decided to halt, refuel, to rest and to wait for daylight before trying to push on.

Once again his enemies slipped through Sharon's fingers. The main body of the Shazli Division, which Sharon had set out to destroy, was already haring back towards the Giddi Pass and the Egyptian rearguard slipped away while the Israelis sat the night out at the edge of the minefield. Nearly all the infantrymen from the brigade which had been holding the position where Sharon had called a halt had also piled into their trucks and headed towards the Suez Canal (although few of them got away because they ran into Yoffe's Centurions at the Mitla Pass, or were bombed out of existence by Israeli aircraft). Consequently

when dawn broke on Thursday morning Sharon's troops faced an empty position; the only evidence of the Egyptians being abandoned tanks and guns.

So Sharon resumed his advance towards Nakhl, where he hoped to intercept the second brigade of the 6th Division. The latter had been deployed around Kuntilla but it had pulled out during the night, and set off back for Suez along the Pilgrims' Way. Sharon arrived at Nakhl before the Egyptians, blocked the Pilgrim's Way east of the town with a battalion of Shermans, and lined the eastern approach with concealed Centurions and mechanised infantry. The Egyptians drove straight into the ambush and were caught in criss-cross fire on the ground. Behind them followed the Israeli independent brigade which had faced them across the border opposite Kuntilla, so there was no going back. From above the relays of Israeli aircraft, which had pursued them from the moment they abandoned their defences, bombed, napalmed and strafed them. In desperation the Egyptians tried to fight their way past Sharon, but time and again they were beaten back. When night came and the fighting died down, the road between Thamed and Nakhl had taken on the now familiar appearance of the major defiles in Sinai, and was choked with destroyed and abandoned guns and vehicles.

So the Egyptian Army in Sinai was defeated. Sharm-El-Sheikh was captured by a combined naval and

Left: Air supply to the Sharon Ugda near Kuseima.

Above: An Egyptian SAM-2 missile abandoned in its emplacement.

Right: Suez town under fire.

paratroop operation and the Israeli flag was raised there on the Wednesday morning (the third day). As military operations go, this one was of little significance since the Egyptians had withdrawn all but one company of infantry before the Israelis arrived. When the UN soldiers evacuated Sharm-El-Sheikh on 23 May they had destroyed the desalination plant and the Egyptian garrison sent in to take over was faced with the problem of getting fresh water. The few wells which existed were inadequate for the numbers of troops sent to Sharm-El-Sheikh and water had to be shipped in from Suez. Until hostilities broke out this was feasible, but when war began the Israeli Air Force and three Israeli Motor Torpedo Boats operating from Elat stopped water boats.

Following the occupation of Sharm-El-Sheikh, sailors from the Israeli MTBs landed on Nas Nazrani and found it to be deserted. The Straits of Tiran, whose closure had precipitated the war, were now open to Israeli shipping and Elat could breathe again. Finally, on Wednesday afternoon, a detachment of paratroops was flown in helicopters from Sharm-El-Sheikh and set down at El Tur, a small oil centre in the Gulf of Suez, on the west coast of Sinai and about fifty miles from its tip. From there the paratroops moved north to link up with the Israelis on the Canal.

On Thursday 8 June, Israel's flag flew all along the Suez Canal, and the Straits of Tiran were open. After only four days' fighting the Egyptian air and land forces had been crushed; the sands of Sinai were strewn with the burnt-out wrecks of hundreds of armoured vehicles; about 300 tanks, 500 pieces of artillery, 10,000 trucks and vast quantities of other equipment had fallen into Israeli hands. Much of this equipment of Soviet origin, such as the T-55 tanks and SU-57 self-propelled guns, was of considerable interest to the NATO countries — as was the equipment and layout of the SAM missile site which was overrun between the Mitla Pass and the Canal.

Egyptian casualties ran into thousands: how many thousands is still a matter for speculation. Egyptian figures published at the end of June 1967 stated that 5,000 soldiers had been killed in action. Some months later Nasser said that some 1,500 officers and 10,000 soldiers had been killed and that 500 officers and 5,000 soldiers had been taken prisoner. On these figures the number of wounded could run as high as 50,000 or even more. Prisoners, to the Israelis, were an embarrassment and they shuttled most of the hordes of men who succeeded in tramping through the desert across the Canal. Only the officers were held in captivity, and at the end of the war the Israelis announced that they had some 3,000.

Israeli casualties in Sinai were given as 275 killed and 800 wounded. The greater proportion of these were probably incurred in the 'break-in' battles on the first and second days of the war when the Israelis' concern for success in battle outweighed consideration of the cost in terms of lives. On these two days also many Egyptians stood their ground and fought extremely well. Subsequently, when the Israeli Air Force had completed its prime task of destroying the Arab air forces, and turned to the ground support of Israeli troops, the Egyptians' morale suffered and they did not fight so hard. The fact remains that the totality of the Egyptian defeat, and the brilliance of both conception and execution of the plan which brought about Israel's victory, almost defy belief.

Below: Egyptian PoW.

THE JORDANIAN FRONT

Right up to the time the first Jordanian shells crashed down on the suburbs of New Jerusalem the Israelis had been hoping that Jordan would stay out of the war. It was a rational hope, but in the Middle East the rational things are least likely to happen.

What was to be the final appeal for peace was made shortly after the outbreak of war with Egypt. In a message addressed to King Hussein which was sent via General Odd Bull, the UN Commander at Government House in Jerusalem, the Israeli Government promised that if Jordan would keep the peace, so too would they. This was a political promise to which Israel's military commanders gave their full support, for they had no desire to open a second front at this stage of the war. Faced by Jordan's seven infantry and two armoured brigades — five of which were deployed on the west bank of the Jordan — Israel's military resources could stretch only to the modest provision for a holding action until the battle for Sinai had been resolved. And there was good reason to suppose that Hussein would hesitate before entering the war. Despite his recent pact with Nasser, the experience of 1956, Nasser's constant hostility right up to signing of the pact and the fragility of the Jordanian Army, all provided grounds for believing that Hussein would opt for caution.

Unfortunately the emotional build-up in Jordan had swept pragmatic considerations aside and the optimistic Israeli conjectures were shattered at about 1100hrs on 5 June. Until then Jerusalem was relatively quite, and life went on much as usual. There were few signs of Israeli soldiers or military vehicles on the streets of New Jerusalem and the supermarket at the corner of the Avenue George V and Goshon Agron Street was so crowded and noisy that nobody heard the first shells. From the Arab heights above Jerusalem, Jordanian artillery and mortars rained down on targets in the Israeli sector of the city, while long-range guns reached across Israel's narrow waist to hit the outskirts of Tel Aviv. Syrian artillery on the hill overlooking the Sea of Galilee was also firing on towns in northern Israel. But it was New Jerusalem which suffered the worst damage and most of its residents spent the next two days sheltering from the constant bombardment. Only those who were compelled to do so ventured above ground; yet more than 500 civilians were killed and wounded by Jordanian shells. None of the Jewish areas of the partitioned city were spared and the houses of the Prime Minister, the Israeli President, and the Mayor of Jerusalem were all damaged by Jordanian shells. When the glass panels of showcases in the Israel Museum were shattered the Isaiah Scroll — the most complete of the Dead Sea Scrolls — was hastily moved to an underground vault. One of the famous Chagall stained-glass windows in the Hadassah Medical Centre's Synagogue was smashed, but the remainder were removed to safety before the tempo of the shelling increased. From France, Chagall wrote: 'I am not worried about the windows, only about the safety of Israel. Let Israel be safe and I will make you lovelier windows'.

The Israelis did not return the Jordanian fire for two hours. But as the shelling, mortar and small-arms fire steadily got worse it was clear that an ugly situation was developing. Up to about noon on the Monday morning the Israelis clung to the belief that Hussein was merely trying to show Nasser that he was fulfilling his side of the military pact, and that he had no intention of putting up a serious fight. If he was determined to throw Jordan into the fight, however, Israel would not remain on the defensive. Israeli army intelligence had a shrewd idea of the Arab plan for 'recovering' Palestine and Jordan's role included a thrust west to link up with an Egyptian drive east across the Negev. If these attacks were to succeed Israel would be cut into three; and while the Negev attack might be contained, the geography of Israel gave a Jordanian thrust a passable chance of victory. From the Jordan border it was only 12 miles to the Israeli coast at Tel Aviv — a determined armoured column could smash across that in a few hours. Israeli plans were therefore based on preventing the Jordanians' armour from rolling down to Tel Aviv, although the key to the opening stages of the battle was a political one — the Old City of Jerusalem. For a people to whom Jerusalem had such spiritual concern, this was the most precious goal. Without Jerusalem as its capital Israel could be compared to a body without its soul. But there were also good strategic reasons why the partition arrangement of 1948 should be amended. With Jerusalem and a wide access to the sea the Israelis would be able to consolidate their foothold in the Judean heartland, and there would no longer be the danger of their state degenerating into a coastal enclave clinging to the Mediterranean.

In essence the Israeli plan was to isolate the battle for Jersualem, while concentrating their main effort on the destruction of the Arab Legion formations along the entire length of the west bank of the Jordan. The plan was put into effect when the Israelis realised that Hussein was not going to be satisfied with a token gesture of support for the Arab cause.

It was an attempt to occupy Government House that triggered off the battle for Jerusalem. If only because Government House was in demilitarised territory and about 100 UN personnel were sheltering there, this was asking for trouble as it brought King Hussein into direct conflict with the United Nations. General Odd Bull, the UN commander, called for a cease fire but the Jordanians ignored the appeal, and by 1300hrs they had occupied the tiny wood which separated Government House from the adjacent farm. At this point the Israelis reacted.

Command of the Israeli troops in Jerusalem had been entrusted to Brigadier Uzi Narkiss, a veteran of the Israelis' War of Independence. In 1948 he had fought as a battalion commander under Brigadier Yitzhak Rabin to hold Jerusalem, and it had been his sad duty to order a company under the command of Mordecai Gur to fall back from the Zion Gate. Rabin was now Chief of Staff, and Gur a brigade commander who was shortly to find himself again under Narkiss's command. All three — Rabin, Narkiss and Gur — were men born in Jerusalem who had always hoped they might see the Wailing Wall again. And now they might.

At 1430hrs on Monday afternoon, two companies of Israeli infantry and six Shermans crossed the 1948 armistice line and advanced on Government House. These

Operations on the Western Bank and in Jerusalem, 5-7 June 1967.

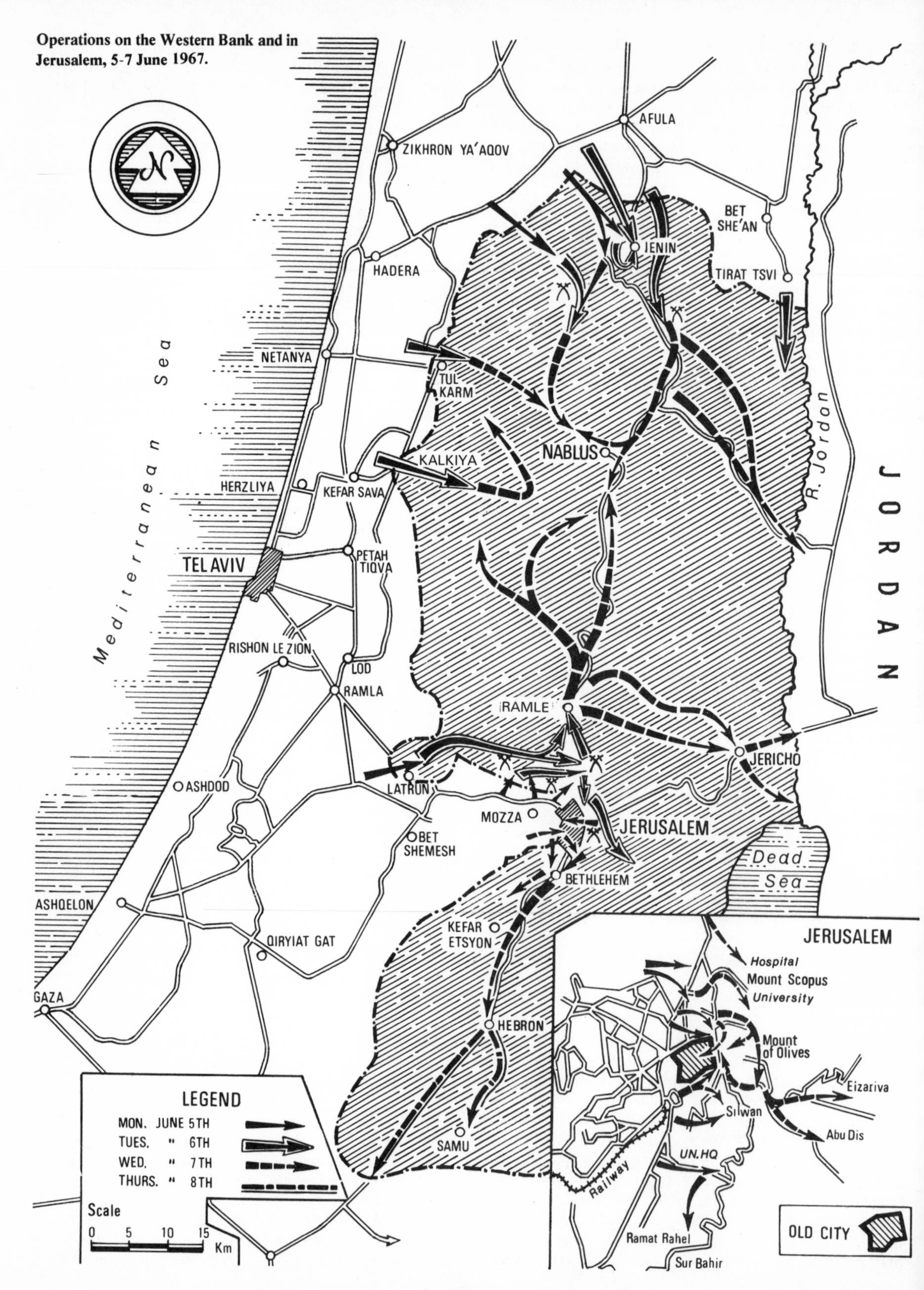

troops were from one of the three battalions of the only Israeli brigade which Narkiss could call on at that time. Like the rest of the brigade the men were all reservists who lived and worked in the Jerusalem area — a fact which was to confer and immense advantage in the street fighting which was to come. By 1500hrs, following a brief and bloody encounter which cost the Israelis eight and the Jordanians 18 dead, the Israeli flag was flying above Government House. This enabled General Odd Bull and the remainder of the UN personnel to be evacuated to Tel Aviv.

Meanwhile Jordanian forces in Samaria — the area which constituted the northern province of Jordan on the West Bank — had been reported by Israeli aircraft to be moving south. What the reconnaissance aircraft had seen was the 60th Jordanian Armoured Brigade trundling from Jericho towards Jerusalem, and its replacement, the 40th Jordanian Armoured Brigade, on its way from Damiya Bridge to Jericho. General Riad, the Egyptian general who was now directing Jordan's war against Israel, had persuaded Hussein to ask Syria for troops to block any Israeli sallies into northern Jordan and the West Bank. Confident that these reinforcements would soon be on their way he had ordered the 60th Brigade to move to the Ramallah Ridge, the sausage-shaped plateau which dominated the northern approach to Jerusalem and part of the Jewish quarters of the city. Realising that if the Jordanians succeeded in establishing themselves on the ridge they would be able either to hit the Israeli forces in Jerusalem in the flank or to encircle them, Narkiss resolved to seize the ridge first. Now that battle was joined and the situation in Jerusalem promised a hard and tough fight Narkiss had been allocated more troops. The three battalions of a reservist armoured brigade which had assembled at Ramle was already on its way towards Jerusalem; and a parachute brigade, consisting of one regular and two reserve battalions of paratroopers, which had been briefed for an airborne attack on El Arish was hurriedly diverted to Jerusalem. The paratroopers had no armoured vehicles, but they were tough and self-sufficient infantrymen ideally suited to tasks which Narkiss had in mind for them. Two other infantry brigades — one of which had concentrated near Latrun on Israel's geographical waist, and the other near Kalkiya — were also placed under Narkiss's command about the same time.

As soon as the armoured brigade arrived from Ramle, Narkiss threw it straight into the fray. Its objective was the Ramallah ridge, on which a three-pronged attack was mounted. As the approaches to the main ridge were heavily mined and the brigade had no flail tanks, Israeli infantrymen had to walk in front — probing and clearing a path for the Shermans which followed. Only six tanks were put out of action in the course of this advance, but it cost the lives or limbs of 40 Israelis. Beyond the minefields the Jordanians were established in a number of concreted strongpoints: Radar Hill, Abdul Aziz Hill and the village of Beit Iksa. Each was tackled in succession, with the Shermans firing at point blank range into individual strongpoints until all Jordanian resistance ceased. By midnight the three Israeli columns had converged on the first crest of the main Ramallah Ridge. After clearing Biddu, a fortified village on the main ridge, the whole brigade turned east and moved along the road to Nebi Samuel — the burial place of the Prophet Samuel, which Christian pilgrims throughout the ages have called the Hill of Joy. Aided by flares the Israeli tanks enveloped Nebi Samuel in a pincer movement, overran the key village of Beit Hanina and then swept on eastwards.

South of this road junction a battalion of Jordanian infantry was holding positions on the road leading to Jerusalem. As these positions blocked the way south to the Israeli enclave at Mount Scopus north-east of the Holy City, one of the Israeli armoured battalions was ordered to break through. However, just as the Israeli Shermans were getting into position to assault the outlying Jordanian position at Shafat, a battalion of Jordanian Pattons was seen to be heading towards Tel El Ful. It was one of the battalions of the 30th Armoured Brigade, en route from Jericho, which had been detailed to secure Tel El Ful. Swinging round, the Shermans just had time to gain the Ramallah road and get into ambush positions before the Pattons arrived. A bloody tank battle then ensued, with both sides slogging hard at each other at close range. When the Jordanians broke off at about 1000hrs, six Pattons had been destroyed and 11 others were abandoned on the battlefield. Israeli casualties included three Shermans.

With Tel El Ful indisputably in their possession the Israelis now turned their attention back to Shafat. Following a combined armour and infantry attack Shafat quickly fell. The positions covering the defile of Givat Hamivtar were the next objective. These, and the defences of French Hill, completed the Jordanian defensive arc shielding Jerusalem from the north, and they were vital to the Jordanians. Tough resistance was met at Givat Hamivtar which had to be assaulted three times before the Jordanian defenders were overhelmed. Even tougher resistance was met at French Hill, where five Israeli tanks were knocked out by Jordanian anti-tank weapons and both sides sustained many casualties in bitter hand to hand fighting. By 1700hrs however, the Israelis had smashed their way through to their enclave on Mount Scopus, and the battle for Jerusalem was approaching its military climax.

In other sectors of the central front the Israelis were bent on smashing the Jordanians along the entire length of the west bank. While his armoured brigade was forcing its way up to the Ramallah Ridge in the north, Narkiss decided to cut the Jordanian road south from Jerusalem to Bethlehem. The battalion which had taken Government House was ordered to advance south along the spur on which Government House stood and to secure the Jordanian village of Sur Behir, which dominated the road to Bethlehem. But the village was defended by two strong-points, and although the Israelis gained a foothold in the village on the Monday night, they were driven out by a Jordanian counter-attack. Next morning the Israelis returned to the offensive and during the course of the morning the Sur Bahir ridge was slowly and painfully cleared. Then, at noon, another Israeli battalion, supported by Shermans, crashed through the barbed wire fence of the 1948 Armistice Line between Government House and Mount Zion to clear the warren of houses forming the Abu Tur

Above: Israeli border police calling on the inhabitants of Jenin to remain calm.

Above right: The Arab population of Jenin returning to their homes after the fighting.

district of Jerusalem proper. Progress was slow, the house-to-house fighting was bitter, and the advancing Israelis came under increasing mortar fire from the Old City. By 1900hrs a small area near the Pool of Siloam had been cleared but casualties were such that Narkiss decided to pull the battalion back to Abu Tur.

While Narkiss's armour was rolling up the heights towards Ramallah another Israeli Ugda swung into action against the northern section of the Jordanian front. Commanded by Brigadier Elad Peled, Director of Israel's National Defence College, this Ugda of one armoured brigade, one infantry brigade and a number of independent infantry units, had been formed to deal with any hostile moves by the Syrians. When it was clear the Syria was not going to attack anywhere and that Jordan presented the more immediate and important threat, Peled was given fresh orders. While a battalion of infantry created a diversion by marching southwards from Tirat Tsvi along a track on the west side of the Jordan River, two separate armoured columns set off from Mediddo (in Israel) crossed the border at Moshav Ramon and headed for Jenin. A battery of the 'Long Toms' which had been shelling Tel Aviv was overrun en route, and at 0300hrs on the Tuesday morning (the second day) the Israeli armour closed in on Jenin.

Within minutes the Israeli Shermans were halted by a battalion of Jordanian Pattons concealed in the olive groves round the town and waiting for them. The Israelis quickly recovered and a second assault was attempted. But when this failed they decided to try a ruse. Turning, the Shermans moved slowly back the way they had come, leaving their disabled vehicles behind and leading the Jordanians to the conclusion that the Israelis were withdrawing. Breaking cover the Pattons gave chase. This was a fatal mistake, which ended with the virtual annihilation of the whole Jordanian battalion. Once this tank battle had been resolved the Israelis turned back to Jenin, and although the Jordanians fought hard the town was in Israeli hands by 0730hrs.

About this time, however, Israeli aircraft reported about 60 Jordanian Pattons approaching Jenin from the south-east along the Nablus road. These were, in fact, two battalions of the 40th Jordanian Armoured Brigade returning to their former position after a fruitless journey to Jericho to relieve the 60th Brigade. To counter this sudden new threat the Israeli tanks had to go back through Jenin before they could turn south, and when the inhabitants saw this happening, they assumed that the Israelis were withdrawing. White flags fluttering from the windows of

houses were hastily pulled in, rifles, machine guns and bazookas which had been concealed during the Israeli advance reappeared and the shooting flared up. This second round of fighting temporarily made life difficult for the Israelis who were trying to get out to meet the approaching Pattons. But the Israeli infantry who were left behind systematically broke this resistance, and by 1pm the shooting had been quelled and the town of Jenin was quiet.

Meanwhile Peled's Shermans had met the Jordanian Pattons, which were advancing in two columns — the first being 15 miles ahead of the second. When the first Pattons spotted the Israeli Shermans they sheered off the road and deployed in positions they had occupied previously in the Kabatiya Hills. The Israelis charged on, only to run into an ambush staged by the second lot of Pattons, in which 17 Shermans were destroyed. Reforming, the remaining Shermans turned to charge through the ambush and suffered more casualties. Two Israeli air strikes were launched during the afternoon but they failed to dislodge the Jordanians and when night fell the tanks of both sides still faced each other across a valley dominated by the Kabatiya Hills. Next day, however, when the overwhelming power of the Israeli Air Force was put to use, the Israelis' fortune changed. Wave after wave of Mystères and Mirages skimmed over the battlefield between Jenin and Nablus or dived into the valley of the River Jordan beyond. Rockets and napalm rained down on the Jordanians and after eight hours the resistance was broken. The battle for Jerusalem had not been resolved by Wednesday afternoon (the third day) but Jordan was already beaten. The whole of the West Bank was as good as in Israeli hands and the famous Arab Legion had almost ceased to exist. At 1330hrs King Hussein told his troops that Jordan would continue to fight 'to the last breath and last drop of blood'. But the Security Council's call for a cease-fire was now his only chance of holding his crumbling nation together.

Before turning back to the sequence of events in Jerusalem, brief mention must be made of the capture of Latrun, the strategic village between the coastal plain and the inland mountains. The terra cotta roof of the massive stone Trappist monastery at Latrun can be seen for miles. This was built in 1890 next to a Crusader fortress, the Touron de Chevaliers, which had been built to guard the road to Jerusalem; the village stands on a little rise above the monastery. Near the top of a Jordanian salient which jutted into Israel, Latrun was on the old Jerusalem-Tel Aviv road, twenty miles from Tel Aviv and fifteen from Jerusalem. In 1948 the Latrun defile constituted the gateway to Jerusalem and it had witnessed some desperate fighting. Because the Israelis had repeatedly failed to capture the defile they had had to reroute a 20-mile stretch of road to Jerusalem round the Judean foot-hills, and for 19 years the old road was barred with a sign 'Stop'. 'Frontier'. So Latrun was a place of bitter Israeli memories and its capture on Tuesday afternoon (the second day) by an Israeli infantry brigade made a prestige gain. There was little more than token resistance and most of the Jordanian garrison withdrew. Fanning out from Latrun the Israelis cleared the salient during Wednesday morning, and an armoured column drove east towards Ramallah. That the Jordanians still had teeth and were prepared to use them was evident when the Israeli column ran into a road block, which was taken only after a brisk battle. Once this obstacle had been cleared, however, the Israeli infantry from Latrun were able to drive on and by late afternoon they had linked up with Narkiss's armoured brigade holding the Ramallah road junction. The setting for the vital battle for Jerusalem was now complete.

The inhabitants of Jerusalem were still taking cover. News of Israeli victories in Sinai were beginning to percolate into the shelters of New Jerusalem, although Radio Damascus was still ranting about the 'hours of revenge' and exhorting 'Arab brothers' to 'get on to Tel Aviv'. But Radio Cairo and Radio Amman were less belligerent now, for defeatism had begun to set in at the headquarters of the UAR and Jordanian High Command. Shells and mortar bombs continued to fall in Jerusalem, however, and bursts of machine gun fire swept the streets near the walls of the Old City when Narkiss issued his order for a night attack to seize the Mount Scopus Ridge from which the Israelis would be able to look down on the Holy City.

The 27th Infantry Brigade of the Arab Legion were manning the formidable concrete and stone emplacements along the 1948 Armistice Line. In front of these defences a wide stretch of open ground had been literally strewn with mines and other obstacles. Bangalore torpedoes and explosive charges were used to clear paths, but the Israeli infantry suffered heavy casualties in the process. And once through the minefield they were plunged into desperate hand-to-hand fighting for the strong points which lay behind. Every yard of communication trench was contested, and when once these had been cleared there still remained the houses in which the retreating Jordanian troops took refuge and fought back. This was the biggest and fiercest infantry battle of the whole war; casualties were heavy on both sides, and it was here that the Arabs inflicted the worst damage on the Israelis.

Perhaps the toughest nut to crack of all the Jordanian defensive positions was Ammunition Hill, near the Police Training School. This was held by about 200 of the Arab Legion and the five-hour battle to evict them is generally acknowledged to be the fiercest engagement in all the Arab-Israeli operations so far. There were no glorious charges by tanks here — Mordechai Gur's paratroopers who took the position had to fight from bunker to bunker. And when they emerged from the maze of trenches, battered but triumphant, Ammunition Hill had cost them about 50 dead and three times as many wounded. Behind them lay 106 dead Jordanians, and every man of the remainder of the garrison wounded.

The paratroopers' task was not completed yet. The Police School stood at the entrance to the warren of houses known as the Sheikh Jarrah district, which for 19 years had threatened the northern suburbs of New Jerusalem and cut off the road to the Mount Scopus enclave. More bloody house-to-house fighting took place before it was overrun.

Meantime more of Gur's paratroopers had crossed the Armistice Line near the Mandelbaum Gate — the UN-controlled 'gate' between Israel and Jordan. In two columns the sweating paratroopers systematically battered their way through the buildings of the district known as the American Colony. Progress was slow, but it would have been slower still without the support of the artillery, tanks and Israeli aircraft which were called to assist. Two searchlights mounted on the tall Histradut building in New Jerusalem were used to indicate targets at night, and by day the Israelis hung flags from the buildings they had captured to show the limits of their advance. Houses that could not be overwhelmed by infantry fire-power were dealt with at point-blank range by Shermans, and covered lanes were blasted through the houses for the evacuation of casualties and replenishment of ammunition.

With the capture of Sheikh Jarrah and the American Colony districts there came a lull in the fighting, broken only by the occasional sniper's shot or the explosion of a grenade. The Jordanians, soldiers and civilians alike, had evacuated the streets and houses outside the walls of the Old City and fled eastwards. For the Israelis who badly needed a breathing space to rest and replenish the relative calm was a welcome respite. It did not last long; from behind Jerusalem's ramparts the Arab Legion rallied and returned to the battle. From the high walls of the Old City Jordanian snipers picked off Israeli troops, and any movement which could be seen from the walls attracted a barrage of mortar and artillery fire from weapons sited on the Augusta Victoria Ridge behind the Mount of Olives. So

Left: Moshe Dayan, General Rabin and Brigadier Uzi Narkiss enter the old city of Jerusalem.

Right: Israeli bazooka team in Jerusalem's old city.

Below: Israeli officer with a Greek Orthodox priest in the Holy City, 7 June 1967.

Below right: Dayan, a keen archaeologist, in the old city.

the paratroops, who by now had reached the Rockefeller Museum, were ordered into action again.

The first attack was a failure. As the paratroops advanced across the open ground towards their objective, the Augusta Victoria Ridge, they were met with a hail of mortar bombs and small-arms fire. They could not move, and the Sherman tanks which attempted to force a passage forward were driven back to the shelter of the built up area by accurate and effective Jordanian anti-tank fire, bazookas fired from the Old City wall and guns located on the ridge. When two air strikes on the ridge failed to silence these guns Narkiss decided to wait until dusk and the attack was called off. The second attack was no more successful. Within minutes of the Shermans crossing the start-line three of them had been knocked out, and casualties among the paratroopers were mounting at an alarming rate. So Narkiss again called off the attack; he would wait, he decided, until 2300hrs. By that time he would be able to organise and coordinate a more powerful assault.

In the event the attack never took place, for in this particular sector things did not now seem to be going so well for the Israelis. Heavy fighting had brought them considerable gains, and the Old City was virtually surrounded. But the failure to seize the Augusta Victoria Ridge was a distinct set-back, and there was some reason to suppose that the Jordanians were preparing for a counter-attack down the Jericho road. To the Jordanians, however, the situation looked very different and any pessimism in Jerusalem was more than matched by gloom in Amman. Literally nothing had gone as King Hussein and General Riad had planned. The first brigade of Iraqi reinforcements which was to take over from the Arab Legion in the Jordan Valley had been spotted by the Israeli Air Force and bombed to pieces on its journey across the border. Three other brigades had been promised but by the time they reached Jordan's border President Aref realised the war was not going well for the Arabs, and his three brigades were ordered to halt. The Syrians had also failed Jordan; they had no air cover, they said. And the Egyptians, with problems enough of their own, were far from helpful. After talking to his master, Field Marshal Amer, in Cairo, General Riad told Hussein that there seemed to be only two courses of action open: to ask the Israelis for a cease-fire, or to pull the Arab Legion back across the Jordan.

For Hussein these alternatives were too terrible to contemplate at first. Unlike other Arab politicians — and most Egyptian generals — the King had spent much of the war in the forward areas, racing from one unit to another urging his troops to hold their ground. Nasser had called him 'a traitor to the Arabs' before the war, and he did not wish to lend substance to this accusation by being the first Arab leader to sue for peace. Nor did he wish to abandon the West Bank, which he might never recover. (Arab jealousies die hard and no doubt Hussein harboured a suspicion that some of his Arab allies would not be sorry to see the richest part of his kingdom lopped off — even by the Israelis.) Early on the Tuesday morning (the second day) Hussein made his famous conversation with Nasser about foreign intervention. At 1330hrs he told his troops

that Jordan would fight on; yet within half an hour he had come to accept the conclusions of the Egyptian commander-in-chief of his forces and started to think about a cease-fire. Meantime Riad was working on the basis of the King's determination to fight on, and at 2200hrs he issued an order for all Jordanian forces to pull back to the East Bank. About half an hour after this the UN called for a cease-fire, and although the Jordanians chose to ignore this particular appeal its effect was coupled with the withdrawal order. As it looked as if there might be some advantage in the Arab Legion staying where it was, Riad's order was countermanded, and Jordanian units ordered to stand fast if they had not moved or to go back if they had. Order, counter-order, disorder: in several places the Arab Legionnaires had to fight to get back to the positions they had evacuated; in others the countermanding order did not reach the units concerned until it was too late. This is what happened in Jerusalem, where two battalions packed up and slipped away during the night. Finally in the early hours of Wednesday morning Hussein called on his troops to obey the UN cease-fire, provided the Israelis did the same. It was at this point that the morale of the bewildered and long-suffering Legionnaires began to falter. Because they were moving in accordance with the order to withdraw or the second order to go back, it was a long time before the order to stop shooting reached them. In any case the UN appeal could not have been effective because the Israelis had chosen to ignore it until they had occupied their ancient capital and regained the most vital landmark of their existence, the Wailing Wall.

Above left: Entering the old city through the Lion's Gate.

Above: Rabbi Shlomo Goren, the Israeli Army's chief rabbi, blowing the 'Shofar' — the traditional ram's horn — at the Western Wall shortly after the capture of Jerusalem's old city.

Not knowing that the greater part of the Jordanian garrison of the Old City were pulling out the Israelis spent Tuesday night licking their wounds and waiting for a counter-attack which never materialised. Next morning, however, when the pilot of an Israeli aircraft making a dawn reconnaissance reported seeing troops and traffic moving away from Jerusalem and none towards it, Narkiss ordered a resumption of the offensive. Preceded by an artillery barrage and an air strike, Gur's paratroops again assaulted the Augusta Victoria Ridge. Apart from a token rearguard, which fled downhill as the Israelis approached, the ridge was deserted. Most of the Jordanians had left before dawn and when the paratroops swept south to take the El Tur district and the Mount of Olives they met only scattered opposition. So, once again these areas had been secured, the Jerusalem-Jericho road blocked and Gur assembled his force for an attack on the Old City from the east.

In the early heat of the Mediterranean sun a battalion of paratroopers followed a section of Shermans down the Jericho road towards St Stephen's Gate, known to the Israelis as the 'Lion's Gate'. There they stopped for what was to be the final assault, while mortar fire was put down on the Moslem Quarter near the gate and recoilless guns blasted the ramparts. Over the intercom radio in his half-track, Gur, speaking in a voice charged with emotion, announced '...we are about to take the Temple Mount. This is an historic task. The Jewish people are praying for our victory. All of Israel is waiting for it... I wish you success...' Then, roaring up to St Stephen's Gate Gur's vehicle charged through into the Old City. The nail studded door of the Gate had been damaged by a shell and it collapsed as he drove through. Turning left Gur headed towards the Temple Mount, with his paratroops running behind. It is 150 yards from the St Stephen's Gate to the majestic Mosque of the Dome of the Rock. The Israelis covered the distance in minutes, dodging in and out among the ancient olive and pine trees covering the crest of Mt Morjah, the Temple Mount. As they ran, bullets fired by Arab Legionnaires manning a post behind the Al-Aksa Mosque sang past them. But the sole remaining battalion of Jordanian troops had slipped through a gap in the Israeli ring while the paratroops were forming up for their attack.

The first paratroops reached the Wailing Wall about 1015hrs, and soon after that the Governor of what had been Arab Jerusalem approached Gur in the Temple Square. The Jordanian troops had left, he declared, and resistance would cease. Meantime the paratroops were making sure that there would be no more shooting. As they fanned out to search and occupy the Old City, loudspeakers summoned the survivors to come from their homes and surrender. But bullets were still flying when the Chief Rabbi of the Israeli Army, Brigadier Shlomo Goren, arrived at the wall to lead an ecstatic gathering of sweating paratroopers and government ministers in prayer. Holding his Scrolls of the Law in his right hand, and a ram's horn brought to Israel by a survivor of Belsen in his right hand, the Chief Rabbi solemnly sounded a call for rejoicing. For many Israelis it would not have mattered now if the war had gone further, for this act signified complete victory. What was happening in Sinai was more sensational and certainly far more important militarily than the capture of the Holy City. But the Wailing Wall had symbolised Jewish national hopes for 1,897 years, and the Israelis' attitude was summed up by Gur when he stood before its great boulders: 'None of us alive has ever seen or done anything so great as he has done today'.

General Dayan was among the first Israeli VIPs to contemplate the ancient stones of the Second Temple. Troops beside him, carefully cradling rifles and bazookas under their arms, stood with heads bowed as he offered up an intransigent prayer: 'We have returned to the most sacred of our shrines never to part from them again'.

If Dayan believed in divine providence for the fulfilment of the 2,000-year dream, events to the north of Jerusalem had already established that he was not leaving Jordan's defeat entirely to the Almighty. By the early hours of Wednesday morning Peled's armour was poised for an assault on Nablus. Pattons of the Jordanian 40th Armoured Brigade and men of the 25th Infantry Brigade blocking the road south from Jenin were routed and scattered at Kufeir, by a combined air and tank assault in an operation which was a textbook demonstration of the modern and bloody employment of air power. As the Pattons withdrew they were picked off individually by Israeli aircraft. Akkaba and Tubas were taken without opposition and the Israeli tanks roamed on south to the junction of the road leading from Damya Bridge to Nablus. Here the column divided, one armoured battalion driving south into the Jordan Valley while the remainder of the brigade turned towards Nablus. At the outskirts of the town they received an unexpected welcome. The war had moved too quickly for the inhabitants of Nablus. Peace and quiet prevailed in the town and the Israeli tanks were mistaken for those of the Iraqi who had been expected to pass through on their triumphant march to Tel Aviv. When the real identity of the visitors became apparent and the true situation dawned, however, the cheering stopped and the townsfolk dispersed to lock themselves in their houses. Sniping started, and it was several hours before Israeli infantrymen finally nailed down control of the town.

Peled's armour did not stay to see this operation completed. From Nablus the Israeli tanks headed west along the road to Deir Sharaf and Nathanya. Israeli aircraft had seen Jordanian Pattons, retreating from the previous day's action below Jenin, moving south along the road from Arraba. When the two forces clashed a tank battle ensued in which Israeli AMXs knocked out 10 Pattons at close range. The Israeli Air Force which joined claimed 15 more. With this action on the Thursday morning the fighting in the northern sector came to a complete stop. At Damya Bridge the Israeli tanks stood back from the river bank to allow hordes of fearful refugees and disorganised bands of Arab Legionnaires to cross unimpeded to the East Bank. All the Jordanians were on foot by this time as Israeli aircraft attacked any vehicle identified as Jordanian with rocket and cannon-fire or napalm.

South and east of Jerusalem other Biblical towns fell to the advancing Israelis — Bethlehem, Hebron, Jericho — until they had seized all of Hussein's kingdom west of the Jordan River and the Dead Sea. As in Sinai Israel's

absolute mastery of the air meant ultimate Arab defeat. On Thursday morning (the fourth day) Hussein, unshaven and hollow-eyed, returned sadly to Amman to announce that his men could fight no longer, and to send a message to U Thant telling him that Jordan would accept a cease-fire.

In New York on Wednesday evening (the third day) delegates of the United Nations were treated to the curious spectacle of the Soviet Ambassador urgently presenting a resolution calling for an absolute cease-fire in the Middle East by 2000hrs GMT. It was already too late to save Egypt, but Moscow was anxious to stop the war before Israeli troops could consolidate Sharm-El-Sheikh. Unless the Israelis could be halted and driven back the Arabs would suffer a humiliating defeat. Israel said that she would cease fire if all the Arab states did the same, but 2000hrs came and went with the combatants still fighting. And next day the combatants continued to pound each other in defiance of the UN mandatory order. In Sinai the Israelis were fighting the crucial battles to block the Egyptian escape routes to the Suez Canal, and in Jordan the fighting had also reached its climax. In the north there was little fighting but Radio Damascus was still ranting about 'hoisting the Palestinian flag in the skies of Tel Aviv'.

Overnight the Syrians' attitude seemed to change, since they agreed to a cease-fire on Thursday morning: when Egypt followed suit a few hours later it looked as if the war was over. But it was not. The Israelis had a long standing and bitter score to settle with their northern neighbours. For years Syria had maintained a constant stream of abuse and propaganda against Israel; invented the slogan of the 'Popular Liberation War'; recruited, armed, trained and financed the Palestinian guerillas and then sent them into Israel to burn, wreck, ruin and destroy. It was Syria who had been the cause of the war, and the Israelis intended that Syria should pay for its sins.

Left: Israeli half-tracks advancing.

Above: Repairing an Israeli AMX-13 damaged on the Jordanian Front.

Right: When possible mobile showers were brought for the troops — a welcome interlude during the battle.

THE SYRIAN FRONT

The border between the two countries ran north-south, and stretched for 20 miles from the kibbutz of Tel Dan in the north to the shores of Lake Galilee in the south. On the Syrian side a slope rose steeply some to a crest three miles away, which dominated the Israeli plain below. Over the years the Syrians had constructed a strongly fortified belt of defences, 10 miles deep. Some 265 guns were dug into the hills behind the crest, and the infantry positions on the height itself were concreted and interconnected with underground trenches. The front itself was heavily mined and anti-tank guns were sited in depth. These forward defences were manned by three infantry brigades, each supported by T-34s and SU-100s. Scattered among the front-line defences there were also 30 German Panzers of World War II vintage, and some 75mm guns. A week or two before the war started three other infantry brigades were sent up to reinforce the defences. All in all, on 5 June there were over 40,000 Syrian soldiers with 260 tanks and self-propelled guns in three armoured brigades and five infantry brigades on the Golan Plateau. Tactically they were in a very strong position. But it was an inefficient army which was preparing to drive the Jews into the sea. Vehicles were badly maintained, weapons were filthy and there was no sanitary discipline in the fixed defences. The Russian advisers and instructors, who had come to teach the Syrians how to use the sophisticated armaments which the Soviet Union had provided, were exasperated.

On 5 June (the first day) the northern front was unusually quiet, and the only evidence of Syrian hostility was a bomb dropped by Syrian aircraft on the little town of Tiberias (before the Israeli Air Force struck at Syria's air bases). But early in the morning of the second day of the war — encouraged perhaps by Radio Cairo's false claims of successes in the south — the Syrians put down a heavy artillery barrage on the frontier kibbutzim at Shear Yashov and Tel Dan. When the barrage lifted at about 0700hrs, two companies of Syrian infantry crossed the border under cover of fire from tanks on the Banias Ridge above Tel Dan with the obvious intention of enclosing the settlement in a pincer movement. The attack was held up by Israeli militia-farmers, shopkeepers, and the local bus driver; and when Israeli aircraft arrived on the scene at 0720hrs their cannon fire and napalm induced the invaders to beat a quick retreat.

Throughout the second, third and fourth days of the war the Syrians intermittently bombarded all the Israeli settlements within range of their guns — from Kibbutz Dan and Kfar Szold in the north, through Gadot and Rosh

Right: Operations on the Golan Plateau, 9-10 June 1967.

Below: Damage caused by Syrian shells at Rosh-Pina on 5 June 1967.

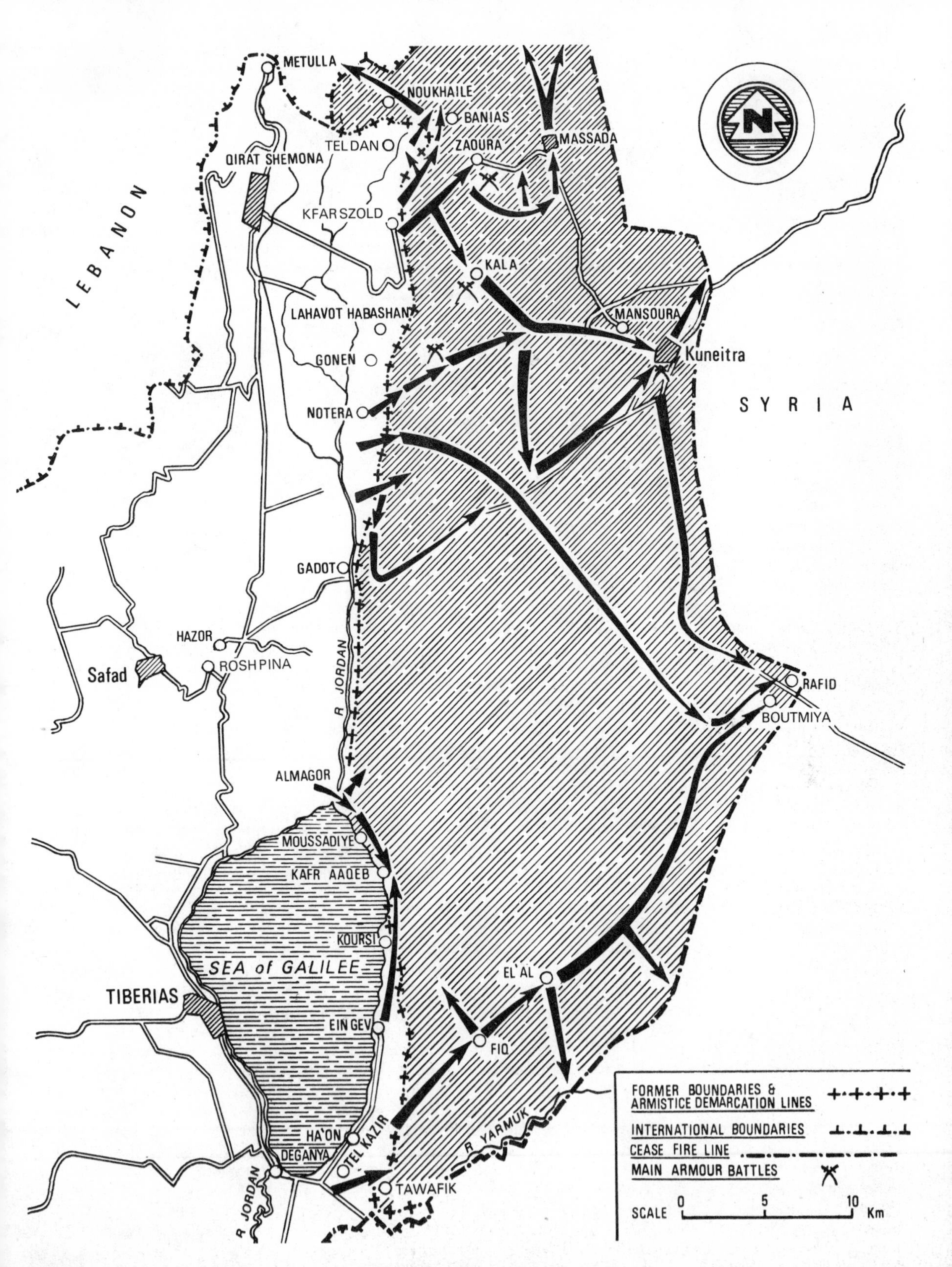
METULLA
NOUKHAILE
BANIAS
TEL DAN
ZAOURA
MASSADA
QIRAT SHEMONA
LEBANON
KFAR SZOLD
KALA
LAHAVOT HABASHAN
MANSOURA
GONEN
Kuneitra
NOTERA
SYRIA
GADOT
HAZOR
Safad
ROSH PINA
R JORDAN
RAFID
BOUTMIYA
ALMAGOR
MOUSSADIYE
KAFR AAQEB
KOURSI
SEA of GALILEE
EL AL
TIBERIAS
EIN GEV
FIQ
TEL KAZIR
HA'ON
DEGANYA
R YARMUK
TAWAFIK
R JORDAN
N
FORMER BOUNDARIES & ARMISTICE DEMARCATION LINES
INTERNATIONAL BOUNDARIES
CEASE FIRE LINE
MAIN ARMOUR BATTLES
SCALE 0 5 10 Km

Pina in the middle, to Ein Gev, Haon and Tel Kazir in the south. There were casualties, but most of the farmers stayed in their shelters and most of the damage caused by the shelling was to their crops.

Syria's agreement to a cease-fire on Thursday morning (the fourth day) brought a five-hour lull in the shelling. Then it started again and Radio Damascus announced that Syria was not bound by any cease-fire. Believing that they were holding impregnable positions, the Syrians were emboldened by the fact that the Israelis had not attempted to attack. Israel's troops had overstretched themselves on the southern and central front they calculated. Furthermore they reckoned that Israel would not wish to further provoke the Soviet Union. But the Syrians were wrong. Israel's army still had the power to deal with Syria, and was more than keen to do so. The Israeli cabinet was divided on the issue, and there was a good case for holding off an attack. A proposal had been received from the Russians that if Israel would let Syria off the hook, then the Soviet Union might allow to emigrate those of Russia's three million Jews who wished to do so. It was a bait, bribe and blood money. But it was a cogent reason for leaving Syria alone. After a long argument however, the Israeli cabinet decided that the Russians could not be trusted, and that Israel might never again be presented with the opportunity to sweep away the menace of the formidable Syrian Western Wall. Israeli troops must show the Syrians that even with Russian advice, guidance and equipment, Israel could overcome them.

Orders went out to that effect at about 1800hrs Jerusalem time, and Israeli troops began to concentrate for the offensive. In the north two of the armoured brigades which had been fighting the Jordanians as part of the Peled Ugda, and the paratroop brigade which had been in action with Uzi Narkiss were put under command of Brigadier David Elazar. The infantry brigade which had made a feint move south into Jordan on the Tuesday and which had reassembled south of the Sea of Galilee was also put under Elazar's command. So too was one of the last of the reserve brigades which had not yet seen any action and which had concentrated near Givat Haem in the north. The three mechanised infantry battalions of the famous Golani brigade, commanded by Colonel Yona, and another infantry brigade completed the force which was to smash through the Syrian defences. Its total strength amounted to about 250 tanks — almost as many as the Syrians — and about 20,000 men.

Elazar's orders were simple. The Syrian armour was to be drawn into battle, the Golan plateau was to be seized and the artillery which had harassed the Israelis for the past two years was to be destroyed. The road to Damascus was to be forced open to show the Syrians that topographical advantage did not guarantee their immunity. Once these objectives were accomplished the offensive would stop; in victory Israel would demonstrate magnanimity.

The Israeli plan was bold but extremely conventional. The attack was to be made on four fronts, the main thrust being directed against the northern sector, where the terrain was hardest and the Syrian position least strongly defended. The Golani brigade, which, with two companies of Shermans, was designated for this task, was given Banias Ridge as its objective. Still in the northern sector but slightly south of the Golani brigade's operation one of the armoured brigades starting from Kfar Szold would force a passage through the first line of Syrian defences to seize Zaoura. It would then turn south-west and smash its way through the second and third lines of Surian positions to seize the town of Kuneitra, where the Syrians had their headquarters. These attacks were complementary. In the centre sector one of the armoured brigades which had returned from Jordan was to attack towards Rawye, after a path had been cleared for the tanks by infantry. When the tanks went in the infantry would follow and exploit towards Dardara, a village on the lower road to Kuneitra. In the

Left: Israeli half-tracks carrying reservists passing through Tiberias en route for Golan, 5 June 1967.

Right: Border patrol.

Below: M-50 Super-Shermans passing a disabled Israeli AMX-13 on the way up to the Golan Heights.

south central sector infantry would advance from Almagor and exploit down the eastern side of the Sea of Galilee. And finally, in the very south the paratroop brigade from Jerusalem would break into the Golan plateau near Tel Kazir. In all these operations the paramount aim was to seize Kuneitra.

The ground attacks were scheduled to start at 0700hrs on Friday morning (the fifth day) and from dawn that day until the final cease-fire came into effect at 1830hrs on Saturday Israeli aircraft pounded the Syrian positions. Their bombs did little damage to the concrete and stone emplacements, and the napalm which was dropped was channelled away in the gutters which the Syrians had providentially fixed to their overhead cover. But many of the defenders were stunned by the blast of bombs and their morale was shaken by the continuity and persistence of the Israeli strikes. Israeli sappers started to clear paths through the minefields before first light. Clearing lanes through their own minefields proved to be more difficult than the minefields of the Syrians. On this part of the border rains washed many mines away, necessitating the minefields being resown periodically. The Israelis had done this conscientiously, but the Syrians had not bothered, so there were great gaps in their minefield belt. In anticipation of their own advance to Tiberias and Tel Aviv, the Syrians had also lifted many of the mines they had sown round the Beni Yakov bridge across the Jordan.

The first Israeli formation to cross the Syrian border was the armoured brigade which mounted the heights in two columns from the vicinity of Kfar Szold. As they crossed no man's land on the two sides of the frontier the Syrian artillery laid down a heavy barrage and although the Israeli Air Force screamed down on these guns the men and vehicles suffered many casualties. At the border eight bulldozers went into the lead to clear the mines which the sappers had not been able to reach; five of these were knocked out before the armoured columns were through the minefield.

Nine hours elasped before the tanks reached the crest, and the Israelis took heavy casualties all the way. Meantime the Golani brigade did not cross the border until 1400hrs. The Syrian guns had created havoc in the initial phases of the attack and when the infantry did reach the first line of Syrian positions, the defenders were ousted only after bitter hand-to-hand combat inside the positions. Fortifications, such as those at Tel Azzaziat, had already acquired a notorious reputation from the many border incidents of the years before. The fights here lasted until 1830hrs and this battle is regarded with the battle for Ammunition Hill, as one of the two most hard fought and costly engagements of the whole war. When it was over, 60 Syrians had been killed and 20 others captured; the cost to the Israelis was 30 killed and about 70 wounded.

About ten miles further south AMX tanks raced across the border about noon. They were not supported by infantry and they took the Syrians by surprise. By the time the latter could call down artillery support the tanks were already on their foward positions on the first crest of the plateau. Bulldozers and infantry came up in a second wave to clear a passage through the barbed wire and fashion a rough road passable for wheeled vehicles. Then the third wave went in, consisting of infantry in buses, lorries and furniture vans. Panicking, the Syrians radioed for tank support; in doing so the location of the tanks was disclosed to the Israelis who were monitoring the Syrian wavelengths. The information was passed to the Israeli Air Force, and the Syrian tanks never arrived.

By Friday evening the Israelis had established a bridgehead five miles wide on the top of the Golan escarpment between Zaoura and Kala and had penetrated the northern part of the Syrian defensive wall in five other places. When night fell they were on the outskirts of Masada. But it had not been an easy day for the Israelis. They had not been as successful as they had hoped, and their programme was behind schedule. Organisational problems, preparation, reconnaissance, briefing and re-supply had all been more difficult than expected. So too had the terrain, and the Syrians had shown an unexpected resilience — generally standing fast and fighting back until their posts were physically overrun.

Left: Israeli AMX-13 at the Syrian frontier on Golan.

Above: Evacuating a tank crew casualty.

Right: Syrian soldiers surrendering on Golan.

Throughout that night, the first with a full moon and for the Israelis the Sabbath, Elazar's men regrouped and waited for a counter-attack which never came, while helicopters landed in the foward areas and removed the wounded. At dawn the offensive was resumed in all four sectors of the front. From Zaoura and Rawye armoured columns set out for Kuneitra, while a third force headed south-east towards Boutmiya.

The Syrians put up a stiff resistance until about noon. Then their opposition began to crumble, and the Israelis took one position after another. From Banias in the north to Tawafik in the south the Syrian troops were throwing down their weapons and taking to their heels. Discipline had gone and the morale of the Syrian soldiers had disintegrated. The conflict had turned into a rout, as the Israeli armour set out in pursuit of the fleeing Syrians. Tanks and positions which had not been abandoned were destroyed en route, and at 1430hrs the Israelis entered Kuneitra. It was a ghost town where tanks had been abandoned with their engines running and radios on. Leaving the mopping up operations to the infantry of the Golani brigade, the Israeli armour pushed on southwards towards Boutmiya.

Meanwhile Syrian resistance in the south had also collapsed, and when the Israelis moved in to attack the fortified ridge stretching from Tawafik through Kfar Hareb to El Al at 1400hrs the defences were found to be empty. It appeared that the Syrian defeat was complete. However, as it was not known whether the villages and positions behind the defensive belt had been abandoned a rapid advance was called for. A helicopter was sent out to reconnoitre and when it reported that the entire Golan Heights appeared to have been abandoned a paratroop force was put into helicopters and set down at key points ahead of the tanks and infantry. As the tanks and infantry advanced over the rough terrain eastwards and north towards what was to become the cease-fire line, the helicopters leap-frogged the paratroops forward — until finally they landed at the deserted Boutmiya crossroads. Here at this junction there was a reunion of paratroops, tanks from Kuneitra, tanks from Dardara, tanks from Kfar Harib, and tanks and infantry from Tel Kazir.

By 1830hrs when the cease-fire came into effect the Israelis were in complete control of the Golan Heights and were driving round the deserted eastern shores of Lake Galilee as if they were on the Dizengoff Boulevard in the heart of Tel Aviv. The road to Damascus was open and at a cost of 152 killed and 306 wounded the Israelis had achieved all they had set out to achieve. The war was over.

Cease-fire — and time for a welcome meal.

8 The War at Sea

Israel's stupendous victory was won in the air over Egypt and on the battlefields of Sinai, Jerusalem and the Golan Heights. At sea the Israeli and Egyptian navies went into action, but their achievements were unspectacular and relatively uninfluential. Apart from landing a party of sailors at Sharm El Sheikh on Wednesday 7 June, Israeli naval operations were limited to two sorties against Egyptian naval bases and the interception of three submarines. A combined naval and air assault on El Arish, planned to take place on the first night of the war, was called off, partly because Jordan had joined battle, and partly because Tal's troops had done better than expected. Consequently the Israeli Navy had little chance to show its mettle and gain glory. With the Israeli Air Force, however, it could share the credit for the freedom from bombardment of Israel's long and vulnerable coastline throughout the course of hostilities.

As darkness fell on 5 June, an Israeli flotilla slipped down the Israeli coast and sailed along the shores of Sinai towards Port Said. The commander of the Israeli ships knew that the Egyptian Air Force had virtually ceased to exist, while the Commander-in-Chief of the Egyptian Navy, Rear-Admiral Soliman Izzat, was blissfully unware of this fact. As the Egyptian High Command had not yet dared to reveal to Nasser the extent of the disaster, it is scarcely surprising that Izzat was left in ignorance. He had no reason to disbelieve the extravagant claims broadcast by Radio Cairo, and every reason therefore to be confident that the very existence of the Egytian Air Force would deter offensive action in Egyptian waters by the Israeli Navy.

Consequently the Egyptians were not expecting the Israeli flotilla, which was within 15 miles of Port Said before there was any Egyptian reaction. The Israelis then spotted two Osa class patrol boats heading towards them at high speed. When the Egyptian vessels were less than a mile away and closing in rapidly, an Israeli destroyer opened fire. Several shots were seen to strike the patrol boats, which veered off, turned about, and made off into Port Said harbour..

This action was incidental to the Israeli main operation, which then continued. First at Port Said and a later at Alexandria, two small parties of frogmen were put ashore with orders to do as much damage as possible to Egyptian naval vessels and installations. Four of the Osa patrol boats and three frigates were known to be in Port Said and the Israel hoped to be able to put some, if not all of them, out of action. In the event the frogmen succeeded in getting into the harbour but were unable to find any of the ships they were looking for. A couple of laden oil tankers tempted them as alternative targets, but the Israelis decided that if they did blow them up, the resultant explosion would probably devastate not only the dock area but the town itself. So they slipped back to the rendezvous where boats were waiting to take them home. Their mission, efficiently performed but unspectacular because it did not achieve its objective, was not a success.

The other operation was more successful, but the men who took part were less fortunate. Taken by submarine to a point just off the Ras El Tin naval base, six Israeli frogmen rowed ashore in a small dinghy and successfully made their way into the main anchorage. There they damaged a number of vessels and sank several, among them a missile craft of the Osa class. With their task completed the frogmen then tried to return to the rendezvous where the submarine which had brought them to Alexandria was supposed to pick them up. Arriving late at the rendezvous, all six men had to lie up until the next night when the submarine would return if they had failed to turn up first time. According to the Israelis the submarine went back and waited on both nights, while the Egyptians claimed that they had detected the submarine soon after it had put the frogmen ashore and had fired on it. Hoping that it would return they had also had a naval force lying in wait, but the submarine failed to show up. In the event the six Israeli soldiers were captured on Tuesday afternoon, and were eventually repatriated when the war ended.

Meantime the Israeli flotilla which took the frogmen to Port Said had withdrawn from Egyptian territorial waters. The Egyptian Air Force still had some serviceable aircraft, and Brigadier Erell did not want his ships to be caught napping. As soon as the Egyptians realised that the force blockading their harbour had gone, however, the ships which the frogmen had been looking for slipped away westward along the coast to Alexandria. Alexandria was a comparatively safe haven, but the Egyptian patrol boats were not in a position to sally out and bombard the Israeli coastline and sneak back to harbour without fear of retaliation. Their range was limited by the fuel they could carry, and refuelling at sea in daylight would make them sitting ducks for the Israeli Air Force. Only from Port Said was it possible for the Osas to reach Israel and return to base during the short hours of darkness.

On Wednesday and Thursday, the Israelis spotted submarines near Rosh Hanikra close to the Lebanese-Israeli border, and Haifa. Israeli destroyers attacked them and the submarines submerged. Oil slicks, which appeared on the surface later, were a sign that the submarines were damaged if not sunk. Perhaps the most interresting facet of this action off Haifa was the subsequent Egyptian denial that any of their submarines went anywhere near Haifa or the northern Israeli coast during hostilities.

Another mysterious casualty of the war was the American naval communications ship USS *Liberty*, a converted freighter crammed with electronic equipment. Chugging along at about five knots on a west-northwest course about 12 miles off the Sinai coast, the *Liberty* was sighted by two Israeli patrolboats on Thursday afternoon. Believing it to be an Egyptian vessel in disguise, the patrol boats' commanders reported their conclusion by radio and asked for air support. The message was duly passed to the Israeli operations room at Jerusalem, where all requests for air support were monitored and coordinated, and the patrol boats were told to take another look at the *Liberty* and confirm that it was an enemy ship. Yes, came the reply, it was probably the Egyptian supply ship *El Quesir* . . . but there was the possibility that it might be a Soviet vessel. Meanwhile the United States and Soviet embassies in Tel Aviv were asked if they had any ships operating in the area where the suspect vessel had been sighted; both said that they did not.

So a strike was authorised and shortly after 1400hrs three Mirages took off to home on the *Liberty*. Sweeping across the ship's starboard bow they raked the American vessel with machine gun and cannon fire, riddling its hull and superstructure in half a dozen strafing runs. When the planes flew off the waiting Israeli patrol boats closed in. Making for the *Liberty* with all machine guns firing, they launched two torpedoes. One of these found its mark and tore a gaping hole in the *Liberty* squarely amidships and below the water line. Thirty-five minutes later the Israeli attack ended as abruptly as it had begun. The flag at the *Liberty's* masthead had been shot away during the strafing runs, but the patrol boats had got close enough to see the English lettering on the ship's stern and the 'holding ensign' that had been run up to replace the lost flag.

Once they had realised their mistake the Israeli patrol boat commanders stopped astern of the *Liberty* to signal 'Do you need assistance?', and when they radioed the news back to the shore an Israeli helicopter was put at the disposal of the United States naval attaché. He flew out to the *Liberty* but was refused permission to go aboard and flew back to Tel Aviv after dropping his visiting card on the deck of the stricken ship. Refusing all offers of Israeli assistance, the captain of the *Liberty*, Commander William McConagle, patched up the hole in the side of his ship and steamed away north. The *Liberty* was listing heavily to starboard but its watertight compartments kept it afloat. In due course it was joined by the cruiser SS *Little Rock* which escorted the *Liberty* to Malta where it was put into dry dock for repairs.

Thirty-four officers and men of the *Liberty* crew were killed and 70 others wounded in this action. And as might be expected there was a storm of controversy about the incident. Israel offered an apology and full compensation, claiming that it had mistaken the ship for an Egyptian vessel. The United States accepted the apology but a secret court of inquiry was set up to investigate. Why a sophisticated American 'spy ship' should be cruising so close to the battle zone was a question which has never been publicly answered. In the absence of official explanations theories proliferated. Perhaps the most interesting, if not most outrageous, of these was that the Israelis attacked the *Liberty* because she had monitored communications proving that Israel had started the war. Another maintained that the ship's American flag was seen before the Mirages commenced their attack, but it was thought to be an Arab ruse.

Ironically, the court of inquiry reported that on the morning of the attack the United States Joint Chief of Staff had ordered the *Liberty* to move further away from the coast 'even though such a move would partially degrade her mission' — whatever it was. Moreover only three days earlier the Israelis had asked the Pentagon what ships it would have in the area in the coming week. Beause of some mix-up they got no reply; which lent credence to their later belief that no United States ships were operating in the area and that the *Liberty* must therefore be an Egyptian ship flying an American flag in order to get close to bombard El Arish, which had been captured by the Israelis. The only clear facts about this mysterious episode were the grim casualty figures.

9 1967 Aftermath: The War of Attrition

gypt finally accepted the United Nations Security ouncil's call for a cease-fire on Thursday evening 8 June, ıd President Nasser delivered a radio and television ldress to the Arab world on 9 June. He had made no ıblic utterance since the beginning of the war. The only ficial voice had been Radio Cairo, broadcasting the ɔtimistic communiques of the UAR High Command and e fatuous rhetoric of commentators who were still ɔasting of Arab victories at a time when the Egyptian my was no longer capable of defending the Suez Canal ıd the road to Cairo was open. The Arabs could have arned the truth from foreign radio stations, but until the mnants of the Egyptian army began to find their way ɔme, the Egyptian public did not begin to grasp the full tent of the disaster. So when Nasser announced the ase-fire after his long silence, the news came as a shock. eople were angry and bewildered by the fact that the army ɔpeared to have given up so soon. Despite the accusations American and British air support for the Israelis there as not the excuse of 1956 that Egypt had had to face an tack of two great powers as well as Israel.

It was Nasser's darkest hour, for the defeat was far orse than in 1956. Israeli troops had not only occupied e whole of Sinai but also held the east bank of the Suez anal for which Egypt had run such risks to regain control ıd had made such efforts to develop. Egypt's allies had ɔllapsed, and Nasser's work of 15 years — ousting reign troops from Egypt, establishing control of the Suez anal, and restoring self-confidence among the Arab world – all seemed to have been brought to ruin in a few isastrous days. Now the Arab world faced the prospects f a humiliating capitulation, for there was no hope as in 956 of snatching diplomatic victories from military defeat. orld opinion was no longer overwhelmingly on Egypt's de as it had been in 1956.

The prewar picture of Israel as a beleaguered fortress, reatened by a ring of hostile Arab armies bent not only n her defeat but the actual annihilation of her people had rned the Israelis wide international sympathy, especially Europe and the United States. In other countries too, in sia, Africa, Latin America and even within the ommunist countries of Eastern Europe, there was now reater sympathy for the Israelis who were deemed to have it back only after unreasonable provocation. Moreover, y the discrepancies between their threats and their erformance, the Arabs had invited world derision. Over the centuries the Jews have learned to extract a laugh from almost any event, tribulation or triumph. By the end of the war people were chuckling over jokes about the Israeli 'blitzkrieg', in which a crack regiment known as the Bagel Lancers had taken part. In the *New York Times* a full-page advertisement recommended *Visit Israel and See the Pyramids*. Unofficial humour of this nature added lustre to officially inspired Israeli propaganda which stressed the poor performance of Arab soldiers — Egyptian soldiers in particular.

Faced with this situation it is hardly surprising that Nasser came near to a nervous and physical collapse, and it was a gaunt and seemingly broken man who stood before the television cameras on 9 June 1967. 'We cannot hide from ourselves the fact that we have met with a grave setback in the last few days', he told his audience. The enemy plan to invade Syria had been the cause of the war, he said: 'It had been Egypt's duty not to accept this in silence'. The United States and the Soviet Union had both insisted on Egypt holding her fire. But the enemy had struck with a stronger blow than had been expected, showing that 'there were other forces behind him which came to settle their account with the Arab Nationalist Movement.' Nasser then declared that he was ready to assume entire responsibility for the 'setback'. He had decided to give up all his official posts, and every political role, and become an ordinary citizen. He was, he said, handing over the Egyptian presidency to Vice-President Zachria Mohieddin. 'The forces of imperialism', he said, 'imagine that Abdul Nasser is their enemy, I want it to be clear that it is the entire Arab nation, and not Gamal Abdul Nasser'.

If the Egptian leader's speech was intended to turn ignominy into personal triumph it certainly worked. As soon as they heard him announce his resignation people in Cairo began to pour out of their houses shouting for Nasser to stay. Sobbing men ran through the streets wailing 'Nasser, Nasser, don't leave us; we need you'. Thousands of people travelled into Cairo by car, bus and train to join the crowds which massed along the five-mile stretch of road from Nasser's house to the centre of Cairo. In Algeria mobs who had been shouting 'Lynch Nasser', suddenly changed their tune. From Damascus President Aref telephoned Cairo, urging Nasser to reconsider his decision; in the Lebanon President Helou is said to have broken down and wept when he heard that the Egyptian

Left: Israeli retaliation: Kantara burning after an IAF raid, March 1969.

Below: UN truck damaged by Egyptian shelling, May 1969.

Right: Burning tanker in the Gulf of Suez, following an Israeli retaliatory artillery bombardment.

leader intended to resign. From Baghdad to Beirut Arab mobs swept into the streets to demonstrate for Nasser. Nearly all these demonstrations showed an ugly anti-American and anti-British bias; most of this was restricted to the shouting of slogans, but in Beirut a mob set fire to a Coca Cola bottling plant on the grounds that it belonged to the 'US Imperialists'.

If, as it now seems probable, a group of the senior Egyptian army officers were hatching a plot to depose Nasser, their chances of success were very small. Zacharia Mohieddin, whose policies were known to be pro-American, quickly announced that he would refuse to take over the presidency; the Egyptian Cabinet voted not to accept Nasser's resignation, and the Egyptian National Assembly did the same. As he had probably calculated all along, the Egyptian leader was able to '. . . bow to the voice of the people', to withdraw his resignation and to keep his job.

The other Arab political leaders also managed to survive in the immediate wake of the war. Like Nasser, King Hussein broadcast a public reckoning; unlike Nasser, however, he offered no alibis, made no excuses, and used no intemperate language to explain Jordan's defeat. Israel had won, he said, 'with overwhelming strength . . . It is apparent that we have not yet learnt well enough how to use the weapons of modern warfare'. Amid all the fantasies, delusions and confusion pervading the Arab world in the wake of the war, Hussein's voice was the most realistic. His country had fought the hardest and lost the most, but Hussein's personal reputation in Jordan and the Arab world was higher than ever. A cheering crowd in Amman converged on his Cadillac, picked it up and carried it five yards to demonstrate their adulation.

Stunned beyond belief, the Arab world appeared unable to comprehend the disaster which had overtaken it. It could no longer make war, but refused to make peace; it had lost its armies but was desperately determined not to lose its face. Throughout Islam, Moslem mullahs proclaimed American and British products unholy. 'Defeat exists only for those who admit it', said Cairo's semi-official newspaper *Al Gumhuria* a week after the war. 'We do not admit it.' Two weeks later another Cairo Newspaper *Al Ahram* told its readers: 'The battle is still going on. Victory is ours'. In Damascus slogans newly painted on the walls of public buildings promised 'We shall destroy the enemy'. In both Beirut and Cairo the Arabs demanded that the name of the American University should be changed to Palestine University, and Algeria compiled a list of 'pro-Zionist' cinema stars, including Sophia Loren, Elizabeth Taylor and Harry Belafonte, and banned their films. Libyan mobs destroyed wine and liquor stores symbols of US 'imperialism', and King Idris demanded that the United States abandon its Wheelers Field air force base. Egypt and Syria closed their ports to American and British ships; Sudanese and Iraqi dock labourers refused to unload them. Behind these exercises in extended solipsism there was plenty of evidence of the realities of defeat, however. What was left of Jordan was swarming with refugees from the West Bank; Amman's normal population of 300,000 was swelled by at least 100,000 refugees, most of whom arrived destitute and hungry. Although schools, mosques and public buildings were hurriedely converted to provide sleeping accommodation, thousands of refugees had nowhere to go. They foraged for food, which rapidly became scarce and impossibly expensive. Hussein's government established two refugee camps, and other Arab nations sent emergency supplies of food, clothing and money. But these were barely sufficient and the problems of organisation and distribution were exacerbated by inefficiency and national jealousies. For example Syria detained one Lebanese convoy for 12 hours before allowing it to proceed to Amman.

Cairo presented another grim picture of confusion, hysteria and dismay. Guards on the Nile bridges, government offices and important installations were doubled in the immediate aftermath of the war. Periodical air-raid alerts sent people scurrying for shelter, and the Egyptian Government issued a warning that watches, cigarette packets and fountain pens found in the streets were probably booby traps dropped by Israeli aircraft. In the absence of information regarding casualties and the extent of the debacle, Cairo's bazaars buzzed with rumours. Soldiers returning from Sinai blamed their misfortunes on their officers, and it was a long time before Egptian Army officers could venture into the streets of Cairo in uniform without running the risk of being spat on.

In human and economic terms Jordan suffered more than Egypt from the war. Hussein's tough little Arab Legion fought hard, as is witnessed by the official casualty figures which listed 6,094 killed out of an estimated 50,000 soldiers who fought on the West Bank. How many men were wounded has never been disclosed, but 5,000 were said to be missing, although some of these turned up later among the refugees who stole back across the river. Three-quarters of Jordan's tanks were lost in the fighting; so too were three-quarters of the army's guns, and the Royal Jordanian Air Force was left literally without planes. Territorially the cost was even greater. With the loss of the

West Bank went most of Jordan's richest source of foreign-currency earnings, estimated at 35 million dollars a year.

Egypt lost at least three-quarters of its air force, 800 of its 900 tanks — 300 of which were abandoned intact — and enormous quantities of other vehicles. The Israelis also claimed to have taken 400 field guns, 50 self-propelled guns, and 30 155mm guns. The Russians mounted a massive airlift to replace some of these losses, but disenchantment with their Arab proteges slowed this rearmament programme. The Arab defeat brought the Russians diplomatic and political loss of face, and with the Suez Canal out of action they faced frustrating logistic problems in building up the Soviet Navy as an 'instrument of diplomacy' in the Indian Ocean. Nasser had failed the Soviet Union and the Russians were not over-anxious to replace the entire one billion of dollars worth of lost equipment — preferring to give the Egyptians the wherewithal for defence without making them capable of launching an attack on Israel.

With the occupation of Sinai, Egypt lost 20% of its territory and its economy was in deplorable shape. Industrial output had slowed before the war started. By some estimates many new factories were operating at less than half capacity, owing to lack of spare parts and raw materials. Now, the four main sources of foreign exchange were either sick, dead, sunk, or in Israel. Because of the war tourism, which ordinarily brought in 78 million dollars a year, had dried up; the Suez Canal, which earned Egypt 260 million dollars a year, was clogged with sunken ships; and the wells in Sinai, providing nearly 80% of Egypt's oil production, were in Israeli hands. At the same time the cotton crop worth 300 million dollars a year and mortgaged to the Soviet Union was threatened by the worst plague of cotton leaf worms since World War II.

With the economy in a mess and the morale of the Egyptian army at an all time low, Nasser's pampered officer corps provided the scapegoats. Eleven generals were dismissed, including the army, navy and air force commanders and Field Marshal Amer; hundreds of other officers were cashiered for desertion in the face of the enemy. The Russians, disgusted with the performance of the Egyptian Army and air force, insisted on a complete reorganisation of the military in return for replacing the lost equipment.

Similar conditions were imposed on Syria, which had lost six of its MiGs, 110 of its tanks and about half of the other armoured vehicles in its possession. President Atassi and the ruling Baathist party had been unmasked as paper tigers for championing total war and then limiting their offensive to shelling until the Israelis turned on them. So the Soviet Union was in no particular hurry to replace the lost equipment until the Syrian defence forces were purged. Syria had also lost some territory but as she had no oil or tourist industry she suffered much less economically than Egypt or Jordan. In effect the Israeli invasion of Syria united the Syrians and gave the Baathist government a new lease of life. Among all the belligerent Arab states Syria's attitude of 'No peace until Zionism ends', has been the most extreme.

The two brigades which Iraq sent to Jordan took heavy casualties in men and equipment, and the Israeli Air Force destroyed 17 Iraqi planes. But President Aref's moderate socialist regime emerged from the war without too many scars. Aref's troubles stemmed less from the war with Israel and his country's economy (80% of Iraq's revenue is derived from oil), but from internal dissension caused by the Kurdish minority in the north and the Shiah Moslems in the south.

Right: Kiryat Shmonah, a town in Galilee near the Lebanese border which has long been the target for shells and missiles of the Syrians and the Palestine Liberation Organisation. These pictures were taken after a bazooka attack in August 1969.

Apart from the two Hunter jets trespassing in Israeli air space on Tuesday 6 June, Lebanon did not clash with Israel. But it suffered badly in the war's aftermath. No one expected the Lebanese to fight, but their Christian-Moslem coalition government made belligerent noises, evicted the American ambassador and downgraded the American embassy to a legation. With the ambassdor went the tourists which were the mainstay of Lebanon's economic life. Except for a few Arab diplomats, Beirut's luxury hotels were empty for a long time, and even when the tourists started to drift back their numbers were greatly reduced, owing to the fact that 60% of the prewar tourists used the Lebanon as a stop-over on their way to Jerusalem, and access to the Holy City was now through Israel. Lebanon also suffered as a result of the activities of the Palestine Liberation Movement guerilla groups which insisted on operating against Israel from Lebanese territory. After the war the Palestine Liberation Organisation was taken over by more militant groups, one of which, the Popular Front for the Liberation of Palestine (PFLP), hijacked an El Al plane. Israeli retaliation came swiftly, in the shape of a raid on Beirut international airport.

Saudi Arabia was untouched by the war; the troops it sent to Jordan did not fight and King Feisal stayed well away from the theatre of operations. As with Iraq, oil is the basis of Saudi Arabia's economy and this only suffered from the self-imposed Arab ban on export to the West. When the effect of this embargo, a loss estimated at 300,000 dollars a day, began to be felt, it was lifted as being 'shortsighted and injurious to our overall economic position'. Meanwhile the King and his princes continued to send large donations to help buy new equipment for the shattered armies of the other Arab states.

In South Arabia, both the Yemen and the new People's Republic of South Yemen temporarily profited from the war, because their Arab patrons were forced to leave them alone. The Six-Day War was mainly responsible for the withdrawal of Egypt from the Yemen although the civil war there continued briefly in a somewhat lower key.

Libya was not directly involved in the war, because its offer of troops was turned down by Nasser. But 77-year old King Idris, who demonstrated support for the Arab cause by stopping oil production, telling the Americans to leave Wheelers Field, and the British to evacuate their army

Right: Kiryat Shmonah after a shower of Katyusha rockets in January 1970.

Below: And yet again in August 1971.

bases at Tobruk and Benghazi, was deposed by a pro-Nasser military coup in 1969.

Algeria, on the periphery of the Arab world, was barely affected by the war, since there was no involvement and the fighting was too remote. In the aftermath however, President Houari Boumedienne quickly made it clear he was anxious to replace Nasser as the new leader of the Arab left. Nasser had been closely associated with ex-President Ben Bella whom Boumedienne overthrew, and relations between Egypt and Algeria had never been warm or close since that time. Moreover Boumedienne was keen to attract Soviet assistance for Algeria. When he flew to Moscow in the summer of 1967, the Algerian president became the first Arab leader to stage a summit visit to the Soviet Union since the Arab defeat. President Atassi of Syria, who also had an eye on the Arab leadership, quickly followed him. But neither man had sufficient popular following to threaten Nasser's leadership and by the end of 1969 Boumedienne appeared to have lost interest. Since then Algeria's attitude towards Arab affairs has become one of distant interest, approaching detachment.

Israel's gain and losses from the war proved to be paradoxical. Prestige was her chief gain. But prestige had not been her war aim. The motives for her pre-emptive strike were not those proclaimed on the morning of 5 June, that is, a riposte to an Egyptian invasion. Nor was concern over Elat more than symbolic, although lines of communications were important symbols. The Israelis' real hope was to compel their unrealistic neighbours to accept the Jewish State. And whatever the dimensions of this state might be they wanted security for it. (A complication was the wide difference of opinion as to the location of the frontiers of Israel, and some Israelis seem disposed to accept the newly extended territory as the reality they wished to secure.)

But Israel had won land as well as prestige from her six days of bloody battle. Much of this land, like Sinai, was an empty waste. But some of it was inhabited, and the conquest of people and property brings enormous obligations. 'We have conquered a dung-heap in order to win a pearl', said one Israeli soldier on the West Bank shortly after the cease-fire. 'We've got Jerusalem again — and we've got the refugee camps too.' After the war Israel found that she was responsible for the welfare of 1,330,000 hostile Arabs, more than a tenth of whom were impoverished refugees from the 1948 war. Those Arabs not only had to be fed and housed, but also policed and screened for saboteurs. In Gaza there were refugees who had emerged as commandos during the fighting and slipped back into their warren of tin roofed shacks afterwards. Neither territory nor prestige could produce security. Before 1967 Israel's losses from border incursions had been irregular and small; they were certainly far less than the toll she had periodically inflicted on the Arabs in reprisal raids. After 1967 Israel had to keep a far larger number of her 230,000 army reservists in uniform and the number of Israeli casualties mounted with steady momentum. By 1970 Israel was spending, in hard cash, more than three million dollars a day on defence. For such an expenditure in blood and cash much of the land she had gained seemed to offer a bleak return.

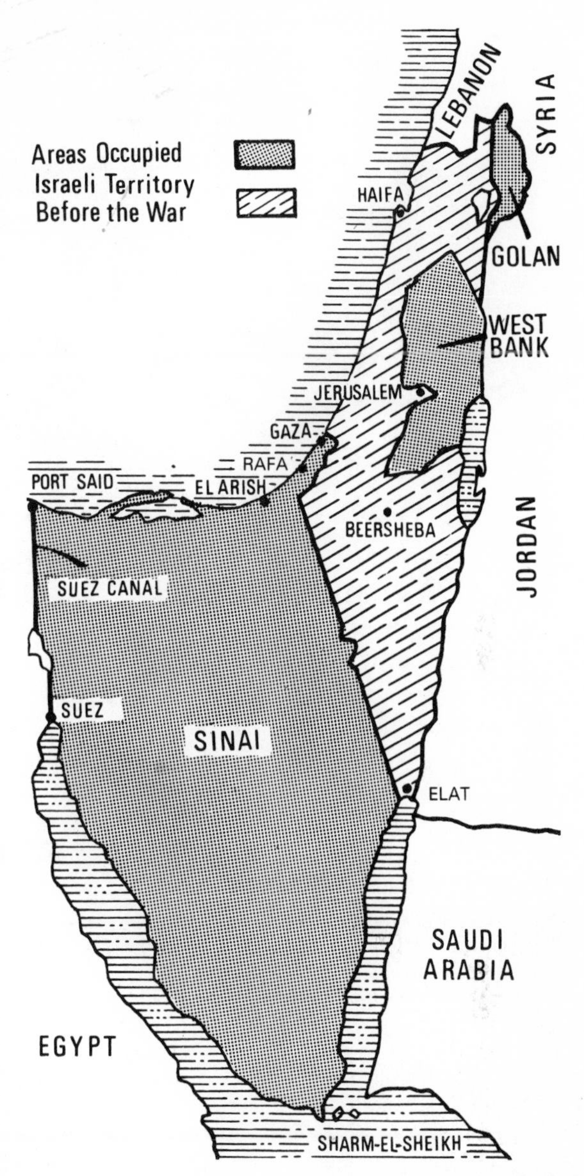

Above: Territory occupied during the Six-Day War, 5-10 June 1967.

Despite such difficulties the Israelis quickly succeeded to an astonishing degree in restoring normality. Following the pattern of the United States occupation of Japan they handed back authority to the mayors and city councils of Arab towns, and Arab officials were encouraged to restore communal services — water, electricity, sanitation — to towns and villages. New currency systems were devised and shops reopened. At the same time the Israelis were prepared to be ruthless when the situation demanded toughness. The more frequent the attacks by the fedayeen the more the reprisals. Homes in which arms were found or reported to have been visited by Palestinian commandos

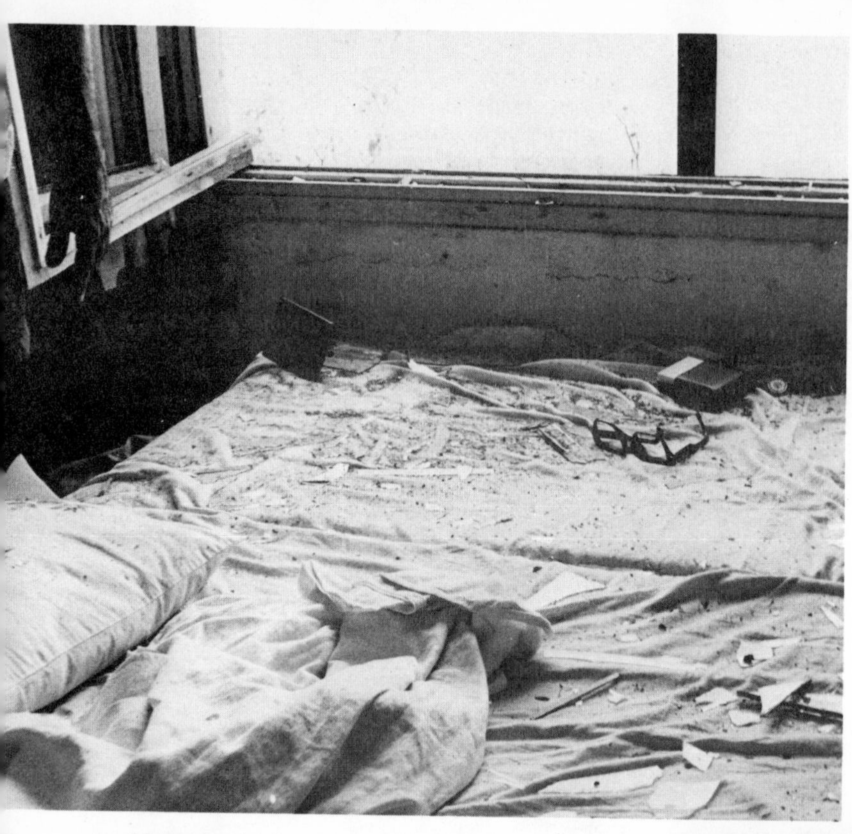

Left: The Jordanians with long range artillery shelled other kibutzim. Kibbutz Moaz-Halm September 1969.

Right and below: Kibbutz Massada December 1969.

were blown up; Arabs suspected of sabotage activities were summarily shipped off to prisoner-of-war camps. In Jerusalem Israeli soldiers evicted Arabs from what was once the Jewish quarter of the Old City; Arabs believed to be associated with the Palestine guerillas were seized and forced across the river into Jordan.

Inevitably these severities of military occupation brought victorious Israel into closer and more bitter contact with the last and most important party of the war — the Palestinians. Before June 1967 most Palestinians had existed on the Arab side of the 1948 armistice line; 300,000 of them were enclosed in the Gaza Strip, many thousands more lived on the West Bank where their activities were supervised and curbed by Hussein's Arab Legion. Fedayeen activities had been on a relatively small scale up to the time of the crisis which provoked the war. But the defeat of the Arab armies gave a new impetus to the Palestine guerilla movement. Arab propaganda had promised certain victory over Israel, and in the humiliation of defeat the Palestinians came to realise, as never before, the bitter fact that for nearly 20 years they had been only a minor factor in the conflict. For the first time the Arab struggle against Israel began to get some sympathy in the west, and the Palestinians began to compare their cause with that of occupied Europe in World War II. Revered by the rest of the Arab world the guerilla attacks mounted from Jordan or Lebanon prompted Israeli reprisals — usually in the ratio of ten to one — which scorched the east bank of the Jordan valley and ultimately turned southern Lebanon into a no-man's-land.

On the whole the armistice lines with Egypt, Syria and Jordan remained reasonably quiet until the end of 1968. But the Six-Day War had left the Arabs a legacy of shame and bitterness and they gazed across the cease-fire line with increasing fury and frustration as Israeli settlements started to sprout in the occupied territories.

The first incident leading to what the Israelis were to dub the 'War of Attrition' occurred in Sinai, and stemmed from differences of interpretation as to the precise location of the dividing line between Israel and Egypt. From Suez in the south the line was supposed to run 'up the Canal' and the Israelis interpreted this as a line passing through the middle of the Canal. They also assumed that if the Egyptians used boats on their side of the waterway Israel had the right to do the same on their side. Consequently when the Egyptians started to use small boats, the Israelis followed suit. When the Egyptians opened fire, the Israelis retaliated and the sitution began to deteriorate rapidly when the Israeli Air Force bombed targets in Suez and other Egyptian towns on the west bank of the Canal. Eventually both sides agreed to stop using boats in the Canal, and for a time the situation seemed to improve although the shooting did not stop altogether.

In September 1968 however, there was another development when the Egyptians initiated an attritional offensive. Egyptian artillery opened fire on Israeli positions along the Canal and as they continued to pound them Israeli casualties began to mount. The Israelis set a high value on human life and Nasser, advised by the Russians, saw this as a means of bringing pressure to bear on Israel. Stepping up the tempo of operations would increase Israel's economic burden but, more important a constant drain of casualties would undermine Israeli morale.

In the beginning it certainly seemed as if the strategy of attrition would work. Ten Israeli soldiers were killed and 17 wounded in the first Egyptian bombardment, 15 killed and 34 wounded in the second. Israeli artillery hit back, bombarding military installations, the Suez oil installations, the villages and towns along the Canal. But it was clear to the Israelis from the outset that merely returning the fire was no answer to the new Egyptian ploy, and the Israeli Air Force embarked on a series of punitive raids.

In the course of the War of Attrition over 8,000 tons of bombs were used and 150 Egyptian pilots were shot down. The MiG-21C and D interceptors flown by Egyptians were no match for the Israelis, it seemed. Moreover the Russian SAM-2 missiles appeared to be wholly ineffective.

There was little the Egyptians could do except to step up the artillery duels and commando raids across the canal. Doing so brought further reprisals and the Israelis extended the scope of their operations beyond the Suez front. On two occasions, in November 1968 and in the following April, Israeli raiding parties were sent by helicopter to attack bridges over the Nile and electricity plants in Upper Egypt. And by the end of 1969 Suez and Port Tewfik had been virtually razed to the ground by Israeli shelling and the Israelis had demonstrated in no uncertain manner their ability to strike far beyond the Egyptian lines without any appreciable opposition.

Encouraged by their successes the Israelis sent the new F-4 Phantom fighter-bombers, which they received from the United States in September 1969, to raid deeper into Egypt. (President Johnson authorised the shipment of Phantoms and other American arms to Israel in October 1968 just before the presidential election when the scale of the Russian rearmament programme became known. When President Nixon took office in January the Phantoms had not yet left, and their delivery was held up until September. Up to the outbreak of the Yom Kippur War American deliveries of military equipment to Israel amounted to less than a quarter of what the Soviet Union poured into Egypt and Syria alone. Altogether 95 Phantoms and 160 A-4 Skyhawks were delivered; Israel also obtained some 850 tanks from Britain and the US.) As the Phantoms were even more powerful than the Mirages the Israelis had been using so successfully, Egypt's President Nasser faced a truly horrifying prospect. In January 1970 therefore he set off for Moscow to beg for more help to defend Egypt against Israeli air attacks and to ask that, until Egyptian crews could be trained in the use of the highly sophisticated SAM missiles, the Russians would allow their own crews to man them.

The Soviet leaders were willing enough to supply more weapons, but they were not at all happy about putting Russians in charge of the anti-aircraft missiles and letting them fire them at Israeli aircraft. The Soviet Government was currently involved in delicate discussions with Washington about a Middle East settlement and they did not wish to provoke a military confrontation with the US. On a visit to Washington for talks with Lyndon Johnson in 1968 Mr Kosygin had been considerably shaken by the depth of pro-Israel sentiment in America, and he had impressed on his colleagues and associates in the Kremlin the need for caution in extending Russian cooperation with Egypt. So Nasser was told that acceding to his proposals would upset the balance of power in the Middle East. The Egyptian President's reply was to the effect that the balance of power had already been upset by America's supply of Phantoms to Israel and that it was therefore imperative for Egypt to have some answer to these deadly weapons of offence.

After a week of argument the Soviet leaders agreed to meet Nasser's demands, and — as they had predicted themselves — their response transformed the strategic situation in the Middle East. Soviet arms deliveries were stepped up and in the course of the following year some 2,500 million dollars worth of military equipment was sent to Egypt. This equipment included improved SAM-2s and new SAM-3 ('Goa') missiles, specially designed to counter low-level attack. Mobile radar-directed four-barrelled 23mm anti-aircraft cannons were also sent, together with hundreds of 14.5mm, 23mm, and 37mm towed anti-aircraft guns. About 15,000 Russians moved to Egypt and Russian troops took over the manning of the SAM missiles while Russian pilots, in a superior version of the well-tried MiG, flew missions in defence of Cairo. In April 1970 Israeli pilots encountered Russian air cover over Cairo for the first time, and discreetly withdrew from it.

It was now obvious that a direct Soviet-American military confrontation would be inevitable unless the tension was relaxed. Thus, when the US expressed concern about Soviet involvement in Egypt, the Russians canvassed the idea of a cease-fire. But this did not stop the anti-aircraft missile defence network, originally set up to cover Cairo and Alexandria, being extended, and missiles sites began to creep towards the Canal. Israel tried to eliminate the sites by bombing them, and on one occasion challenged Soviet pilots flying the six Soviet MiG squadrons in Egypt, shooting down several. But the Israelis were also losing aircraft and partly for this reason in August 1970 they accepted a cease-fire, together with a 'stand-still' in the region 32 miles on each side of the Canal. Despite this the Russian missiles were pushed forward until some 40 or 50 sites, comprising 500-600 missiles, were established up to 19 miles from the Canal. Half of the missiles were SAM-3s and the overall system provided the Egyptians with air cover extending to 10 miles over the Israeli side of the Canal. To counter this the US agreed to supply the Israelis with another 18 Phantoms and to provide electronic countermeasures (ECM) equipment to neutralise the SAMs. Until this equipment was tested there was no way of telling whether it was effective. In the short term, however, there was little doubt that the Egyptians had gained added security.

Safe behind the missile-screen the reorganised Egyptian Army was training hard, for one sole purpose: to cross the canal and recover the territory lost in 1967. Under the direction of Russian instructors, military 'advisers' and technicians, Egyptian officers absorbed the lessons of the Six-Day War and mastered Soviet tactics. Soviet bridging techniques and procedures were practised and plans formulated for a crossing of the Canal and the invasion of Sinai. Appreciating that the Arabs had been unable to compete with the Israelis in tank warfare the Russians proffered supplies of portable anti-tank missiles; first the PUR-61 'Snappers', and later the PUR-64 'Saggers' which were to blunt the cutting edge of the Israeli armour in Sinai during the first days of the coming war.

But the Russians remained anxious to avoid a military confrontation with the US, and this led to problems in their dealings with Egypt — and later with Syria — in 1971 and 1972. These were probably an inevitable development consequent on the intensification of Egyptian nationalism combined with resentment over the presence of the growing number of Russians in Egypt. Friction is said to have developed because the Russians were endeavouring to restrain the Egyptians from embarking on another war with Israel. Whatever the cause, in May 1971 the Russians were peremptorily ordered out of Egypt, and the military advisers and technicians quietly packed their bags and sailed home.

Why the Russians withdrew so politely and meekly is something of an enigma. The commonly accepted theory is that they did so in order to avoid further deterioration of their relationship with the Arab world, which would have an effect on Soviet bases and facilities in Egypt. Another theory postulates that the withdrawal was influenced by Dr Kissinger making it clear to Moscow that Soviet military adventures in the Middle East were incompatible with recent requests for American economic and technical assistance to Russian industry and for grain to feed the Russian people. Whichever of these two theories is correct, the Israelis can be excused for wondering whether the withdrawal was simply a move agreed between the Egyptians and Russians as part of a deception plan to induce the Israelis to lower their guard. If it was, then it certainly succeeded.

Left: Kibbutz Kfar-Rupin August 1970.

Below: Terrorist attacks on 'soft' civilian targets were all part of the War of Attrition. This picture was taken after a bomb had been planted in a School bus in northern Israel.

Right: Kibbutz Hamaduju June 1970.

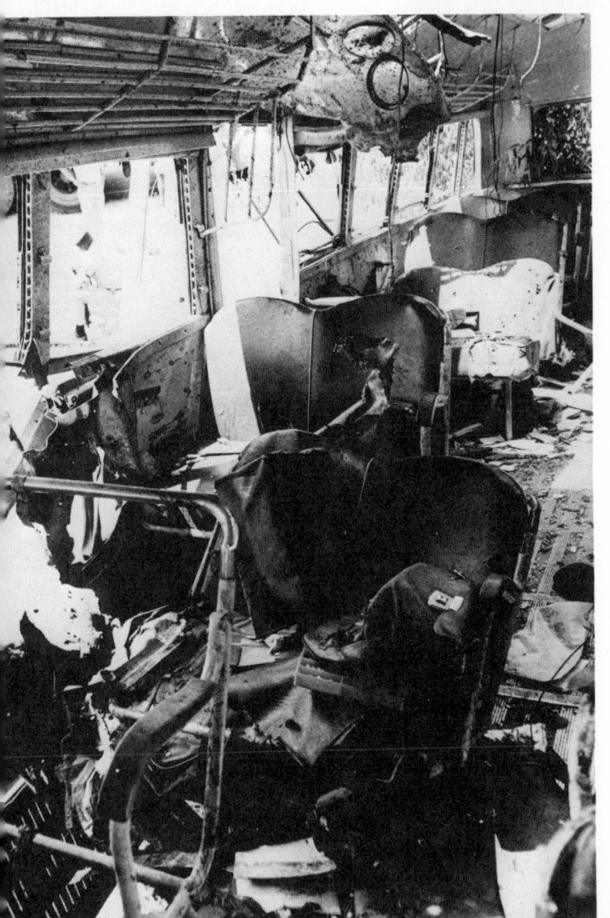

In effect, the Russians were understandably worried that an Egyptian invasion of Sinai might jeopardise the prospects of detente — which at that time were moving along nicely — and, more important, bring a military confrontation with the US. But there can be little doubt that, having armed and trained Egypt and Syria for a war on Israel, they had a shrewd idea of the Arab plan. That the Russians actually planned the war with Egypt and Syria, or even approved it, is not so certain. The Russians can hardly have wanted another war in the Middle East, but they probably found it expedient to refrain from giving the Egyptians an ultimatum or interfering in any way with the plans. Both superpowers are locked into the Middle East by their respective clients. The difference is that the United States cannot afford to write off the goodwill of the Arabs as readily as the Soviet Union can align itself against Israel.

Whatever Moscow's attitude towards the war — and once it had begun the Russians had little choice but to support its Arab clients if they were to keep them as such — it appears that it was the Arabs themselves who decided on hostilities. '1971', said Anwar Sadat who had become Egypt's new president when Nasser suddenly died in September 1970, 'will be the Year of Decision'. But when 1972 had come and gone without any untoward occurrence many Israelis felt confirmed in their views that the Egyptian President set more store by retoric than action. On May Day 1973, however, Sadat transformed his threat into a vow. He was not going to permit the state of 'no war, no peace' to continue for much longer, and in a speech primarily intended for the Arab audience in the Israeli-occupied territories he promised that the 'night will not last for long', and urged them to wait patiently for zero hour.

Yet it looked as if zero hour was going to be postponed until the autumn, for in August Sadat announced that he was embarking on a three-month political offensive to consolidate Egypt's relations with the other Arab 'front-line' states. Saudi Arabia headed the list of the states — not so much because King Faisal's kingdom was in the front-line, but because Faisal's financial and political support was essential to Egypt and Syria's military build-up. But Faisal, nursing dreams of a coalition of Arab States to counter the Arab radicals led by Libya's Colonel Gaddafi, set conditions for increased financial support to Cairo. He was willing to cooperate in stepping up the pressure to secure a settlement of the Palestine question, he told Sadat when the latter visited him during August. But such cooperation would be dependent upon Egypt's rapprochement with Jordan, for the Arab world had fallen apart after the Six-Day War, and Egypt had severed diplomatic relations with Jordan after King Hussein's stern military action against the Palestinian guerillas operating in his country. (The cease-fire of August 1970 contributed to the fate of the guerillas. Israel continued to operate against the guerilla bases and the guerillas came in increasing conflict with the Government of Jordan — one of their main hosts. After the sensational hijacking of four airliners by the Popular Front for the Liberation of Palestine in September 1970 hostilities broke out between the guerillas and the Jordanian army, the former being heavily defeated after an incipient Syrian invasion of Jordan had been repelled. Subsequently renewed fighting, and a further defeat for the guerillas in April 1971, greatly diminished the effectiveness of the surviving guerillas in Jordan.) Once the ties between Amman, Cairo and Damascus had been re-established, the Saudi Arabian monarch promised more money for Egypt, and to exert political pressure on the United States to lessen its support for Israel. The Arab leaders were convinced that the threats of cutting off oil supplies were already beginning to have an effect and that fears of an energy crisis had become a factor which could effect the policy of the West.

With the promise of Faisal's cooperation in his pocket Sadat returned to Egypt and a tripartite summit meeting of the leaders of Egypt, Syria and Jordan was called for the middle of September. As the three Arab leaders, King Hussein of Jordan, President Hafad Assad of Syria and President Sadat gathered in Cairo the Israelis gave a spectacular demonstration of their ability to dominate the skies of the Middle East. Israeli fighter aircraft flying on a routine patrol about 20 miles from the Syrian coast were intercepted by a group of Syrian MiG-21s. The ensuing engagement was short, fast, and violent — and apparently decidedly one-sided. Within a few minutes, according to the Israelis, their Mirages and Phantoms shot down 13 MiGs — at a cost of only one Mirage. The Syrian version of the dogfight was different; they claimed that they had lost only eight of their planes and had destroyed five of the Israelis'. Irrespective of whether the Syrian or the Israeli report was believed, the outcome of this aerial battle could well be interpreted as a warning to the Arab leaders that in another 'confrontation' Israel might still prove to be the predominant military power in the area.

No clarion call for war against Israel was issued by the Cairo summit in fact. Indeed the Arab leaders appeared to have done little more than patch over the differences that existed between them. King Hussein was warmly received by Sadat and the Syrian President Assad. But when he was asked for help in reactivating the 'eastern front' against Israel by permitting commando forces to enter Jordan, Hussein's response was a categorical refusal. Nevertheless when the conference was over, Sadat declared that Cairo would resume diplomatic ties with Amman, and the indications were that Syria would shortly do the same.

In retrospect it is clear that another war with Israel had been decided upon, and the fact that the decision to initiate military action before Sadat's three months of political offensive were over appears to have been motivated by Sadat's own belief that the political climate was ripe for it. The UN General Assembly was in session this time and Dr Kissinger was reported to be intensifying American efforts to bring about a Middle East peace settlement. On the evidence of Kissinger's performance in settling the Vietnam War only after fighting had reached a peak Sadat concluded that an escalation of hostilities might well act as a spur in the Middle East. There was still hope, of course, that a bit of sabre-rattling might promote concrete proposals for peace without the need for actual fighting. But Sadat himself did not think that anything would be resolved, by Kissinger or anyone else, without war. 'Everyone has fallen asleep over the Middle East crisis . . .' he said on May Day, 'The time has come for a shock . . .'. So, as preparations for war were quietly stepped up, the only matter that had to be decided now was when Sadat's promised shock would be administered.

Selection of 6 October — the holiest and also the quietest day in the Jewish year — as D-day for the coming war was based on three premises. First, the Arabs decided, the Israelis would be in a relaxed and holiday mood. Thousands of servicemen would probably be home on leave; people would be fasting and at prayer, and even the Israeli Broadcasting Service would be closed down. Secondly, with an election in the offing, even if the Israelis were to glean any information about Egyptian and Syrian troop movements prior to the opening of hostilities, the odds were that Mrs Golda Meir's Government would prefer to take a chance on it being a false alarm rather than mobilise reservists. To lend weight to this theory both the Syrians and the Egyptians had deliberately created false tension on a number of occasions in recent months. Finally, Israeli attention was known to be focussed on the question of Jewish immigration from the Soviet Union. Austria's decision to give in to Arab terrorists and close transit facilities used by Russian Jewish immigrants bound for Israel had recently brought Israel's Prime Minister Golda Meir into confrontation with the Austrian Chancellor in Vienna, and the Israelis were seething with rage.

So the stage was set and the decision to strike on 6 October was taken. From then on the prelude to hostilities was a mirror image of that which preceded the Six-Day War. In 1967 the Arab news media were claiming that the Israelis were massing troops on the Syrian border; in 1973 it was Israeli newsmen who spoke of Arab troops concentrating on Israel's borders. In 1967 they were ready and opted to strike first; six years later they were neither ready nor prepared to deliver the first blow.

10 Yom Kippur 1973

On Friday, 5 October 1973, newspapers in Israel reminded their readers that the following day would be Yom Kippur, the Jewish Day of Atonement. '. . . From sunset tonight until tomorrow morning', they declared, 'most Jews will be fasting and spending much of their time in synagogues, repenting of their sins and praying for a good year. The country will come to a standstill . . . with only the Defence Forces and the most vital services keeping operational. Traffic will halt this afternoon . . .' As this form of Yom Kippur curtain-raiser had been appearing year after year there was nothing to suggest that the 1973 Day of Atonement would be different from any year since 1967. Earlier in the week Beirut newspapers had reported that Syria was calling up reservists because Israel was said to be massing troops on her side of the border along the Golan Heights. There had also been rumours that Egyptian troops were manoeuvring behind the Canal. But there was nothing especially novel or sinister about such snippets of news; reports of Syrian and Egyptian troops concentrating and manoeuvring were all part of the war of nerves. The Israeli public was more interested in the rumpus over Austria's decision to shut down the Jewish transit camp at Schoenau than in rumours of war. And with retrospective hindsight some Israelis were later to wonder whether the Austrian Chancellor had collaborated in the Arab deception plan — albeit unwittingly.

To Israeli soldiers in the forward areas all was quiet along the Suez and Golan fronts. Along the 103-mile cease-fire line behind the Suez Canal men of a reservist infantry brigade sitting in observation posts in the isolated fortifications of the Bar-Lev Line watched Egyptian troops sunning themselves on the other side of the Canal. Over the past three years not a single soldier had died for his country on either side of the Canal. And except for rare encounters between Israeli and Egyptian aircraft, the confrontation had assumed the look of a 'phoney war' — in which the primary enemy for the troops on both sides was just plain boredom. On 5 October there was no indication of any change. The once-thriving cities of Suez and Ismailia had the appearance of ghost towns; parties of Egyptian troops bathed regularly in the Suez Canal, and nobody seemed to be wearing a steel helmet. Nor did there seem to be any undue movement on the western side of the Canal; certainly no one saw the columns of tanks which might easily have sparked off a conflict.

But, unseen by the Israeli observers in their fortified watchtowers, the Egyptians were completing their final preparations for Operation Badr — code-named after the battle which Mohammed fought and won against great odds during the feast of Ramadan. The Canal banks have always served to shield movement in the immediate proximity of the water-way from observers on the opposite side. And following the cease-fire which marked the end of the War of Attrition the Egyptians had raised the level of these embankments and erected hessian screens to conceal their activities from Israeli observers on the other side of the Canal. Behind this cover they had rehearsed the final stages of an operation to cross the Canal, and stealthily moved up all the equipment necessary for it. Until only hours before it was to take place, however, few of the men who were to take part in the operation knew it actually would take place. The date for D-day was set in September, but this was a secret restricted to President Sadat, President Assad, the most trustworthy members of their political entourages, and a few high-ranking officers of the Egyptian and Syrian Armies. Neither the Iraq Government nor Jordan's King Hussein were in on the secret, yet both were to be involved in the war. At the beginning of October the information was passed down to the Egyptian divisional commanders, and as D-day approached, finally disseminated to battalion level. Many of the troops who took part did not know about it until the actual morning of Yom Kippur, however, although they had been practising attacks on mock Bar-Lev strongpoints for weeks. Secrecy went hand in hand with an elaborate deception plan, in which the Egyptians claimed to have used 65 different measures to distract Israel's attention from their build-up. Soldiers who were in the habit of swimming in the Canal at the same time every afternoon were ordered to continue the practice on 6 October, and some of them were in the water when the first shots were fired. Another ploy was used in the northern sector where Major-General Saad Maamoun commanded the Egyptian Second Army. Maamoun warned his men that anyone putting his helmet on one moment before the attack started would be sent into battle without it.

On the Golan Heights, where the Syrians planned to crush the Israeli defences with a massive armoured attack, preparations were harder to conceal. During the last week of September Israeli reconnaissance aircraft began to report widespread and ominous concentrations of armour and artillery behind the 1967 cease-fire line. With the approach of Yom Kippur these reports and other intelligence information suggested that something unusual

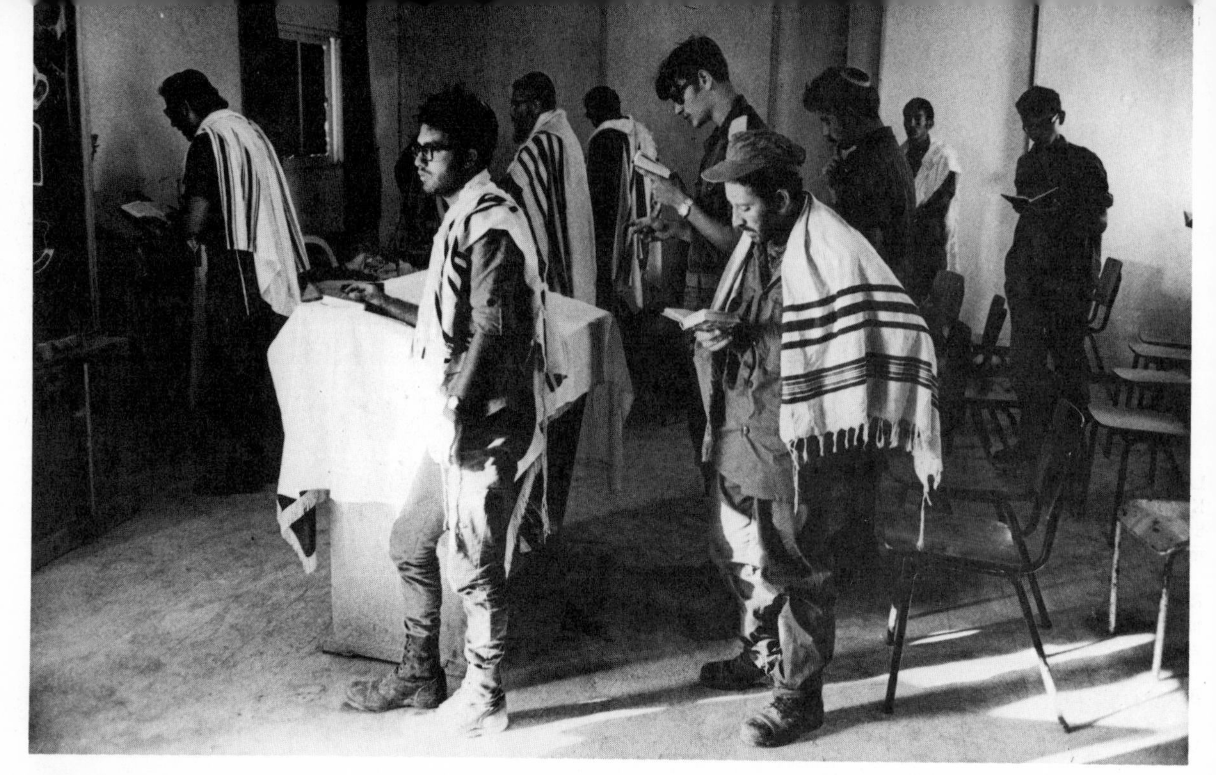

was afoot, and Moshe Dayan, Israel's Minister of Defence, was sufficiently worried to do two things. Ten days before the war began he put the Israeli Army on the alert, and reinforced General Isaac Hoffy's Northern Command with another armoured brigade. (Up to this time Hoffy had only two infantry brigades and an understrength armoured brigade with which to defend the 60 mile Golan front.) But although Dayan himself was anxious, he could not persuade the Israeli Cabinet that the situation was critical. Their view was strengthened when, two days before the onslaught began, Israeli intelligence experts concluded that a war was not imminent. Egyptian troop movement behind the Suez Canal, and Syrians in the area between Damascus and the Golan Heights were essentially 'defensive' in character they opined — experimental perhaps, part of large scale manoeuvres not likely to lead to an immediate confrontation. It was even possible that the Arabs were making preparations to deal with a possible Israeli raid — in retaliation for what had happened in Austria. Thus, although there was no lack of evidence that the Arabs were up to something, this assessment made it clear there was no immediate threat. Political indicators led to the same conclusion. In the Western World recent Egyptian political moves seemed to have been markedly unsuccessful; what was overlooked was that the same moves were almost triumphant in the Arab States. (Within a few days one Israeli source was to say that they might have included the fact that Sadat prayed in Mecca — for victory against Israel and not rain for Egypt.)

On Wednesday 3 October, the Israeli Cabinet gathered in Jerusalem for the only meeting scheduled in the week before Yom Kippur. Its deliberations were concerned almost entirely with the problems of Soviet Jews emigrating to Israel and Mrs Meir's recent face to face confrontation with the Austrian Chancellor. The build-up on Golan and ominous manoeuvrings behind the Suez Canal or the possibility of another war with the Arabs were not even discussed. In retrospect the pre-occupation with what proved to be a distraction may now seem strangely negligent. Various explanations have been put forward but critics who agree on little else agree that the almost incredible victory of 1967 was one of the root causes of the trouble. A blindness to see the facts, it is said, arose from profound conviction that the Arabs would not attack after the terrible defeat which they had suffered, or, even if they did they would make a mess of it and there would be ample time to stop them before they could do serious damage.

How terribly wrong these assumptions were was soon to be apparent. While the Israeli Cabinet was in session, the Syrians on the Golan and the Egyptians behind the Canal were putting the finishing touches to the plans for a simultaneous all-out attack on Israel. Three Syrian infantry divisions had been secretly moved up near the Golan cease-fire line, and two armoured divisions equipped with the latest Soviet tanks were deploying — ready to move through them as soon as the order was given. In Egypt the latest lorry-borne SAM missiles were being driven up from Alexandria to deploy along the Canal, and thicken up the fixed missile sites already there. From Israeli observation posts groups of Egyptian officers were seen reconnoitring along their side of the Canal, and peering through field glasses at the Israeli side. Egyptian sappers were also spotted driving stakes into the ground near the water's edge while bulldozers levelled the approaches to it. But any alarm that such activity might have occasioned among the Israelis was allayed by the air of normality that the Egyptians maintained up to the very hour of attack.

Left: Most Israelis expected to spend Yom Kippur 1973 at prayer or meditating. Spcial *Mussaf* services were arranged for the troops.

Right: on the Golan Heights the troops had been alerted and were standing to when the Syrians attacked.

Below: Israeli children in the kibbutzim near the Syrian border spent most of the war in air raid shelters.

On Thursday night road blocks were set up round Cairo's fashionable suburb of Zamalek, where many foreign residents have their homes. Movement out of the area was strictly controlled while convoys of official cars ferried the families of Russian advisers to Cairo airport where planes were waiting to fly them home to the Soviet Union. A similar scene was enacted a few hours later in Damascus. Meanwhile the Syrian armoured divisions behind Golan were moving up and artillery was redeploying; the 'defensive' posture noted by Israeli Intelligence had changed to an offensive formation.

When reports of these redeployments and concentrations reached him, the Israeli Chief of Staff, General David Elazar decided that the Intelligence assessment of 'a very low probability' of war was no longer valid. Israel's Defence Forces were immediately put on 'the highest state of readiness', all servicemen's leave was cancelled, all Air Force pilots ordered back on duty and the requisite preliminaries for calling up reserves were put into effect. A few key reservists were also alerted, amongst whom was the rumbustious General 'Arik' Sharon, who was to lead an Israeli force across the Suez Canal. General Sharon had retired only three months previously and until August had been in command of the Israeli Army in Sinai. Disappointed with his prospects of promotion, Sharon left the army to go into politics. But he was earmarked for the command of an armoured division in Sinai in the event of war, and it was this appointment he now took up.

Throughout Israel, as dusk fell on Friday evening, the Kol Nidre service signalled the start of Yom Kippur. Four Israeli ministers of the inner group known as 'Mrs Meir's kitchen cabinet' met in Tel Aviv to consider whether the hallowed calm of Yom Kippur should be disturbed by the mobilisation of Israel's armed forces. General Elazar wanted the reserves to be called immediately. But the four ministers — Mrs Meir herself, Yigal Allon, the Deputy Prime Minister, Moshe Dayan, the Minister of Defence, and Israel Galili, the Minister without Portfolio — decided against such a move. Israel must not do anything which could be interpreted as fusing the Middle East powder barrel. For almost two years the Arabs had been threatening war Mondays and Thursdays as the Yiddish saying goes, so this might well be just another instance of Egypt and Syria 'crying wolf'. But if they did break the cease-fire agreement and started a shooting match there would still be time to act. Moshe Dayan had estimated that it would take the Egyptians about 24 hours to get a bridge across the 180 metres wide Canal, even if its construction were allowed to go undisturbed. Similarly in the north, where the Syrians had never shown much professional skill in battles with the Israelis, there ought to be ample time to organise an air-strike to halt them in their tracks. What Dayan had failed to appreciate fully was the significance of the vast and elaborate aerial umbrella provided by Soviet SAM missiles. This was to make long-range Israeli air strikes far more costly than before. Recalling the tremendous success of 1967, and the poor performance of the Arab armies after the Egyptian Air Force had been smashed, Dayan reckoned it would be best to wait for the Arabs to attack. Then the world would see that it was the Egyptians and Syrians who had started the war. So Elazar's demand for an immediate call-up was turned down.

So too, in the early hours of the following morning 6 October, Yom Kippur — was his request for a pre-emptive strike. Israeli Intelligence experts listening to the transmissions of the field radios of Egyptian and Syrian army units had detected changes in traffic patterns which indicated that the Arab preparations for war were almost complete. Elazar believed that an Israeli air attack should be launched without further delay. 'How many friends would we have left if we did that?' Mrs Meir is reputed to have asked the Chief of Staff. Elazar and his predecessor General Bar-Lev — now Minister of Commerce, who had been summoned to this fresh meeting of the Israeli Cabinet's inner group — argued back emotionally. 'Every time we decide to consider the options of others we pay for it in blood', they said. In retrospect, whether it would have made a difference if Israel had snatched the initiative at the last moment by launching a preemptive air attack is questionable. It would not have been possible to surprise SAM missiles or overrun the missile defences. Neither the Egyptian nor the Syrian Air Forces were the real threat in October 1973, and if they had been destroyed as they were destroyed in 1967 it would not have made much difference; they did not contribute much to the Yom Kippur War. But Elazar and Bar-Lev were right when they forecast a heavy price in Israeli blood and bones. Believing that the Arabs were incapable of maintaining complex equipment such as missiles, and that Arab soldiers were incompetent, the Israelis paid dearly for their mistake.

In vetoing Elazar's request for permission to launch a pre-emptive strike Mrs Meir took a calculated risk. But if she was not prepared to strike first, she certainly did not intend to let Israel be caught entirely napping. So Elazar was told that he could call up the reserves. As the orders went out the Egyptians were ushering their first Israeli prisoner back across the canal. He had been pounced on by Egyptian commandos, sent across the Canal during the night of 5/6 October to sabotage an Israeli fire-trap. In the event the fire-trap, an oil-burning device controlled from the forward Bar-Lev strongpoints and which was supposed to turn the canal into a blazing inferno did not exist, and successive accounts of its technicalities are journalistic fiction. The truth is that in 1970 the Israelis tried out a device on a small section of the canal. Oil from tanks in the Bar-Lev line positions was carried in pipes to the water's edge, from where it was sprayed from nozzles at the end of the pipes, in a fine film over the surface of the Canal. The trials soon showed the device was impractical and it was discarded. Subsequently when news of the concept leaked out — deliberately leaked perhaps — the Israelis chose not to deny its existence. Thus the Canal fire-traps may be considered a successful Israeli deception measure. According to newspaper reports published during the war the man who could claim the dubious distinction of being the first Israeli to be captured in Sinai was a sapper sent to inspect and repair and damage he found to one of the oil pipes. He was, in fact, an infantryman — a reservist new to the front and totally unaware of what he was walking into when he left the shelter of his bunker. But for the luck of the draw, he would have been on leave for Yom Kippur.

To the majority of Israelis the first hint of unusual activity came at about 0700hrs when people were awakened by the sound of low flying aircraft. But the war had not started yet, and the first shots were actually fired when most of the Jews of Israel were in their synagogues, reciting the Mussaf prayer *piyut*. Shops and stores throughout Israel were closed and shuttered and streets were almost deserted until wailing sirens shattered the stillness. Traffic then began to build up, and Army couriers appeared at the doors of the crowded synagogues to seek out reservists and hustle them off to their units. In the Sephardi synagogue in Jerusalem one young man rose from his seat when his name was shouted. But his father, sitting next to him, held him until the synagogue's rabbi came up and told the father that his son must go. 'His place is not here today', the rabbi said. At some places the couriers interrupted services and handed over lists of names for the rabbi to read out. In the Beit Hakerem synagogue one of the names was that of the rabbi's own son.

All over Jerusalem and Tel Aviv men wearing prayer shawls and skullcaps could be seen driving cars or thumbing lifts to mobilisation points. Most of them went off hungry, for only a few had time to stop and break their fast which had begun at sunset the day before. In some synagogues rabbis interrupted services to tell men in their congregation that breaking their fast and using vehicles to get to their units was permissible if they were called up.

Reaction to the mobilisation was a mixture of bewilderment and anxiety. Very few Israelis knew that war was coming, but the fact that men were called up on Yom Kippur indicated that something serious was afoot. 'The Arabs must have started shooting' said one man in Jerusalem, 'we would never start anything on Yom Kippur.'

At the offices of the Egged Bus Company in Tel Aviv the Minister of Transport had summoned an emergency meeting of the heads of the company's departments. In normal times Egged operated like any other national or local bus company. In a national emergency, however, Egged buses were regarded as Israel's main 'battle wagons'. In 1948 the first Egged buses had carried men and supplies to the Jewish enclaves in Jerusalem and the Negev. Eight years later other Egged buses ferried large numbers of troops to staging posts and battlefields in the Sinai campaign; in the Six-Day War some of the same buses were used as personnel carriers in Sinai. Now they were called upon to fulfill the same role once again. The only difference was that while the earlier wars had been of relatively short duration, it looked as if this one might run into weeks. or even months. Public transport services would have to be restricted to cope with the military commitment, and the drivers, who were not called up to serve in another capacity would undoubtedly have to work longer hours.

The first job was to get the buses back on the road and operating their normal services so that reservists could get to their assembly points and staging posts. So Egged was hurriedly put on an emergency footing, and at 1430hrs — for the first time since the establishment of Israel — Tel Aviv Central Bus Station came to life on Yom Kippur. Minutes later buses were running, crowded with reservists anxious to join their units. Of the 3,200 buses available and

Below: Above ground many of the buildings suffered severe damage.

normally running on domestic services, no less than 2,600 had been ear-marked as transport and the drivers of these buses were called out so quickly that many left home without even a toothbrush. With thousands of other drivers, mechanics and administrative staff mobilised for duty with fighting units, what was left of the Egged Company had to be reorganised to function with those who had been excused any service because they were too old, too young or too frail. By pressing old age pensioners of the company into service again, putting office staff behind the wheel, and slashing public services and changing routes, a scheme emerged which was to see Israel through the Yom Kippur emergency. Inevitably the individuals concerned suffered hardships. A minimum nine-hour day had to be introduced and overtime bonuses were cancelled in order to enable the Egged Company to pay a full salary to those who had been called up. Problems and arguments about working conditions with the possibility of strike action were forgotten for the duration. Israel was fighting for her existence, and the buses were to run on desert tracks across the scorching Sinai, up the winding mountain roads of the Golan Heights, in towns, on the interurban roads, on special missions and from everywhere to anywhere in Israel.

Israel Radio broke its traditional Yom Kippur silence shortly before the buses started running. When it came on the air the first broadcast was to the effect that Egyptian and Syrian forces had launched simultaneous attacks across the Canal and on the Golan Heights. This announcement was followed by orders for Haga, the Civil Defence Organisation, to go on full alert, and a warning that air raids could be expected. All afternoon a programme of news bulletins and classical music was interrupted by incongruous phrases like 'meat-pie', 'sea-wolf', and 'fleshpots' — coded messages for reserve units. By dusk virtually every Israeli, and much of the rest of the world as well, knew that what Moshe Dayan called an 'all-out war' had started again. For Israel Television the Yom Kippur 1973 was its introduction to war reporting, and it had a difficult time. Television almost always lags behind radio because a radio man with a small tape recorder can get to places that a TV team cannot reach. Nor did the Israeli Army approve of newsmen of any kind being right up in the front line as so many Americans were in Vietnam. The result was that the Israelis saw much of the war on their TV screens by switching their sets to the Cairo or Amman TV channels.

In the cities and the kibbutzim near the borders, the wail of sirens prompted people to turn on the radios and the air raid warning caused those who were not involved in the call-up to seek shelter. In Jersualem thousands of tourists were herded into underground shelters, where older women whose vivid memories of past wars wer etched into their minds, sat down and began to moan. Most of them recovered when sirens sounded the all-clear a short while later, but a few insisted in remaining in the concrete room until the following morning.

Elsewhere carefully prepared emergency plans were being set in motion. Civilian lorries and cars were being requisitioned, and hospitals were clearing their wards of all but the most serious cases. Ambulances and private vehicles evacuated hundreds of non-critical cases to their homes to make the maximum hospital space available for the expected rush of war casualties. Doctors and nurses were ordered to emergency posts in hospitals and clinics. Petrol filling stations, closed for the holiday, reopened during the afternoon; in the meantime several Arab-operated petrol stations in East Jerusalem which had remained open as usual this Saturday had already been doing brisk business.

The suddenness of the war created some curious anomalies in both Israel and Egypt. Orders were issued that Tel Aviv should be blacked out and car headlights masked. When daylight faded, however, lights in the shop windows along the fashionable Dizengoff Street snapped on automatically and it was hours before some shopkeepers could be found to turn them off. In the Egyptian capital also the news that war had actually erupted was as surprising to the man in the street as it was to his counterpart in Jerusalem. In the Islamic world it was the holy month of Ramadan and most Arabs were in the middle of their daily fast when Radio Cairo broadcast the news that Israeli jets had attacked Egyptian installations on the Gulf of Suez. Half an hour later the normal programme was replaced by martial music which was interrupted a little while later by an announcer who broke in to tell listeners that 'Egyptian forces have mounted a successful assault across the Suez Canal in several sectors and seized strong enemy positions . . . '

The news was greeted with little enthusiasm; there was little of the frenzy that accompanied the start of the Six-Day War. People were more concerned about the meal which would break their Ramadan fast when dusk descended. As dusk approached, however, Cairo began to take on the look of a city at war. The airport was closed, and although mismanagement of the blackout arrangment resulted in the main streets being brightly lit for hours after sunset, by midnight Cairo had been dimmed-out.

In the late afternoon Mrs Meir went on the air to assure Israel that 'the government have no doubts as to our victory'. She spoke firmly, with an air of serene confidence in the Israeli cause and the ability to back right with might. 'It is our belief', she said, 'that this renewal of Egyptian — Syrian aggression is an act of madness.' Moshe Dayan, who broadcast a few hours later was even more optimistic. Speaking with a self-assurance verging on cockiness he minced no words about Israel suffering early reverses and having to be on the defence fro some time. However he was sure of the future, he said and his stern injunction 'The Arabs will take no advantge from this war . . . ' promised a *hatima tova* which boded ill for the Arabs.

On the other side President Sadat and the Egyptian Ministers made no public statement, but President Assad addressed and Syrian nation over Radio Damascus that evening. By the usual standard of Arab rhetoric his speech was mild and its message, clouded by references to the Arab martyrs of the Crusades, was difficult to discern. But the gist was that the Egyptian-Syrian attack on Israel was a pre-emptive defensive operation. As described by the Palestinian guerilla broadcasts, however, the Arab aim was what it had always been: to destroy Israel and reconstitute Palestine.

11 The Military Balance 1973

It has long been a military cliché that all armies train to fight the last war. But the Israelis seemed different. After the Six-Day War they had a wide unpopulated buffer zone to protect Israel from an Egyptian attack, a smaller and shallower buffer in the northern Golan sector, and the river Jordan provided a natural obstacle against incursions from the east. Egyptian aircraft were now at least 150 miles from Israeli cities; the Syrians no longer overlooked Israel's northern settlements; Jordan had been emasculated; all in all the new frontiers constitued probably the best natural defensive position that Israel could hope to enjoy. The Israelis could therefore afford to modify their pre-emptive first-strike policy, and a new deterrent formula was devised, adjusted to the changed strategic realities of the situation. With the Soviet presence in Egypt giving a new and dangerous dimension to any offensive strategy, the possibility of being a little less quick off the mark appeared all the more valuable. So what was now envisaged was based on Israel's version of a *force de frappe* — a devasting air strike — followed by a massive armoured counter-attack. Between 1967 and 1973 this was the policy adhered to by the Israelis — although in the War of Attrition they were careful to show that they were willing to bomb Soviet-manned missile sites and to engage Soviet aircraft, at least near the Canal, if their buffer zone was threatened.

For its success the Israeli deterrent depended on an early warning period, during which an Arab offensive would be confined to the buffer zones while the Israelis mobilised. Thus, to provide the early warning of an impending attack the Bar Lev Line was conceived. This 'line' was not as its name may have implied, a fortified line comparable with the Maginot or Siegfried Lines or the Atlantic Wall of World War II, but simply a string of 40 observation posts on the east bank of the Canal. Manned usually by a section of eight or ten men (and rarely more than a platoon of about 30), few of the posts were capable of supporting each other by fire if attacked. Their function was merely to provide information and they were never meant to stand up indefinitely to an all-out Arab onslaught. But the amount of elaborate protective measures provided for the inmates of these concrete and steel bunkers — earth and sand 30 feet thick, walls and roofs of granite blocks, surrounded by minefields — led people to believe that they were tougher nuts to crack than turned out to be the case. As 'strongpoints' they were supposed to be able to hold out individually and for some time. The fact that a few were overrun, and several others were voluntarily evacuated at the beginning of the Yom Kippur War provoked a good deal of adverse comment and the concept of the Bar-Lev line was debunked. For the purpose for which it existed however the Bar-Lev line did not fail.

Behind the thin screen of the Bar Lev line the Israelis deployed in a 'non-war' situation were relying on their tanks and artillery to slow up and eventually halt any Arab offensive. Tank-artillery-aircraft teams had been used with devastating effect in the Six-Day War and the Israelis believed that the same weapons and the same tactics could give them another blitzkrieg victory when war broke out again. What they had forgotten was that the Six-Day War was an offensive campaign from the very beginning; in 1973 they were to fight a defensive battle first — something contrary to both their concept of operations and their psychology.

Between the wars the Israelis did much to improve the cutting edge of their fighting machine. Unlike the Arabs, they fostered the manufacture of their own weapons; they also showed great ingenuity in adapting imported equipment to the conditions of the Middle East and in standardising, for easy maintenance, a heterogenous collection of weapons. But one problem remained, despite vigorous efforts to make Israel more and more self-sufficient. Because the more sophisticated weapons had to be imported the Israelis could not lightly contemplate action that would entail substantial losses unless they had some assurance about the supply of replacements. How the lack of such an assurance or the denial of munitions or spares could constrain the Israeli war effort at a critical phase of the campaign was to become all too apparent in October 1973.

The fact that half the Israeli defence budget (of about 1,250 million dollars) was allotted to the air force is indicative of the priority accorded to the Israeli air arm. Over the years there were many behind-the-scenes arguments as to whether so much money should be spent on aircraft rather than on armoured fighting vehicles. But those who supported the air force got their way and American Phantom F-4 interceptors and Skyhawk A-4 fighter-bombers were purchased from the US to supplement the French Mirage IIIc and Super Mystère fighters.

In 'normal' times, when the pot was merely simmering in the Middle East, the strength of the Israeli Air Force was about 10,000 men, of whom some 1,200 were pilots. The

Above: Israeli airborne troops disembarking from a Super Frelon assault helicopter. / *via Jackson*

Right: S-58 helicopter acquired by the IAF from Luftwaffe stocks. / *Peltz via Jackson*

pilots, taken from the cream of Israeli's young men, were dedicated professionals who enlisted at 18 and trained for three years before qualifying to fly operationally. Although their average age was only 23, all of them had an impressive number of flying hours to their credit and their morale was superb. With a ratio of 2.4 pilots to a plane the Israeli Air Force was better placed than the Arabs who did not have a surplus of pilots. For ground and maintenance tasks in emergencies skilled reservists were called up and when fully mobilised the Israeli Air Force totalled about 20,000. In 1973 Israel possessed about 500 aircraft of all types, including helicopters and its 400 first line combat aircraft were organised into fifteen squadrons — five of interceptors, six of fighter-bombers, two of transport aircraft and two of helicopters. There was no Israeli strategic bomber force, mainly because Israel had no long-range bombers.

Of the individual types of aircraft it was the Phantom which was to become the best known. First produced in 1967 it is described in US parlance as a multi-role fighter. Powered by two turbojet engines the Phantom F-4 can reach a speed of Mach 2.4, has a range of 1,500 miles and carries a diverse and deadly load of weapons. The main armament, mounted in a pod in the nose of the plane, is an M61 20mm multi-barrelled Vulcan gun, which is a modern adaptation of the old Gatling gun and which had a cyclic rate of fire of 6,000 rounds per minute. The rest of the Phantom's armament can be varied to suit the circumstances, by attaching bombs, missiles or containers of napalm to fitments provided under the wings. The single-seater Skyhawk, an older American plane, was also to prove its worth to the Israelis in October 1973. With a top speed of about 600mph and a range of 1,000 miles, the Skyhawk was armed with two 20mm cannon and capable of carrying up to five tons of other weapons and electronic devices — air-to-air and air-to-surface missiles, bombs, or ECM equipment to jam the guidance radars of enemy ground-to-air missiles like the SAM-6. If need be both the Phantoms and Skyhawks were capable of carrying nuclear weapons. (There has been a great deal of conjecture as to whether or not Israel has acquired nuclear weapons. Her best known nuclear reactor, at Dimona, produces each year enough plutonium for two bombs; as the reactor started up in 1964 the Israelis could have enough plutonium for an arsenal of low-yield bombs. But the Israeli Government has never admitted to having nuclear

Right: F-4 Phantom, backbone of the modern IAF. / *via BIPAC*

Below: A-4 Skyhawk fighter-bomber. / *via BIPAC*

Bottom: Casevac duty on the Suez Front for a Bell Iroquois of the IDF. / *Camera Press via Jackson*

weapons, and has steered well clear of making a threat of nuclear action).*

Of the other aircraft the French-built Mirage III fighters, capable of a speed of Mach 2.15 and a maximum range of 750 miles, and the French-built Mystère fighter-bombers have served Israel well since the early 1960s. Until the advent of first the Skyhawks, and subsequently the Phantoms, the Mirages were the only Israeli planes capable of challenging the Egyptian Soviet-built MiG-21s. And even the Phantoms could not get near the latest MiG — the MiG-25 Foxbat reconnaissance plane — when it appeared on the scene. (The MiG-25's immunity is not likely to last long, however, when once the Israelis are supplied with the Phoenix long range air-to-air missile carried by the US F-14 Tomcat.)

Backbone of the Israeli air transport command was the French Nord 1501, the Noratlas. This is a medium transport aircraft with a range of 1,500 miles which can carry 45 fully-equipped soldiers or 18 stretcher cases. Vehicles and freight are loaded through a door in the rear of the plane. The American Boeing 277 Stratocruiser, which was also used to ferry personnel and freight, has a rear loading door too.

Of the helicopters possessed by Israel the largest was the French Sud 321, the Super Frelon. With a maximum range of 600 miles, the Super Frelon can lift 30 fully-equipped troops or 15 stretcher cases. In the initial stages of the Yom Kippur War these helicopters and the smaller Sikorski S-582 were used primarily for casualty evacuation; Westland Whirlwind S-55s and French Alouettes intended

* *A sensational claim that Israel came close to using nuclear weapons during the October War was made in a book entitled* The Plumbat Affair *published in June 1978. (Two of its three authors were London* Sunday Times *journalists — Paul Eddy and Peter Gillman.) While its authors accept that pressure of American public opinion probably forced President Nixon to agree to the airlift of supplies to Israel, they suggest that there was a more deadly reason why he initiated the massive re-supply operation. Kissinger, acting on information gleaned by the CA reported to Nixon that Israel was facing defeat and was considering resorting to the employment of nuclear weapons.*

mainly for communication duties were pressed into the same role.

Because of their confidence in the effectiveness of their fighter aircraft the Israelis had not spent much money on anti-aircraft defences. Israeli strategy was based on Israeli air superiority; the prime role of the air force was to make sure that Arab air raids were defeated outside Israeli territory if possible, and without doing damage if it was not. With air superiority Israel's troops on the ground could operate freely and money would be better spent on armoured fighting vehicles than on anti-aircraft defences. Nevertheless in the 1960s the Israelis bought 50 American Hawk (Homing-All-the-Way Killers) ground to air missiles, half of which were deployed to protect the nuclear plant at Dimona while the other half was set up to give Tel-Aviv token cover. These were supplemented by nine SAM-2s, captured intact between the Mitla Pass and Suez Canal in the Six-Day War by troops under the command of the then Brigadier 'Arik' Sharon.

To outsiders brought up to equate discipline and morale with dress and drill, first impressions of the Israeli Army are rarely favourable. Discipline is paternal, inspection and saluting routines hardly exist; as long as they are clean men are permitted considerable latitude in their standards of dress and turn-out. Yet both morale and discipline in the field are of high standard. An independent spirit is native to the Jew, and he cares nothing for discipline in the sense in which other people used the word. The Israelis' forebears have suffered, and life in Israel even now is not for the soft. A rugged strain of obstinacy has been planted in them, with the result that once the Israeli citizen soldiers get their teeth into a job they will not let go. In war or peace they do not believe that spit and polish discipline is necessary; and they have got on quite well in battle without it. They may be casual, but they are alert.

The fact that Israel has a business-like army into which all citizens — male and female — of appropriate age and physique are automatically conscripted (with the exception of married women and those odd-looking male students of theology in Jerusalem) has astonished the world. In two and a half decades the army which evolved mainly from the Haganah of Mandate times had come a long way. Credit for development in its formative years must go to Mosche Dayan and successive chiefs-of-staff who turned it into the first-class fighting force which so convincingly demonstrated its worth in the Six-Day War.

From this war the Israeli armoured corps emerged with the kind of mystique that took the Africa Korps months to achieve in World War II. Stories of the dazzling dashes of Israeli tanks across the Sinai gave strength to the pleas of the 1967 tank generals that strengthening the cutting edge of the Israeli armoured corps was the best way of adjusting to the new and improved Israeli position in the Middle East. In so far as they did not take sufficient heed of technological advances in anti-tank warfare, the Israeli generals can therefore justly be accused of having prepared to fight the Six-Day War all over again. Believing that armour could smash its way through anything the Israeli tank was allowed to become the prima donna of the battlefield.

Almost every penny of what was left, when the Air Force had taken their cut of Israel's defence budget and maintenance commitments had been met, was put into buying more tanks or improving the ones already in service. In view of their limited manpower resources the Israelis decided to concentrate on armour since tanks and

self-propelled artillery maximised the fire-power in the hands of the troops. More of the latest variant of the British Centurion tank were purchased to supplement the earlier Centurions, M-48 Pattons and Shermans in service: 105mm guns — standard in the new Centurions — were fitted to the older tanks and to the Soviet-built T-54s captured in 1967. The range of the 105mm gun was 500 yards more than the 100mm gun of the Syrian and Egyptian main battle tanks, the T-54s and T-55s, and this enabled the Israeli tanks to engage those of the Arabs without exposing themselves to return fire. The new tanks and their new guns — especially the latter — gave the Israelis a tremendous advantage when they were slugging it out in savage static battles. But in the first few days of the war the commanders in both Sinai and Golan were screaming for more artillery support and more infantry to stem the Arab tide. None was available because the money had been spent on tanks.

Most of the artillery that was available consisted of 155mm and 105mm howitzers mounted on tank chassis. To take advantage of the hard-hitting mobility of an armoured force the supporting artillery needs to be self-propelled. There were also a few self-propelled 175mm howitzers, but the rest of the field artillery was composed of captured Soviet 122mm and 130mm guns. Nine hundred 120mm and 160mm mortars mounted on French AMX tank chassis, and captured Soviet-built 240mm rocket-launchers completed the support armoury.

For anti-tank defence the Israelis relied mainly on their own tanks, but they did have US-made 106mm recoilless rifles on jeeps, together with some anti-tank missiles (mounted on weapon carriers). These were the Cobra and the Nord SS.10 and SS.11 ATGW, hollow-charge

Left: Israeli Pattons during the Yom Kippur War. / *via BIPAC*

Above and right: 155mm howitzers in towed and self propelled (L33) versions.

weapons which, though tiny, were bigger than their Soviet counter-parts — the Saggers and Snappers. With a range of up to 3,000 yards they are very lethal. For anti-aircraft defence the Israeli Army had 20mm, 30mm and 40mm guns in addition to the few ground-to-air guided missiles already mentioned.

Before mobilisation the Israeli Army consisted of four armoured brigades, five mechanised brigades, five infantry brigades, one parachute brigade and three brigades of artillery. But fully mobilised the size was increased by six armoured, four mechanised infantry and four parachute brigades — 75,000 men rising to 275,000 when the 72 hours allowed for call-up had elapsed. There was no formation higher than a brigade in the Israeli Army but from two to six brigades could be grouped together into an Ugda. As in 1967 the brigade remained the basic formation and senior reserve officers such as General Sharon, regional commanders or regular officers whose jobs were temporarily in abeyance like the Director of Training and Commandant of the National Defence College were earmarked in peace to command the *Ugdot* (Hebrew plural of Ugda)

The 32 brigades were roughly equivalent to American regiments and organised on similar lines. Armoured brigades were usually composed of two tank battalions and one of mechanised infantry transported in armoured half-tracks, with the usual reconnaissance, artillery support and supply units. Infantry brigades consisted of three motorised infantry battalions, but only the regular brigades and one or two of the reserve brigades were equipped with armoured halftracks. In the others the infantrymen were carried in wheeled transport — requisitioned trucks and, of course, the ubiquitous Egged buses.

Depending on the situation reservists could be called up in batches or mobilised in toto. As in 1967 key men, including couriers, were summoned first by telephone and collected from their homes; couriers then marshalled the round-up of everybody else. Every reservist kept his uniform at home and the call-up process was accelerated by the use of broadcast code-signs alerting specific units. After reporting to a collection centre near his home the reservist was taken to the camp where his unit assembled; there he collected his arms and equipment. The whole procedure was practised regularly and although a period of 72 hours was allowed for complete mobilisation, many units were ready to move off sooner.

Turning now to the other side of the hill: as Syria and Egypt both kept large standing armies they did not face any of the problems associated with mobilisation. In any case their secret preparations and decision to launch a surprise attack at Yom Kippur gave them the initiative. Egypt, with a population of more than 35 million kept an army of about 285,000 men; Syria with a population of about six and a half million could put an army of 120,000 into the field. Both armies had been almost completely Sovietised since 1967, and all the equipment they had lost in the Six-Day War had more than been replaced by the Russians. The Egyptian Army's fighting element was composed basically of three armoured divisions, three mechanised infantry divisions and five other infantry divisions, all on the Soviet pattern. Sixteen artillery brigades were distributed between these divisions. Additionally there were two elite brigades of paratroops and 28 small battalions of commandos, as well as the usual supporting, supply and administrative services. The nub of Syria's army, also organised on the Russian pattern, comprised three armoured divisions, one mechanised division, and three infantry divisions. Like Egypt the Syrians also had some prestige paratroops and five commando battalions. Both countries had been trained in Soviet tactics and Soviet methods of waging war, the disadvantages of which were that they discouraged individual initiative and were more suited to a European theatre than the Middle East.

But if the tactics taught by their Soviet instructors had shortcomings, there can be little doubt that the Russians succeeded in eradicating many of the underlying problems which brought about the Arab debacle in 1967. With patience and training the Arab can be turned into a good soldier. He lacks imagination and initiative but he is tough and capable of enduring hardship in the conditions imposed by the Middle East environment. Selective conscription has ensured that only the fittest and best men were taken into the Egyptian and Syrian armies — an important factor in countries with an endemic low standard of health. Properly led the Egyptian and Arab soldier responds well, but a wide social gap exists between officer and other rank. This has narrowed over the past decade, and perhaps the Russian instructors' greatest achievement was to impress on the Egyptian and Syrian officers the need to take an interest in their men's welfare and to dispel some of the military uncertainly and unease pervading both armies. Humiliation consequent on the Arab defeat in the Six-Day War combined with a burning desire to strike at Israel was a contributory factor leading to an improvement in the standard of training and, with it, morale.

So too was the provision of first class modern equipment. In 1967 the Arab armies fought with a mixture of standard and obsolescent Russian equipment; but in 1973 they were amply provided with the very best in each class of weapon and in very large numbers. Egyptian and Syrian armoured divisions were equipped basically with the T-54 and T-55 tanks issued to Soviet first line divisions. And although the armour of the T-54 and T-55 is thin in comparison to that of the Centurion and M-48, its angles and curves made its penetration difficult since striking projectiles tend to be deflected, while its 35-ton weight added to a 520hp diesel engine make it a remarkably fast and manoeuvrable fighting vehicle when handled properly. Over and above the T-54s and T-55s the Russians also supplied the Arabs with quantities of their most modern operational tank, the T-62. This tank, a more sophisticated version of the T-54, has a 115mm smooth-bore gun of novel design. Like most Soviet armoured fighting vehicles the T-62 has infra-red night-fighting equipment and was also fitted with a schnorkel device enabling it to cross water obstacles under its own power.

In addition to the tanks the Russians also poured about three billion dollar's worth of aircraft, missiles, guns and other sophisticated weapons into Egypt and Syria. Missiles ranged from the 3-ton 'FROGs' (Free Rocket Over Ground) which the Syrians fired into Galilee, down to the

Left: SAM-2 on its articulated trailer.

Below: SAM-3 low level AA missile.

'suitcase' anti-tank 'Saggers' and 'Snappers' which were to blunt the cutting edge of the initial Israel tank attacks in Sinai. Ground-to-ground Katyusha rockets launched from multi-tube batteries were supplied to the Arabs before 1967. But the 'FROGs' of 1973 are in a totally different class. Carried singly on heavy truck-launchers they are designed to carry a tactical nuclear warhead. They are not accurate, and fitted with a high explosive warhead their value as a bombardment weapon is questionable. In the event it appears that the Syrians intended them not for military targets but as a terror weapon for the indiscriminate bombardment of civilian settlements.

The SAM anti-aircraft missiles destined to become the best advertised weapons of the Yom Kippur War, were also relatively new, and it was to be a mixture of the older SAM-2s, SAM-3s and the mobile truck-mounted SAM-6s — in conjunction with traditional anti-aircraft guns — which provided the dealy umbrella over the Canal and Damascus. None of these missiles, not even the little shoulder-fired SAM-7 with its infra-red homing warhead, were unknown or unexpected. But the Soviet Union supplied them to the Arabs in numbers that are huge by any standard; fired in salvos they were devastatingly effective.

Vast quantities of portable anti-tank missiles were also supplied to the Egyptians and Syrians. The wire-guided PUR-64 'Sagger', the latest weapon of its class, could be carried, launched and directed by an infantryman. They were also mounted on multiple launchers on Jeep-type vehicles, and on the larger armoured troop-carriers also supplied to the Arabs. Used in conjunction with Soviet RPG bazookas and fired in salvos they were to take a heavy toll of Israeli tanks until the Israelis adapted their tactics to cope with a revolutionary situation that has been compared to the battle of Crecy in 1346.

The Egyptian and Syrian Air Forces were to play a comparatively minor role in the Yom Kippur War and it

was the relatively stationary force of anti-aircraft missiles which was to limit the activities of the Israeli Air Force. Nevertheless the Russians re-equipped and re-trained the air forces of the two Arab States. But the only real challenges to Israeli aerial domination of the battlefield were made by the mainstay of the Arab Air Forces — MiG fighters. In the event the MiG-21, a single-seater jet developed from the original MiG-15, was no match for Israel's Phantoms. The MiG-21 carried a smaller complement of armaments than the Phantom and was further limited by its 350-mile fighting range, against the 1,000 miles range of the Phantom. Both planes could fly at Mach 2, and were equally manoeuvrable. But the fact that the Phantom could remain over the battlefield three times longer than the MiG, and deliver a harder punch put the Soviet aircraft at a great disadvantage.

Finally, the navies of Israel, Egypt and Syria deserve mention even though they played a very minor and unspectacular role in the Yom Kippur War. After the allocations had been made to buy aircraft and tanks, little remained of Israel's defence budget for the navy; consequently it was the poor relation of Israel's three fighting services. Its scope was considered to be limited as ships move so slowly compared with aircraft. Nevertheless the Israelis had built up a small, compact and hard hitting naval force of about 35 ships based on the three ports of Haifa, Ashdod and Elat. Spearheading the surface fleet were the 12 untried French-built Saar class missile boats delivered in a daring escape in the winter of 1970, and two new locally-built Reshef (Flash) class vessels of 260 tons displacement. All carried eight of the Israeli-made Gabriel missiles apiece and 40mm cannon.

The remainder of the Israeli navy amounted to three submarines, nine torpedo boats and nine patrol vessels, plus the usual auxiliary craft that accompany a fleet of this size. The most modern of the three submarines, the *Leviathan*, was an ex-British T class vessel which had been fitted with machine gun mountings to enable it to fight on the surface. The other two submarines had also seen service with the British Navy but were of much older vintage, being S class vessels of World War II. Of the flotilla of nine torpedo boats five had been built in France, three in Britain and one in Italy. Each carried two torpedoes, a 40mm gun and two 20mm anti-tank guns. The patrol boats, best described as coastguard cutters, were each armed with two 20mm guns.

By comparison with Israel the Egyptian Navy was large and modern, and even if Syria's fleet of nine missile boats, 16 patrol vessels and a collection of sundries were ignored, its strength was sufficient to weigh the naval odds heavily in the Arab's favour. Egypt's fleet included 16 submarines of the Soviet V and R classes, six destroyers, some 25 missiles boats, 40 motor torpedo boats and an assortment of other miscellaneous floating hardware. Pride of place was given to the Soviet built Osa and Komar class missile boats, armed with the Soviet Styx surface-to-surface missiles. Except for the Nanuchka missile corvettes which had only recently made their debut in the eastern Mediterranean the Osas and Komars were the last word in Russian missile-boat design. Consequently when the war started naval experts throughout the world were watching the exploits of the Israeli and Arab fleets with keen interest.

In the event probably the most spectacular achievement attributable to the Israeli Navy was, in the words of its commander, 'that things did not happen'. Israel's coast, with its many tempting targets of large concentrations of population, power stations and oil installations, was extremely vulnerable. Yet quiet prevailed, and throughout the war freighters and passenger ships continued without interference to dock, discharge and load cargoes at Ashdod and Haifa.

Below: MiG-17, here being examined by Israeli technicians after having been forced down at Bezet. / *via BIPAC*

12 Operation Badr

GOLAN

Up on the barren, bramble-covered plateau of the Golan Heights Syrian tanks rolled across their start lines at precisely the same time as Egyptian infantry 300 miles to the southwest were paddling assault boats across the Suez Canal. The timing was a measure of coordination never before achieved by the Arab states. Yet with the exception of one important outpost the Israelis on Golan were not taken by surprise. Crews of the 90 tanks strung out along the cease-fire line were in their hull-down vehicles, screened by earthen barricades; Israeli infantry were standing to in their fighting positions.

But the Israeli fortified observation post high up on the slope of Mount Hermon was over-run within the first few minutes of the start of the war. From this vital position, the Israelis enjoyed a superb view of the Golan Heights, 'Fatahland' in Lebanon and part of Syria. On Yom Kippur it was manned by two platoons of young soldiers, most of whom are believed to have been off-duty and possibly at prayer. None of then saw or heard the four helicopters which landed a Syrian commando force round the back of the mountain; nobody detected the Syrian's stealthy approach, and when the assault came many of them were still wearing slippers and prayer shawls. Most of the garrison was killed in the desperate hand-to-hand fighting which followed; some of those who surrendered were butchered and their mutilated bodies buried nearby — where they were discovered when the Israelis eventually recaptured the position.

On the plateau, due south of Mount Hermon, the Syrians threw two armoured divisions (600 tanks) and two mechanised infantry divisions (about 30,000 men with another 300 tanks) into the attack. Thus, in armour alone the Israelis faced odds of nearly five to one, and in infantry of more than thirty to one. Covered by a thunderous artillery barrage from massed batteries of artillery which 'crept' ahead of them, Syrian flail tanks battered passages through Israeli minefields and bridged the formidable tank ditch which the Israelis had bulldozed along the length of the 1967 border with Syria. Then, using the main Damscus-Kuneitra road as one axis of advance and the Sheikh Miskin-Rafid road as a second axis, the Syrian hordes swept across the stony plain towards Ahmadiye in the north, Hushniye in the centre and Rafid in the south. The main thrust was towards Hushniye, south of the blitzed town of Kuneitra, where the objective of one of the Syrian armoured divisions was the Bnot Yaakov ('Daughters of Jacob') bridge. Capture of this bridge would sever the sole Israeli supply line into central Golan.

North of Kuneitra the attacking Syrians had orders to split into two columns, with the group circling north to cut off Mount Hermon. Meanwhile the other group was to encircle and capture Kuneitra, and then advance towards the Bnot Yaakov bridge, where it would link up with the column from Hushniye. The aim of the third column, which crossed the cease-fire line at Rafid, was to drive south-west towards the southern end of the Sea of Galilee. The objectives and the lines of attack showed a sound appreciation of where the Israelis were most vulnerable. The rock-strewn Golan plateau is flat open country and generally ideal terrain for tanks. There was no natural obstacle between the cease-fire line and the edge of the Golan escarpment to delay the Syrians' advance. Moreover, while the Sinai desert provided a buffer zone between Egypt and Israel 120 miles wide, from the cease-fire line to the Golan cliffs overlooking Galilee was just 17 miles. The Israelis had little room to manoeuvre; if they could not stop the Syrian advance before it swept them back over the cliffs they had lost the battle for the Golan Heights. From bitter experience in 1967 they knew to their cost that its retrieval would mean they would have to pay a terrible price in blood and bones.

The T-54s and T-55s, moving in groups of six or seven, did not confine themselves to the roads . . . 'they flowed like water, finding their way through wherever possible', said a veteran Israeli colonel afterwards. The task of knocking out Israeli positions isolated behind the advancing Syrian front was left to the Syrian infantry, following up the tanks in Soviet BTR-60 armoured personnel carriers. These were the 'meat-grinder' tactics taught by the Soviet advisers to the Syrian Army. Instead of probing and then concentrating them against one weak spot in the enemy line, as that great exponent of tank warfare, Sir Bazil Liddell Hart, would have recommended, the Syrians simply rolled forward, tank alongside tank, along the whole front from Mount Hermon in the north to Rafid in the south.

The Israeli defenders fought back with prodigious nerve and skill in an effort to halt the Syrian advance, and ferocious tank duels raged across the narrow rolling plain throughout the day. Israel's army was mobilising and long columns of Centurions and Pattons would soon be

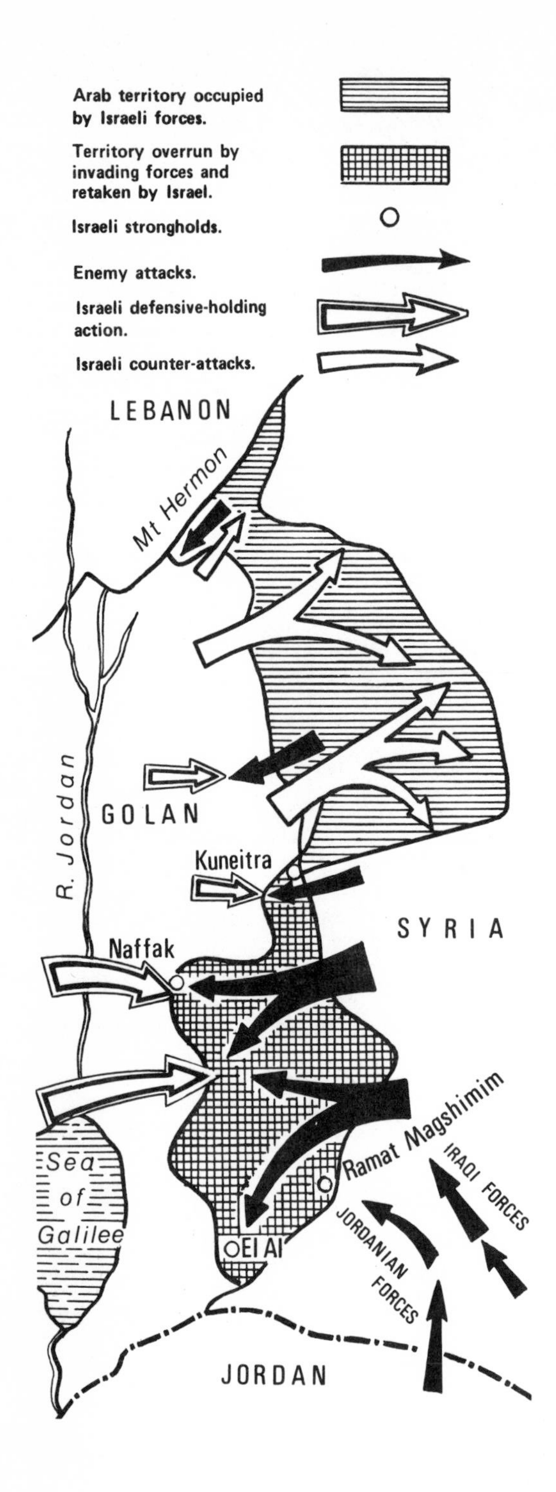

Above: Operations on the Golan Front during the Yom Kippur War.

rumbling up the winding road from Tiberias to the Heights. But the original defenders had to hold on for the best part of two days, and many of the legends of the campaign were conceived in the first 36 hours of the battles on Golan . . . The Israeli tank commander, only 36 years old — or perhaps he was younger — who was credited with the destruction of 15 tanks, or perhaps it was 33 tanks and troop carriers on the Saturday — or perhaps it was the Sunday . . . The Israeli who had been away in Geneva — or was it Paris or London — who arrived at Lod, flew straight up to the Golan to join his unit, where he knocked out five, ten or fifteen Syrian tanks . . . having three tanks shot from under him in the process. Like the fisherman's catch, deeds of heroism tend to grow with the telling, retelling and passage of time.

Whether or not some of the legends are apocryphal, there can be little doubt that the Israelis cut swathes through the Syrian armoured hordes. Once again the Centurions demonstrated their superiority over the Soviet tanks. The Israelis knew that the Syrians had some of the latest T-62s and feared that their Centurions and Pattons would be outgunned and out-manoeuvred by these, the most recent, Soviet main battle tanks. In the event the T-62s were in a minority, and they did not appear until the second day (Sunday) when the Syrians threw in their reserves. All of them were new — one which was knocked out in the fighting on Sunday had only 24 miles on the milometer clock — and in inexperienced Syrian hands their novel smooth-bored 115mm guns and laser-beamed range finders were no match for the Israeli Centurions and Patton 105mms.

T-54s, T-55s, Centurions and Pattons all fired armour-piercing ammunition, and the armour-piercing discarding sabot (APDS) round fired from the 105mm gun was particularly deadly. (Each shell has a hard tungsten core surrounded by a jacket or 'sabot' of a softer material which is squeezed in the barrel of the gun; at the muzzle the sabot drops off and the shot emerges like the cork from a champagne bottle.) Both sides also used HEAT (High Explosive Anti-Tank) ammunition, which directs its explosive blast through a small hole. But only the Centurions were capable of firing HESH (High Explosive Squash Head) shells which flatten on impact and loosen a scab of armour which whirls around the inside of the enemy tank.

The Soviet-built tanks also suffered from the drawback of carrying their shells in the turret, and even a glancing hit frequently managed to turn the T-54s and T-55s into fiery death traps, from which — because there were no safety hatches — the crews rarely escaped.

The Centurion's ammunition was stowed with less chance of fire risk. Its fire-control system was also more effective than that of the Arab tanks. The Israeli gunner was able to find the range to his target with short bursts of machine gun fire; this was automatically transferred to his 105mm cannon, virtually ensuring the certainty of a hit when this gun was fired. The Patton's gun was ranged even faster by means of a fire-control computer. Like that of the Centurion, this system virtually guaranteed a hit and enabled the Israelis to destroy the Arab armour outside the range of the Soviet tank guns.

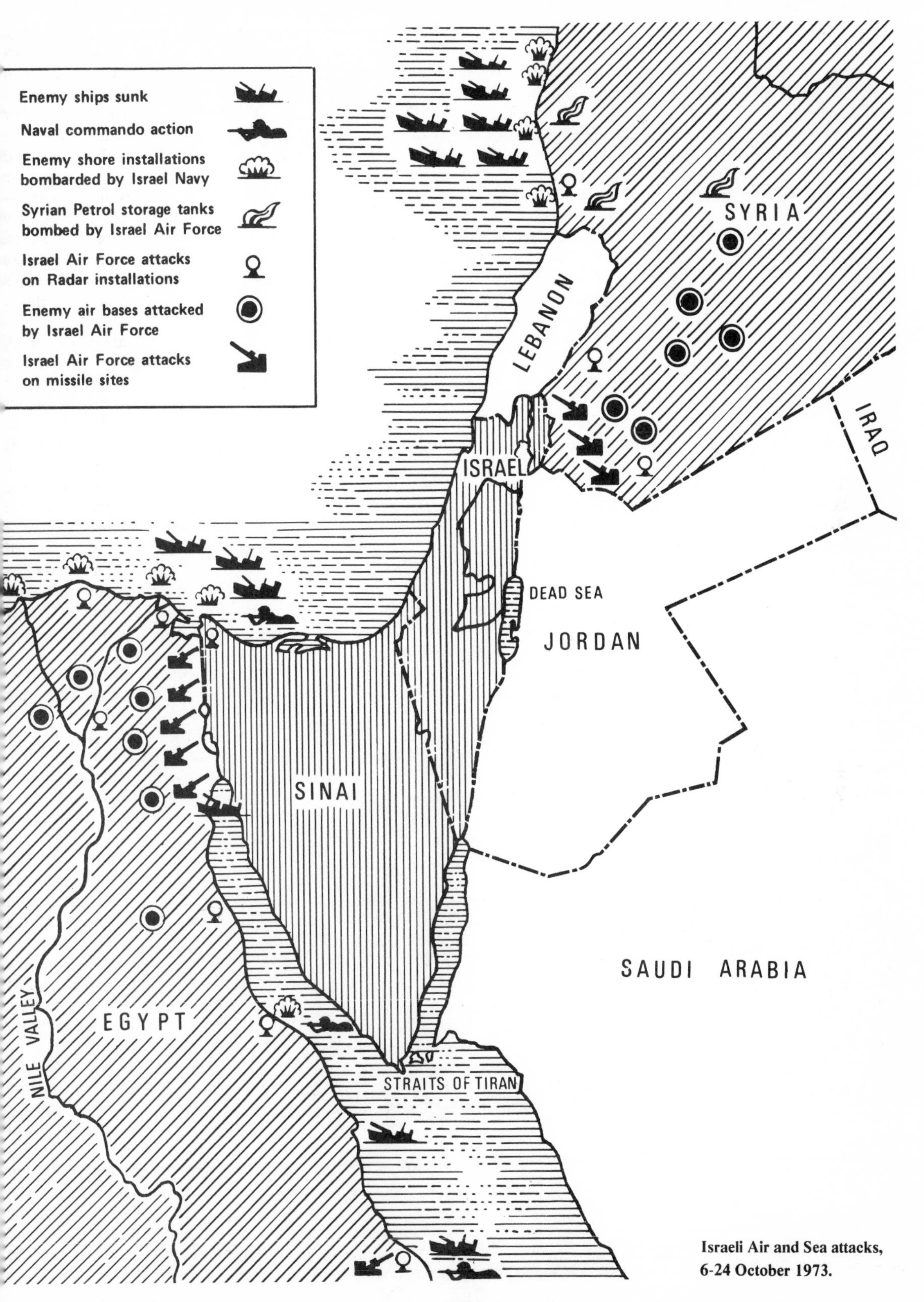

Israeli Air and Sea attacks, 6-24 October 1973.

While the Israelis undoubtedly profited from these technological advantages, their tank commanders were also far more daring and imaginative than their Arab opponents. Time and again — in Sinai as well as on the Golan Heights — the Israelis outfoxed the Arabs. A single Israeli tank would run before a squadron of Arab armour, which was confident of a kill. But the fleeing Israeli decoy would draw them into a trap, and the Arabs would find they had charged into an ambush, where concealed Israeli anti-tank weapons or other Israeli tanks were waiting to strike them with Old Testament vengeance. Yet many individual Syrian tank commanders also showed initiative and elan, and their crews a courage and determination that had rarely been apparent in 1967. Crews of disabled Syrian tanks continued to shoot until their vehicles were literally blown apart, while the commanders of the tanks which penetrated the Israeli defences surged on, through the Golan kibbutzim near Kuneitra, and south of Rafid past the evacuated bunkers of General Hoffy's base headquarters, and on the very lip of the Golan Heights. From there, if the desperate battle now being fought out behind them had not been won by the Israelis, they would have rolled down the hill to the Sea of Galilee.

At this point it must be emphasised that the battles on the Golan Heights were taking place at the same time as a massive war was in progress in Sinai. But for the Israelis the battles on Golan during the first two days of the war were far more crucial than the fighting raging in Sinai. It was not merely a question of the Syrians liberating their occupied land; if the momentum of their attack was

Above: Tank action on the Golan plain.

Left: Israeli reserves deploying.

Above right: Israel's civil hospitals were geared to the war effort and casualties were often evacuated by helicopter from the battlefield direct to established hospitals where every surgical facility was available.

sufficient to carry it beyond the escarpment the Syrians might strike across the River Jordan and Galilee. If that happened Israel would be cut in two For this reason Moshe Dayan decided that the Syrian offensive would have to be smashed before Israel could turn her full attention to the Egyptian incursion in Sinai.

But it took time to assemble the resources needed to turn the tables on the Syrians. Mobilisation was completed quicker than ever before — men sped to their units over empty roads, which 24 hours later could have been chaotically crowded with civilian traffic. Units assembled sooner than expected also. But tanks had first to be prepared for action and then to grind up the cliff road to Golan. It was touch and go who got there first — the Israelis or the Syrians. Only because Hoffy's original Israeli defenders, magnificently supported by the Israeli Air Force, refused to give way, grimly contesting every inch of ground, that the Syrians lost the battle. There was not much option, Major-General 'Rafoul' Eytan said afterwards: 'We just did not have enough troops to do what we wanted. We stopped the Syrians . . . because each man understood that the choice was either to stand and fight it out, or think about the slaughter of loved ones in the valleys behind if the Syrians broke through.'

The Israeli Air Force had been called in as soon as the fighting started, and its Phantoms and Skyhawks hammered clusters of Syrian tanks, personnel carriers and artillery pieces until the tide had been turned and the Golan Heights had became a graveyard of charred vehicles and abandoned guns. But until Phantoms managed to knock out the computer installations controlling most of the Syrian missile screen many of the Israeli planes were shot down by SAM missiles or — flying low to dodge the missiles — by multiple anti-aircraft guns. Batteries of SAM-2, and SAM-3 missiles to hit high-flying jets, truck-mounted SAM-6 missiles and mobile anti-aircraft gun to intercept low-altitude Israeli jets were all integrated into a sophisticated air-defence system of extraordinary complexity. Without the protection of elecronic countermeasures (ECM) devices to jam the frequencies of the radar which directs the SAM rockets, it is difficult even the most skilled pilot to dodge an on-coming missile. The fact that the guidance of the SAM-6 can be switched from radar to a control system operated by a man who can steer the missile to its target, and so make it immune to ECM interference, was an added complication.

Despite the support provided by their air force, the situation on the ground had become so critical by late Saturday that Israeli tank crews from reserve units were being flown to Golan in light aircraft to be thrown straight into the battle. Reservist units were streaming up towards Tiberias and when the first armoured reinforcements arrived, individual tanks were ordered to make their way up the escarpment and to join the battle. Splintering units in this fashion is neither efficient nor wise. But a desperate situation called for desperate and unorthodox remedies.

The Israelis were hoping for a respite at dusk. But the Syrians took the advantage of the darkness to bring up 300 more tanks and to regroup into their broad columns ready for a resumption of the advance. At dawn on Sunday

Left: Israeli strong points on the Golan Heights after the initial onslaught.

Below: One of the fortified Israeli outposts.

Right: After the battles the Golan plain was strewn with the wrecks of knocked out T-55 and T-62 tanks.

morning, with 1,500 tanks crammed into a narrow rolling plain, one of history's greatest armoured battles began. Syrian progress was slow and bloody. Bulldozers had thrown up earth walls to protect the Israeli tanks and the serried lines of advancing armour suffered terrible casualties. As the Syrian tanks passed the Israeli emplacements the Centurions and Pattons swung round and continued to fire. When the battle was over the rocky ground around one such emplacement was littered with the wreckage of 26 T-55s. Nevertheless sheer weight of numbers were bound to carry the Syrian advance forward, and by midday on Sunday their tanks had rolled down the central route to within five miles of the Bnot Yaakov bridge. But this was the turning point, for by now fresh Israeli reserve units were pouring up on to the plateau from the Jordan Valley, and the battle which, as Moshe Dayan said, would teach the Syrians that 'the same road that leads from Damascus to Tel Aviv also leads from Tel Aviv to Damascus' was about to begin.

Elsewhere on the Golan front the outbreak of war was the signal for the bombing and bombardment of the Israeli settlements in Golan and Upper Galilee, and for an outburst of guerilla activity. The Druse villages of Majdal Shams, Masada and Ein Kiniya whose inhabitants were legally and politically Syrian subjects, suffered the most casualties of an air raid on the Saturday afternoon. Kibbutzniks of the frontier settlements, accustomed to their homes being the targets for indiscriminate shelling dived into their underground shelters. At the religious community farm of Ramat Magshimim, five miles from the cease-fire line and only 15 from Rafid, a Yom Kippur service was being celebrated in the shelter when a bus arrived from Tiberias to take the women and children to safety. Leaving

everything behind, the families of the Kibbutzim piled into the bus which drove off while shells and mortar bombs were still falling. Their men followed at dusk and that night Syrian troops occupied the kibbutz.

They did not enjoy their gain for long; within 36 hours they were retreating, and 12 hours later the male kibbutzniks returned. Anticipating booby-traps they had brought a dog trained to sniff out explosives, but the houses were as they had left them. Only the farm had been ravaged by war, and the damage was not as bad as had been expected. Syrian tanks had knocked great gaps in the wire fences through which the cattle had escaped and the orchard had been flattened. But 80% of the cattle were recovered and within two weeks the Ramat Magshimim kibbutz was almost back to its prewar state.

El Rom, a kibbutz further north, was not so lucky. Its poultry sheds were wrecked, its herd of cattle scattered, and the farm buildings were reduced to a shambles during a battle between Israelis and a helicopter-borne Syrian commando. One of the fields close to the Kibbutz, planted with seed potatoes in the week before Yom Kippur, had been the scene of a tank battle; and this sloping tract of land was dotted with the charred remains of 180 Syrian tanks and other armoured vehicles. A 'census' taken a week after the battle put the 'tank harvest' in the whole of Golan at 1,000 of all types. Some of the tanks were still wearing the coating of brown paint given them in the Soviet Union.

North and west of Golan Palestinian guerillas armed with bazookas swarmed across the Lebanese border when the war erupted. In the ensuing week they fired dozens of rockets at Israeli border settlements in the Upper and Western Galilee. There were few casualties and the Lebanese Government was probably more concerned about the provocation caused by the guerillas than the Israelis. Because they feared that Israel was looking for an excuse to annex the fertile region of Southern Lebanon below the Litani River, the Lebanese were anxious to keep out of the war. In the circumstances this was hardly possible and although the Israelis did not retaliate at once Lebanon did not emerge from the first week of the fighting unscathed. Israeli planes destroyed the big Lebanese radar station on Mt Lebanon, and Israeli frogmen slipped into the bay behind Beirut to blow up the submarine telegraph and telephone cables linking Lebanon and Syria with Egypt and Europe. Neither operation was a punitive measure, the Israelis claimed: the radar station was providing information to Syria while the telegraph cables were an efficient and speedy means of communication enabling Syria and Egypt to coordinate their war effort.

Apart from the intermittent disturbances caused by the guerillas the Lebanese-Israeli border stayed calm throughout the war with Israeli farmers working in their grapefruit orchards on the one side of the frontier and Lebanese farmers toiling in their fields on the other side. What disturbed the Israelis was not so much the puny bazooka rockets but the Syrian FROGs, ground-to-ground missiles which could hurl half-ton high-explosive warheads to a range of 40 miles. (Both the Israelis and the Egyptians had more sophisticated long range rockets but none was used in the Yom Kippur War. Egypt's Zafir, or Triumphant, developed in the 1960s by German scientists in Egyptian employ was said to have a range of 200 miles. The Israeli Jericho rocket has an estimated range of 350 miles.) On Sunday evening two FROG rockets hit the town of Migdal Haemek in Western Galilee, injuring 10 people and leaving 200 others homeless. Another FROG slammed into the Gevat kibbutz, destroying half a dozen school and domestic buildings. Luckily the children who usually slept in the dormitories at Gevat were spending the night in shelters honeycombed under the camp.

The distinction between soldiers and civilians and regard for civilian lives in warfare is by no means an untarnished tradition even in the West. The bombings of Warsaw, of Coventry, London and Dresden, are still fresh in the

memory of the older generation. But the distinction exists and when it is broken a sense of shock ripples round the world. In Israel the distinction is virtually unknown. *El adu*, the enemy, has been the Syrians' most common synonym for Israelis and, long before the Palestinian guerilla organisations were heard of, Iraeli settlements in the Jordan and Beisan valleys were targets for Syrian and Jordanian terrorists. Throughout the years also the Syrians have acquired a reputation for torturing prisoners. All this has been reflected in the Israelis' desire for vengeance — a desire which has not been apparent on the Egyptian front. On this occasion the instrument of vengeance was the Israeli Air Force whose fighter-bombers bombed Damascus in addition to military and economic targets elsewhere in Syria. In Damascus there were heavy civilian casualties — 100 killed or wounded, according to a Syrian government spokesman — and the Soviet cultural centre was among the buildings which were heavily damaged. In two other raids on the city of Homs Syria's oil refinery and a power station which supplied 20% of Syria's energy requirements were reduced to ruins. The ports of Tartus, the Banias oil terminal, and Latakia were also bombed and heavy civilian casualties were reported at both places.

The two ports were also the scene of venomous encounters between Israeli and Syrian missile and patrol boats, in the course of which the entire Syrian Navy was virtually wiped and the Russian, Japanese and Greek freighters were sunk. From these actions it became clear that the low-flying Israeli-built Gabriel missile was superior to the Soviet Styx.

Back at the front it was an anxious time for the Syrian Commander-in-Chief, General Youssef Chakour. The Syrian advance which had rolled past Kuneitra had been halted, and many of the tanks which had rolled line abreast across the cease-fire line had been destroyed. The Syrian armour had forced the Israelis back along the roads and the flat country through which they ran. But the Israelis

Left: Battered Syrian vehicles on the Golan.

Above: A Syrian infantryman surrenders.

Right: The cost of war.

84 9239

had clung tenaciously to the craggy hillsides which overlooked them. The Syrian infantry, following the tanks, should have stormed these positions. But they had stayed in the shelter of their armoured carriers near the roads and when the Israelis knocked out the tanks the whole Syrian army ground to a halt.

On Sunday Chakour tried to break the impasse in the centre with a flank attack from the north. 1,800 Moroccans — the first troops of Egypt and Syria's other Arab allies to see action — had taken over the Israeli positions on Mt Hermon captured by the Syrians in the early days of the war, and a Syrian Druze battalion was ordered to move south along the lower slopes of the mountain under cover of the Moroccans. But the Druzes had no stomach for a fight, and Colonel Omar Shalash, their commanding officer shot himself when he learned that his company commanders had no intention of obeying his order to advance. More serious from the Syrian point of view was that the Druzes' failure to move forward meant that there was a gap between Majdel Shams on the lower slopes of Mt Hermon and the Syrian spearhead bogged down round Kuneitra. With General Rafoul Eytan's Israeli troops already probing the Syrian line for just such an opening, General Chakour decided to call off his offensive and orders for the Syrian troops to consolidate were issued instead.

Meanwhile the Israelis were organising themselves for a counter-attack which would drive the Syrians back and see the destruction of the entire Arab army on the northern front. Israeli stragglers, many of them wounded, were limping back from behind the Syrian lines. One young officer, who had survived the destruction of his tank, had

Above left: Israeli briefing before a counter-attack.

Left: Welcome interlude.

Above: Crossing the Syrian border. Israeli armour advancing on the Damascus road.

Right: Israeli armour moving through a deserted Syrian village on Golan.

taken cover until the battle swept past him, before trying to make his way back to the Israeli line. En route he had come across a knocked out Syrian tank and climbed in to look for water. He found the water, and something else — a badly wounded Syrian, the sole survivor of the tank's crew. Despite his own wounds he pulled the Syrian clear of the tank and together they started back for Israeli occupied territory, stopping only to share swigs of water or to take cover when shells began to fall. After 10 hours the two were spotted by an Israeli half-track which picked them up and took both of them off to hospital.

The Israelis' first attempt to make a come-back on Golan was staged on Monday (8 October 1973), and the initial assault quickly showed that they faced a grim and bloody slogging match before the Syrians were beaten. So tactics were adapted accordingly. First the Israeli Air Force would bomb, strafe and plaster the Syrian positions with napalm — the weapon which broke King Hussein's crack troops in the Six-Day War; and a ferocious Israeli artillery bombardment would follow. Finally the Israeli tanks would move in. 'It's not our sort of war', one tank commander commented. Nor does it seem to have been the Arabs' sort of war. The Syrians tried to hit back, and some of their counter-thrusts caused the Israelis to pay a bitter price for the ground they regained.

It was Monday evening that Iraqi troops joined the battle. In common with the rest of the Arab world, neither the Iraq Government in Baghad nor King Hussein of Jordan had been told that Egypt and Syria would attack Israel on Yom Kippur. However, as soon as the news reached Baghdad the Iraqis ordered partial mobilisation and prepared for action. Two MiG squadrons of the Iraqi Air Force were despatched to Syria and by Monday morning tanks of the Iraqi Third Division were rolling on their tracks towards Damascus. Both airmen and soldiers were to get a baptism of fire they would not forget.

On arrival at the Syrian airfields the Iraqi pilots were briefed for missions in the forward areas and in due course they flew off towards the Golan front. Unfortunately nobody had thought to tune the electronic IFF equipment (Identification Friend or Foe device) in the Iraqi aircraft to respond to the radar controlling the Syrian SAM missiles. As a result, when the Iraqis flew over the missiles sites they rapidly lost four MiGs to Syrian SAMs. The Iraqi Third Division was equally unlucky. Arriving on Monday evening, the Iraqi commander went straight to General Chakour and asked for orders. Told simply to 'fight', the Iraqis drove on down to the battlefield without any real idea of what was happening, without tuning their radio and without checking call signs. And when they met the Israelis they paid a heavy price for their incompetence.

King Hussein was less keen than the Iraqi Government to be drawn into the war. In 1967 his army had been severely mauled and he did not intend to let it happen again. Told on the Saturday (6 October 1973) that the war had started he telephoned President Sadat and President Assad to discuss Jordan's role. Clearly he could not afford to be left out of the war if Egypt and Syria were winning, for the Arab world would brand him a coward. But if he opened a third front and the fighting went against the Arabs, the Israelis could be expected to wreak a terrible vengeance. In the event Hussein decided on a form of compromise solution. Jordan's reserves were called up and Jordanian anti-aircraft batteries fired on Israeli aircraft violating Jordanian air space. (When the Israelis started their counter-attack on Golan, their Mirages flew in a northward curve low over Jordan, up and across Golan to attack the Syrians in the flank and rear. Jordanian anti-aircraft fire, combined with Israel's desire not to provoke Hussein, stopped this manoeuvre, and compelled the Israel Air Force to attack the Syrians head-on — with greater danger and consequent greater losses.) But Jordan's attitude was essentially 'defensive', the Hashemite monarch informed the Israelis. To Israelis it did seem that the King was doing the minimum he could avoiding the wrath of the Arabs and the Israelis alike. Certainly there were no indications that Jordan was intending offensive operations yet; and the Allenby Bridge on the West Bank of Jordan stayed open — even though the local bus service became erratic. 'Where is our bus, Abu Yasser?' one Israeli soldier shouted across the bridge to his opposite number on Jordanian soil after a particularly long delay. And the bus eventually arrived.

As the fighting began to go against Syria in the north and to turn against Egypt in the south, Arab pressure on Hussein began to mount. Moroccan and Iraqi troops were already fighting alongside the Syrians, while Kuwaiti, Tunisian and Sudanese troops were joining the battle on the Egyptian front. Apart from Libya, whose volatile President Gadaffi said that he did not think the Egyptian offensive would achieve anything, Jordan was the only 'first-line' Arab State not to be actively involved in the war. 'It was time', President Bourguiba of Tunisia said at a meeting called by Iraq to discuss the role of oil in the conflict, 'for Jordan to enter the war'. Radio Baghdad voiced the suggestion in more definite terms: 'All eyes', said a Palestinian announcer on 12 October 1973, 'the eyes of the little ones, the eyes of the girls, the eyes of the men in the holy fire and in every inch of the vast flaming homeland — all those look up to the men in Jordan who are holding their arms but only listen to the news. How long will the Jordanian Army remain listening without seeing.'

Hussein responded by announcing his decision on 13 October 1973 to send his elite 40th Armoured Brigade to Syria.

By this time the Israelis in Golan were clearly in the ascendant. After a long and bloody counter-attack the Syrians had been pushed back off the Heights and all but a few Syrian troops had been thrown back. Charred and twisted wrecks of burnt-out vehicles and Syrian corpses rotting in the sun were evidence of the bitter battles that had taken place; battle-weary Israeli soldiers were combing the area and rounding up Syrian prisoners. The fighting had been nothing at all like 1967. There had been none of the dashing armoured thrusts or deep-penetration infantry attacks like those of the Six-Day War; this time the Israelis had had to fight by the book. Their tanks had avanced behind a heavy artillery barrage and then slugged it out at close range. When a position was taken it had been consolidated and then the artillery had begun to pound the next objective. In the air the performance of the Israeli Air Force had been significantly limited by the SAM missiles which the Arabs did not have in 1967. But now the Israelis were back on the cease-fire line and long columns of Israeli tanks, many with 'Damscus Express' and 'Nonstop to Damascus' chalked on the sides, were rumbling to advance down the Damascus road.

Yet the war on the Syrian front was far from over. Although the Syrian Army had suffered staggering losses in being pushed off the Heights it stubbornly refused to give up. Two days after breaking through to the old border the Israelis were still battering their way down the Damascus road towards the village of Sasa. And there they were brought to a halt. Somehow or other the Syrians managed to regroup and convert what was tantamount to a rout into an orderly withdrawal. On the high ground before Sasa the Syrians organised a defensive line which held, and where for the rest of the war on this front two well entrenched armies pounded each other.

The Syrians attempted to mount counter offensives at several points during the week, and for hours at a time shells and mortar bombs thundered down on Israeli positions. At first light on Tuesday 16 October 1973, a combined Syrian, Iraqi and Jordanian attack was launched, the objective of which was to sever the Israeli lines of communication to their forward positions in front of Sasa. In an operation directed towards Kuneitra the newly arrived Jordanian 40th Armoured Brigade was given the task of breaking through the Israeli crust, and King Hussein drove up from Amman to watch his Bedouins give battle. In doing so he became the only Arab Head of State to go anywhere near the front. (President Idi Amin of Uganda, whose offer to contribute Ugandan troops was received without enthusiasm by the Arab leaders, spent a good deal of the war in a tent near the end of the runway at Amman airport.) In accordance with the tactics they had copied from the British the Jordanian armour attacked on a narrow front to smash a passage for the infantry. With all the traditional dash and daring of the Arab Legion, Hussein's Centurions surged forward, with the tank commanders in their red and white chequered *keffiyehs* standing head and shoulders out of the turrets. Such tactics were new on the Syrian battlefield and they were surprisingly successful. At a cost of 14 tanks out of the 150 that went into the attack, the Bedouin armour punched its way through the Israeli line. Only then did things start to go wrong. Thirty minutes after the attack began the Iraqi guns began to fire the barrage which should have preceded the assault half an hour before, and the Jordanians found themselves under heavy artillery fire. Then the Syrian fighters and fighter-bombers called up to support the Jordanians began strafing the Iraqis who were coming up in support. Matters were getting so out of hand that the Syrian officer commanding the attack, Colonel Rafek Hilawi, called off the whole operation.

The Israelis continued to fight to get past Sasa and seize the ground where the rugged Golan terrain ends and open rolling country begins until 21 October 1973. They failed to do so, already because they could not afford to devote more resources to the northern front. They had not succeeded in routing the Syrian Army as in 1967, but they had smashed its capability for another offensive, and the situation on the Egyptian front was more pressing. Indeed the transfer of troops, equipment and air effort had started on Saturday 13 October 1973, and although Israeli Mirages, Skyhawks and Phantoms still flew occasional ground-support missions and came up from time to time to deal with Syrian MiGs, the air activity over Golan was markedly reduced after the first week of the war. According to an American intelligence estimate the Syrians suffered 8,000 casualties — killed, wounded or taken prisoner in the course of their abortive offensive, whose path was now marked with the hulks of scarred and battered vehicles. But the Israelis, sitting on 200 square miles of new territory, had also suffered losses — small in comparison with those of the Syrians and their allies, but heavy in relation to Israel's overall population. There was no question of a swift, relatively painless victory over Syria, and the advantages of ground gained in an advance 'downhill to Damascus' had to be weighed against the cost of men and material.

Below: Israeli artillery in action.

Israeli held territory occupied by Arabs.

Arab territory occupied by Israeli forces.

Territory overrun by invading forces and retaken by Israel.

Israeli strongholds.

Egyptian city.

Enemy attacks.

Israeli defensive-holding action.

Israeli counter-attacks.

Port Said

SUEZ CANAL

EGYPT

Kantara

SINAI

Ismailia

Suez

Above: Operations on the Sinai Front during the Yom Kippur War.

SINAI

The Egyptian invasion of Sinai began with an air strike and a massive artillery bombardment. As upwards of 200 tons of high explosive shells, from 2,000 guns concealed among the dunes on the west bank of the Suez Canal, crashed down on previously registered targets, Egyptian MiGs screamed up and down the Bar Lev line bombing, strafing and rocketing. At zero hour, 1400hrs on Yom Kippur, simultaneous explosions also rocketed three places on both banks of the Canal. Egyptian frogmen had planted dynamite charges in the sand walls on the Israeli side, and similar charges had been placed on the west bank. The detonation of these explosives was the signal for Egyptian assault troops to pick up the assault boats and the outboard motors which had been positioned behind the gaps the night before. Within minutes they were racing down to the Canal and chugging across the 180m of water, to fan out and establish a bridgehead as a preliminary to the next phase of the attack. Each assault party had been provided with an Egyptian flag and as soon as it landed the banner was planted on the far bank. 'As the banners began to rise', said Brigadier Abu Saada, the commander of one of the assault brigades in the centre sector near Ismailia, 'It seemed as if a powerful electric current ran through the troops . . . Allah is with us', they cheered.

Despite the evidence of surreptitious Egyptian activity, intensified over the past three days, the absence of Egyptian lookouts, and the suspicious silence which had fallen over the whole West Bank at noon, the men garrisoning the Bar Lev line were stunned by the onslaught. Nobody wanted to believe that an attack was pending; only the godless would choose to attack during a religious festival and the Arabs were celebrating Ramadan. Bored, and fasting for the Day of Atonement, the Israelis were suffering the flies that prey on desert armies and following their routine duties. It was a warm sunny afternoon, and when the Egyptian barrage opened up some were washing clothes, some were resting or relaxing — reading, or writing letters; a few, at the post opposite the southern suburbs of Ismailia, were desultorily kicking a football about. The shelling soon sent everybody scurrying to action stations however and a flurry of telephone and radio messages began to flow in to the Israeli Sinai headquarters at Tasa. Until news started to filter back and the plight of some of the other posts became apparent from the frantic pleas for and artillery support radioed to Tasa, many of the isolated Israeli garrisons assumed that they were involved in some local affair. In the 'jetty' strongpoint close to Port Tewfik at the southern end of the Canal few of the men ate or drank that day. They 'did not want to violate the sanctity of the day' said one of the survivors.

Surprise combined with unpreparedness on the Israel side, and the unexpected skill and ferocity of the Egyptian attack made nonsense of the Israeli plan to defend Sinai. The plan was based on the Bar Lev strong points delaying an attacking force and acting as observation posts for the Israeli artillery and tanks behind them. Safe behind the minefields and barbed wire, and protected from artillery and sniper fire by concrete and sand, the garrisons of the strongpoints should be able to hold their own while the artillery pounded the attackers and the tanks mopped up

Above left: All Egyptian soldiers must have felt like this after crossing the canal.
/PR Dept, Embassy of the Arab Republic of Egypt

Above: Using ladders to scale the sand walls.
/ PR Dept, Embassy of the Arab Republic of Egypt

Left: Egyptian troops move into Sinai.
/PR Dept, Embassy of the Arab Republic of Egypt

any that were left. But even if the strongpoints were not expected to fall so quickly, nor the Egyptians to possess such effective anti-tank weapons, the key element in the Israelis' plan — a sufficiency of artillery and a substantial body of tanks nearby — were missing. In the event there was only one brigade of tanks, the 14th Armoured Brigade — a regular brigade of 200 Pattons, commanded by Colonel Amnon Resheff — on the spot when the war started.

The first assault troops crossed the canal almost unscathed. Scrambling up the steep sides of the sand wall screening and protecting the Israeli line, they fixed ropes and scaling ladders for those coming behind to climb. 'It was like an attack on a Crusader castle' said one of the Egyptians. Wave after wave of Egyptian infantry crossed over; so too did a number of Russian-built PT-76 amphibious light tanks, propelling themselves through the water at a fast speed... Encircling the Israeli positions near the crossing points, the Egyptian infantry plastered the trenches leading to the underground bunkers with flamethrowers and grenades. Then the PT-76s moved in to bulldoze their way up to the strongpoints and fire into them at point-blank range. By 1530hrs the first of the Israeli forts — located south of Port Said — had fallen and in the next six hours 14 others were captured. Ten more held out for another six days, and on orders of the Israeli Sinai HQ a further 10 were evacuated subsequently.

Although each man carried a 60 to 75 pounds load, the Egyptian assault troops took no heavy equipment with them across the Canal. Handcarts were the only transport ferried across for their use, and these were piled high with ammunition and large quantities of the latest portable Soviet anti-tank weapons. Apart from RPG-7 bazookas (literally Rocket Propelled Grenade), there was a surfeit of 'Snapper' and 'Sagger' wire-guided missiles — the tiny sophisticated weapons with a range of between 2,000 and 3,500 yards, which could be packed into light metal containers resembling weekend suitcases. These weapons would enable the assaulting infantry to destroy the Israeli tanks and artillery dug in just behind the Bar Lev line and ward off the expected armoured counter-attack. In the event about half of Resheff's tanks were deployed in static positions, and when the other half roared down towards the Canal they were rapidly brought to a dead stop by a hail of these anti-tank missiles. Repeated efforts to charge through the Egyptian infantry screen, in order to get down to the assistance of the hard-pressed defenders of the Bar Lev strongpoints still holding out, met with the same fate. Attempts to do so at night proved as costly as the daylight attacks.

The situation was analogous to that of June 1942 when the British 8th Army, trying to halt Rommel's Panzers at Gazala, frittered away its armour in piecemeal attacks which accomplished nothing. So the Israelis sought a similar solution to that which had turned the tables on Rommel at Alam Halfa and led eventually to Montgomery's victory at Alamein. Logically, once they had established their bridgeheads across the Canal the Egyptians' main objective would be the vital Ismailia, Gidi and Mitla passes. With this in mind, Major-General Shmuel Gonen, the commander of the Israeli southern front, had ordered his infantry to dig in on the high ground covering the passes, and for the bulk of Resheff's armour to wait in a counter-attack role.

Left, right and below: The Bar-Lev line after the fighting.
/ PR Dept, Embassy of the Arab Republic of Egypt

Above: Storming the Bar-Lev line.
/ PR Dept, Embassy of the Arab Republic of Egypt

Left: Egyptian forces in Sinai.
/ PR Dept, Embassy of the Arab Republic of Egypt

Right: One of the gaps in the Canal sand embankments cut by the Egyptians with high pressure hoses.

In the event the Egyptians did not attempt to seize the passes — much to the disgust of some of their tank commanders who believed that there was nothing in front of them on the second day of the war. Egypt's Minister of War and Commander-in-Chief, General Ahmed Ismail explained this away later by reasoning that the advance was necessarily slow because he did not wish his troops to venture beyond the umbrella provided by the SAM missiles across the Canal. In any case, he claimed, the Arab objectives were limited to the capture of a strip of Sinai on the East bank of the Canal in order to provide 'The Spark' — President Sadat's codename for the war — to transform the situation in the Middle East. In fact this was not so. Egypt's aim was to recover the whole of Sinai, and if they had succeeded in overrunning the passes and the opportunity had been present the Arabs would have gone on to demolish Israel as a state and hand over the country to the Palestinians. Such hopes were destroyed and a chance to win the war was missed when the Egyptians failed to exploit the surprise and successes of the first two days of the war. Just as the Six-Day War had made the Israelis over-confident, so it had made the Egyptians over-cautious.

Yet no lack of dash was apparent among the assault troops who followed their allotted parts in a well-orchestrated plan confidently and professionally. Leaving detachments to reduce the Bar Lev strongpoints close to the areas selected for the laying of pontoon bridges, the bulk of the Egyptian infantry swept on into Sinai. Dragging their handcarts of equipment with them they fanned out along a line in the desert 10-12km beyond the Canal. There they dug in, unloaded their handcarts, assembled their anti-tank missiles and produced another new and sophisticated weapon. This was the little SAM-7 'Strela', a Soviet anti-aircraft missile, hand-held and fired from the shoulder like Britain's Blowpipe. Fired in the general direction of a plane, the 6lb missile is guided to its target by an infra-red device which homes on the heat emitted by the aircraft's engines. In Vietam the SAM-7 had already proved remarkably effective, and it was to do so again in Sinai and Golan. With this formidable armoury the task of the Egyptian infantry was now to stop the Israelis from interfering with the next phase of the operation — getting tanks and heavy weapons across the Canal. This in fact was the crucial period during which the Israeli High Command had reckoned they would be able to crush an Egyptian attack. Getting infantry across the Canal was a comparatively simple operation; but armour and heavy artillery would need bridges, and Moshe Dayan had reckoned that their construction would take 48 hours during which — if the Israeli Air Force failed to blast them out of existence — the Israelis should be able to concentrate a powerful armoured counter-attack force. But Dayan's calculations were upset by an unexpected factor, which cut his timing by more than half. On both sides of the Canal the sand embankments were an obstacle too steep for tanks to climb; before a bridge was thrown across gaps had to be made in them. Bulldozers were of no use — they could get no purchase on the Canal side; explosives would do the job, but clearing a sizeable gap took a long time. (Making a single gap 20ft wide — the minimum to get tanks through — meant shifting about 1,500 cubic yards of sand, and the Egyptians planned on creating 60 such gaps in the east bank, and an equivalent number on their own bank of the Canal.) However, the Egyptians had perfected a means. Patient research had shown that high-pressure jets of water would break the banks better than bulldozers or bombs. So water-cannons were brought up, and within five hours the requisite gaps had been hosed through the canal ramparts and the canal banks trimmed with explosives and bulldozer tanks.

Laying the bridges was made easy by the use of bridging equipment designed by the Russians for crossing rivers in Western Europe. This was the first time such equipment had been used in war, and as a combat trial the Suez Canal crossing certainly proved the worth of the PNP bridge, as it is called. The bridge consists of a series of box-shaped pontoons, each carried on a tracked vehicle. The first of these vehicles drives down to the water's edge and then — by means of hydraulic arms — off-loads the pontoon into the water. A second vehicle then drives on to the first pontoon to lower its pontoon which is slipped to the first, and so on. The procedure is quick, and it is said that the PNP can be laid at 15feet a minute. As Israelis in one of the strongpoints still holding out near one of the crossing points reported over the radio. 'The bridge is growing across the water like an extending arm.'

In the event the bridging operation went better in the northern sector than in the south, where the water-cannon took longer to bore gaps through the embankments, because the sand granules were bigger and more cohesive.

Left: Across the canal.
/ PR Dept, Embassy of the Arab Republic of Egypt

Below: Bridges across the Suez Canal: note hole in sand wall.
/ PR Dept, Embassy of the Arab Republic of Egypt

Right: Israeli PoW.
/ PR Dept, Embassy of the Arab Republic of Egypt

This put back the carefully formulated time schedule of Major-General Abdel-Moneim Wassel's 3rd Army, and Wassel was forced to send his troops up to Ismailia to cross the Canal by one of the 2nd Army's bridges before hurrying south to link up with his infantry. The Egyptians had ten bridges across the Canal and were operating 50 ferries by dusk on Saturday evening. Nevertheless the southern of the two Egyptian armies lacked maximum armoured strength just when it was needed to strengthen the bridgehead. Meanwhile the infantry screen was holding off the Israeli counter-attacks, and under cover of darkness five Egyptian divisions and some 500 tanks poured across the Canal — a tremendous military achievement, which from the Israeli viewpoint was disastrous. Countering thrusts along the 100 miles of front Resheff's squadrons of Pattons had not managed even to dent the Egyptian bridgeheads; pockets of Israeli infantry were fighting gallant little actions and holding isolated positions; and the Israeli artillery in response to urgent requests for fire support was blindly shooting pre-recorded programmes on areas where their shells were often having no effect. There was little coordination of effort; in the words of one Israeli officer too many people 'were doing their own thing'. This was a situation which did not last for very long, however. Barely 10 days later Israel was winning the war in decisive fashion.

On the Sunday morning (7 October) Phantoms and Skyhawks of the Israelis swung into action on the Sinai front, swooping in to attack the Egyptian bridges. They ran into a withering barrage of anti-aircraft fire from the Egyptian missile defence network, and in the initial raids three out of five Israeli aircraft were being hit. (The toll on Golan, where the Israelis lost 34 planes on the Saturday afternoon, was worse. About 80 of Israel's total losses of 115 planes were incurred on the Syrian front.) Forced to bomb from higher altitudes and to try to take the bridges

out with artillery fire the Israelis were less effective. As fast as they damaged the PNP pontoons the Egyptians replaced or repaired them.

Just as the mass use of the new wire-guided anti-tank missiles had made the tank seem as vulnerable on the battlefield as the armoured French knights were to the English archers at Agincourt, so the SAMs defending the bridges over the Canal seemed to put definite limits on the use of aircraft in close support of ground troops. Electronics had transformed the war, and this was especially apparent in the air. Once a missile had been fired and its complex tracking and guidance system had selected and 'locked on' to its target there was very little that a pilot could do to evade it. Only electronic devices capable of outwitting those which operated the missile could save him — and the Israelis were shocked to find that their technology had lagged behind in this field. Devising electronic countermeasures (ECM) takes time and, usually, some knowledge of what is to be countered. The Israelis knew quite a lot about the older SAM-2 and SAM-3 missiles. But the SAM-6s were new to the Middle East and had never been used until the Yom Kippur War.

The amount of manoeuvring which a jet plane flying at Mach 1 or more can do is constrained by the pilot's ability to withstand the powerful g-forces to which he is subjected if he flies too fast. If he turns his aircraft to dodge a missile he may 'black-out', and as the missile has no such problems it is always likely to outmanoeuvre him. The only real solution is to confuse the missile's guidance system, and the simplest way of doing this is by flying very low, so that the missile radar systems are confused by radio wave echoes from the ground. But low flying brought an additional hazard by way of fire from multiple radar directed anti-aircraft guns, integrated in the Arab air defence systems. The other method of defeating electronically guided missiles is to equip the aircraft with ECM devices which will confuse the missile radar by swamping it with signals of the same frequency as that of the guidance system. However this method will work only until improved guidance systems are substituted for the ones that are jammed; consequently the race between improved missile radar systems and more sophisticated ECM devices to outwit them is a progressive and escalating business. With the SAM-6s a subsidiary control system was an added complication. If the radar control was blocked, the operator could switch to a remote control and steer the missile to its target by eye. This system was not new but developed from the German Henschel Hs283 ship-to-air missile of World War II.

As a result of their experience in the Six-Day War the Israelis had come to believe that aircraft and tanks combined with the qualitative supremacy of the Israeli over the Arab armies would guarantee their success in any future war. In 1973 however, the advanced technology reflected in the Soviet SAMs and anti-tank missiles showed the limitations of the two weapons which the Israelis hitherto regarded as the most suitable for an Israeli counter-offensive even in the face of alerted opposition. Fortunately for Israel the Arabs followed the somewhat cautious Soviet military doctrine that dictates one should defer the exploitation of victory until one's position has been consolidated. And while the Egyptians were consolidating the Israelis were absorbing the lessons they learned in the first 24 hours of the war when their first unconsolidated counter-attacks failed. Instead of using their armour, as in the Six-Day War, to storm enemy positions and break through them they were beginning to see advantages in occupying commanding positions and relying on superior markmanship and weapon-handling to shoot it out with the Syrians and Egyptians.

In the face of the missile defences the Israeli Air Force lost a good deal of its freedom of action over the Canal

Left and below: Israeli aircraft wreckage. */ PR Dept, Embassy of the Arab Republic of Egypt*

Right: Israeli self-propelled artillery in Sinai.

Zone. But outside the SAM umbrella it reigned supreme, as the Egyptians found to their cost when they sent helicopter-borne commandos to attack Balzna in the north and Bir Gifgafa, the main forward Israeli air base in Sinai, in the centre. All the helicopters were shot down and most of the commandos were killed. Another sea-borne commando attack on Sharm-El-Sheikh on the remote southern tip of Sinai was also driven off with heavy losses, following a furious engagement.

Heavy fighting continued in Sinai throughout Sunday and Monday (8 October) with what was left of Resheff's tank brigade endeavouring to contain Egyptian efforts to extend their bridgehead area. The Israeli tank commanders had come to realise by now that charging into a hail of anti-tank missiles was suicidal, and they were adopting new tactics. Smoke, which they had tended to disdain till now, was used to screen their manoeuvring; and prophylactic machine gun fire was sprayed ahead of an advance to deter Egyptian infantry concealed among the sand dunes. Many desparate little actions were fought out and the starkness of the early clashes may be gleaned from the accounts of two young Israeli tank commanders. The first, who was wounded when his own tank was set on fire by an Egyptian RPG rocket, switched to the second tank of his troop and ordered the driver to charge into the area from which the bazooka had been fired. The Patton roared forward, but as it reached the line of Egyptian infantry it too was hit by bazooka shells, and the officer, wounded for a second time, was blown back into the hull of the tank. Calling the driver to turn left, to run along the Egyptian line, he shouted 'Crush them, crush them'. The second Israeli, 'Eyal', was with a squadron which was ordered on the Saturday to counter-attack in the Kantara area of the northern sector of the Canal. Eyal's tank was hit along with two others and

unable to move. However, as the fire control system was still working, he kept on shooting in support of a Bar Lev strongpoint about 50 yards away. Eventually the tank was surrounded by Egyptians and three of the crew surrendered. But Eyal hid in the tank pretending to be dead until nightfall, when he crawled to the strongpoint. Later that night the garrison was ordered to evacuate the strongpoint and move to a point where Israeli half-tracks would pick them up. Moving to the pick-up point was easier said than done, however, as the Egyptians appeared to have anticipated their route. And to reach safety the party had to spend a day in hiding in Kantara cemetery before taking a circuitous path through the Egyptian lines.

Fear of the outcome of an Israeli counter-offensive in Sinai was largely responsible for Egyptian caution and apparent reluctance to exploit their initial successes. Fifty-five year old General Ismail, the Egyptian Commander-in-Chief was, in the words of one British officer, 'a brilliant classroom soldier', and he had fought in four wars — including that of 1967. But he was not the stuff that Napoleons are made of. Memories of the Six-Day War haunted him, in the same way that memories of the Somme haunted Allied generals during World War II. Ismail remembered that Egypt had lost an army and been left defenceless in 1967, and he was not prepared to risk a repetition. General Saad Shazli, Ismail's Chief-of-Staff, was made of sterner stuff. A capable and aggressive field commander, he too remembered 1967, having seen an army melt around him, and walked back across the desert to Egypt through Israeli lines. At 51 he was one of Egypt's 'Hawkish' generals, and considered by some to be Egypt's Moshe Dayan. Shazli was all for a mobile and adventurous thrust into Sinai; Ismail considered there should be no move until an overwhelming Egyptian force had concentrated on the east bank of the Canal, and the missile screen brought forward. Shazli's strategy would have faced high odds. But Ismail's caution was to prove fatal.

The expected Israeli counter-offensive began on Monday (8 October) with a twin thrust by two armoured brigades. Some 700 armoured fighting vehicles manoeuvred for advantage among the dunes in a desert plain 60 miles by 20 before the Canal. The manoeuvrings were punctuated by thunderous bombardments from guns on both sides. Then came the battle which ended, to the astonishment of Egypt as well as Israel, in a stunning Egyptian victory. One regiment of Reshef's armoured brigade, commanded by Lieutenant-Colonel Assaf Yakouri, was completely routed and a crestfallen Yakouri — captured with 25 of his tanks — was displayed on Cairo television that night. That night also Radio Cairo claimed further gains in Sinai, including the capture of Kantara East where, said the announcer, the inhabitants had rushed from their house to greet their liberators. At that moment the few Arabs who had chosen to stay in Kantara when it was over-run were in El Arish 100 miles to the east — where they had been since 1968 when the Israelis evacuated them.

A few days later Radio Cairo scored another propaganda success, when they announced the surrender of the Israeli 'jetty' strongpoint on Port Tewfik pier. Its garrison had held out until the Israeli headquarters at Sinai told its commander, a young lieutenant, to give up. Five of the original 42 men had been killed in the first hours of the war and he had been cut off for eight days — under constant attack. With 15 of the remaining 37 men wounded, medical supplies finished, ammunition low and food running out, the Israelis had little hope of achieving anything more. The surrender was conducted in a blaze of publicity in the presence of Red Cross delegates. The Egyptians were puzzled when one of the Israelis emerged from the strongpoint carrying a large red Torah, but when Arnaud de Borchgrave, the *Newsweek* representative, explained that the Torah contained holy scriptures like the Koran, they agreed to let it accompany the men into captivity. The Israeli flag flying over the fort was hauled down and the prisoners ferried across the Canal before the Egyptians decided to extend the ceremony. So the Israeli lieutenant was ordered to pick two men to go back with him across the water to salute the Egyptian flag as it was raised on the last redoubt of the foremost section of the Bar Lev line.

For four days it had been the Arabs' kind of war. The Syrians on the Golan Heights were now in retreat and

Kuneitra had been retaken. But on Golan and in Sinai the Arabs had compelled Israel to fight huge grinding battles that had chewed up hundreds of tanks and thousands of men. This was not the sort of war that Israel wanted to fight — nor one she could afford for long. With both sides pouring reinforcements into Sinai it was obvious that major battle was pending. This started at 6am on Sunday 14 October with a 90 minute artillery bombardment and was to be a crucial turning point in the war. Egyptian tanks, supported by MiG and Sukhoi fighter-bombers then rolled into action, heading for the vital Mitla, Gidi and Khatmia (Ismailia) passes, and the tank battle which followed was the first of a series of week-long conflicts which overshadow in scale every armoured battle to date— including those of Alamein and Stalingrad. The Egyptians were repulsed with terrible losses: the Israelis claim to have destroyed 250 Egyptian tanks. But the Israelis also suffered heavily — 150 tanks the Egyptians said. (Neither Arab nor Israeli communiqués were very reliable. 'They've learnt to fight from us', went a current Israeli joke, 'we've learnt to handle information from them.') And among the 656 Israeli casualties was Major-General Avraham Mendler, the recently appointed commander of the Israeli Armoured Forces in Sinai, who was killed when a shell landed on his half-track. Mendler had captured Kuneitra in the Six-Day War, and before his death he had promised his troops they would see a comparable victory in Egypt.

This battle, coming at a time when the Israelis had just started to divert their resources from the northern front can now be seen to be the turning point of the Sinai campaign. The Egyptian effort had passed its climax and the Israeli Air Force — outside the range of the SAMs — had wrought terrible havoc among the Egyptian tanks. A new anti-tank weapon, the TOW missile, airlifted to Israel in US Galaxies, had also proved deadly. The Egyptians had missed their chances and from now on they were on the defensive.

Below: Surrendering the flag.
/ PR Dept, Embassy of the Arab Republic of Egypt

13 Replenishing the Arsenals

In 1967 the Soviet Union did not attempt to re-supply the arsenals of its Arab clients until a cease-fire had been announced. In 1973, however, the Russians mounted the biggest airlift since the Allied re-supply of Berlin in 1948 — in a clear bid to reinforce what appeared at the time to be an Arab victory.

Starting on Tuesday 9 October a fleet of 80 military transport planes, supplemented by 20 Aeroflot commercial cargo planes, set up a shuttle service ferrying supplies from Soviet bases in the Caucasus, the Ukraine and Southern Russia to Syria and Egypt. Giant Antonov freighters landed at the Syrian military airfield near Palmyra, north-east of Damascus and at Aleppo; longer range Antonov An-22s touched down at the airfields round Cairo. The planes flew over Yugoslavia, Turkey and Cyprus. With 50 to 60 extra flights a day crowding the air space above Nicosia and Famagusta, the pilots of civilian airliners flying their scheduled routes were worried. 'Coming in from Cyprus is getting to be like Piccadilly Circus — in fog and with the traffic lights out' one pilot is reputed to have said when he landed at Beirut during the second week of the war.

By Monday 15 October it was calculated that some 4,000 tons of military supplies had been airlifted to the two Arab States. The bulk of the supplies consisted of artillery, ammunition, SAM-6 missiles and anti-tank weapons. To begin with there was little point in sending new tanks to Syria because the Syrian Army was running out of tank crews. But as the war moved into its second week, ships from Black Sea ports carrying T-54, T-55 and T-62 tanks, and MiG-21 fighters started to arrive at Alexandria in Egypt and Tartus and Latakia in Syria. The weapons had been taken from Soviet stockpiles in Russia and Eastern Europe. The Russians were even reported to have stripped Hungarian units of equipment in order to send their weapons to the Arabs.

The Russians gave their best, although the weapons they provided did not suffice to prevent the Syrians from being defeated nor keep the Israelis from crossing the Suez Canal. In 1967 the Arab armies fought with a mixture of standard and obsolescent Russian equipment; six years later in an 'era of detente' they were amply provided with the very best in every class of weapons, and in very large numbers.

The most advertised weapons of the war were the anti-tank missiles which repulsed the Israeli counter-attacks in the first days of the war, and the SAM anti-aircraft missiles. The FROG bombardment rockets, and the SCUD missiles sent to Egypt attracted less attention. Yet both FROGs and SCUDs were specifically designed to carry nuclear warheads. Using them to deliver high explosive warheads, as was the case with the FROGs fired by the Syrians, is like chartering a jumbo jet for a newspaper round. Mercifully the Egyptians did not launch any of the 30 SCUDs they are believed to possess. Fitted with the warhead it was designed to carry, one of these weapons fired from Egypt could have done at least as much damage to Tel Aviv as Hiroshima suffered in 1945.

What made the high-altitude SAM-2s, SAM-3 'Goas', SAM-6 'Gainfuls' and the little, shoulder-fired SAM-7 'Grails' so effective in keeping the Israeli Air Force at bay was not just their design but the fact that the Russians supplied these highly complex weapons in numbers that are huge by any standards. And it was in respect of these weapons that the effect of the Soviet airlift was most important. None of the SAMs are cheap and the Russians were said to have a limited stock of them. Nevertheless they shipped them to the Middle East in quantities which enabled the Arabs to shoot them off like shot-gun cartridges. Their sheer numbers negated evasion tactics; Israeli fighters dodging one missile and then another and then a third would be hit by a fourth. At low altitude there was the menace of the SAM-7, and automatic weapons such as mobile radar-directed quadruple 23mm anti-aircraft cannons and hundreds of 14.5mm, 23mm and 57mm towed guns. (A complete battalion of Iraqi 57mm guns was caught on a bridge near Kuneitra and totally destroyed by Israeli fighter-bombers.)

With all these modern weapons still being poured into Egypt and Syria the Israelis were in danger of being overwhelmed — the Syrians alone had more tanks than Britain and France combined; in other cases they were in danger of being outclassed. Faced with the bitter realisation that the Israelis were fighting to no purpose since their losses were being countered by an unending flow of Soviet munitions, Mrs Meir telephoned an appeal to the United States. Israel wanted at least 75 aircraft — including 15 Phantoms — tanks, mobile artillery and missiles, she told President Nixon officially. The Nixon Administration would only say that Israel's requests were under consideration; privately officials let it be known that America would not let the Israelis down, and small supplies of ammunition which had been ordered before the war were hurriedly assembled at US bases — where Israeli cargo planes covertly picked them up and rushed them to Israel.

Although the Americans supported Israel they hesitated to risk an escalation in the Middle East conflict until it was certain that the United Nations threatened the very cornerstone of President Nixon's foreign policy — the fragile rapprochement that he and Dr Kissinger were nurturing with the Soviet Union — as well as the prospects of any genuine peace settlement in the Middle East. The Arabs knew this and already they probably realised that they would never succeed in driving the Israelis into the sea; they were hoping that a short war — terminated by a cease-fire brought about by the force of world opinion — would bring them a psychological victory, and increase the pressure on Israel to return the territory she had captured in 1967. For their part the Israelis had also recognised that another clash with the Arabs would be as much a political and diplomatic battle as a military struggle. This was why there had been no pre-emptive strike or premature mobilisation, declared the Israeli Ambassador in Washington. 'We wanted everyone to be sure that Israel had done everything to prevent war.'

By Thursday 11 October 1973, when the war was in its sixth day, there were still no signs of a cease-fire formula emerging from the United Nations. A British attempt to persuade the Arab States to agree to a meeting of the Security Council had been rebuffed, and a meeting of the General Assembly had ended in a stormy scene when accusations by the Syrian delegate that Israel had started the war with simultaneous attacks on Egypt and his own country brought counter-accusations of Arab mendacity from the Israeli delegate. But it was Russian reactions that concerned the Americans most, and these were a curious mixture of restraint and belligerence. Official statements from the Kremlin did little more than give what US commentators called 'minimal' support for the Arabs. And the fact that the Russian technicians and advisers had been pulled out of Egypt and Syria just before the war started, seemed to demonstrate the Soviet Union's desire to stay at arm's length from the conflict. Assurances that the war would not be allowed to interfere with the nascent US-Soviet state of detente pointed in the same direction. Behind the scenes however, Soviet diplomats in the Middle East were exhorting the leaders of Lebanon, Algeria and Jordan to join in the fighting. With no evidence of any real effort by the Russians to persuade Egypt and Syria to still their guns, and reports that their massive airlift of military equipment was tipping the scales against Israel, President Nixon approved the Washington Special Action Group's recommendation to send arms and munitions to Israel.

The air supply operation got under way next morning, and by Sunday 14 October 1973, Galaxies were taking off from bases all across the US and ferrying their 100-ton payloads via the US air base in the Portuguese Azores to Lod airport in Israel. There the arms they carried were transferred to Hercules transports which flew them on to forward airfields where they were unloaded and sent straight up to the forward troops. The battlefield's appetite was voracious, for it is estimated that no less than 16,500 tons of weapons were fed into its maw by the two super-powers during the first two weeks of the fighting. This served to underline the fact that while the Arabs and Israelis were doing the actual fighting it was the United States and Russia that were supplying most of the firepower.

Many of the new American weapons, especially the TOW anti-tank missiles, were needed in Sinai where the Israelis were still waiting for the Egyptians to exploit the advantages they had won on the first two days of the war. Aircraft were a more urgent requirement, so the Americans withdrew 36 Skyhawks and 32 combat-ready Phantoms from US Air Force fighter squadrons and flew them off to Israel. On arrival at Israeli airfields the Star of David was hastily painted over the Stars and Stripes insignia and they were quickly in action. This, said the Egyptians — blandly ignoring the Russian airlift — clearly amounted to active American participation in the war.

The new Phantoms arrived in Israel already fitted with ECM equipment designed to jam the signals of the tracking and guidance radars of the SAM-2s and SAM-3s (SAM-6s were new to the field and it was not possible to design ECM equipment specifically to cope with them until a SAM-6 missile was captured.) With the Phantoms also came a wide range of American 'smart' bombs — including Rockeye cluster bombs, Walleye television-guided bombs and laser-guided devices — Shrike anti-radar missiles to confuse the SAM-6 radars, and Sparrow and Sidewinder air-to-air missiles.

All these new weapons were to have a tremendous impact on the war — the extent of which has been assessed and will be re-assessed time and again. But in the Middle East the human element proved to be as important as it ever was and the stolid courage of the Egyptian and Syrian soldiers did not suffice. In 1973 as in 1967 Egypt and Syria were saved only by the cease-fire procured by the Soviet Union. Beyond the Middle East one of the most important outcomes of the war was that it gave the Russians a chance to test their latest weapons in Sinai and Syria — just as the Americans had tested theirs in Vietnam.

14 The Israeli Breakthrough

On the second day of the war an ugly situation was developing at the Israeli Southern Command Headquarters, from where its commander, Major-General 'Gorodish' Gonen was directing the battle in Sinai. The situation was rapidly deteriorating and the Israeli High Command had issued a directive saying that the Northern Front was to have priority; turning on the Egyptians would have to wait until the Syrians had been repulsed.

Gonen, a pedantic strictly religious man, had held his command for only three months, and he did not command much respect from his brother officers. Neither his bravery nor his efficiency was in question — he had shown plenty of both during the Six-Day War. But he did not have the panache of his predecessor, the swashbuckling paratrooper General 'Arik' Sharon. Forty-five, tough, out-spoken and ambitious, Sharon was a dedicated soldier, who had fought in all the Arab-Israeli wars. As a platoon commander in the War of Independence he was wounded at Latrun; as a major, commanding the commando *meshugeners* of Unit 101, he led a controversial reprisal raid against the Jordanian village of Kibya; as a parachute brigade commander in the Sinai campaign of 1956 he defiantly captured the Egyptian positions covering the Mitla Pass — although he had been specifically ordered not to attack. And in the Six-Day War it was Sharon's Ugda which battered a way through the Mitla Pass. Appointed to the command in which he was succeeded by Gonen, Sharon had retired from the army only when he learned that he was not going to be promoted and would never be appointed Chief of-Staff. (This was largely because his right-wing political inclinations were distrusted by Mrs Meir's Labour Coalition Government.)

In civilian life Sharon took up farming, but in the three months which elapsed between his relegation to the reserve and the outbreak of war, he had maintained close links with his old headquarters. As a reserve officer earmarked for the command of an ugda in Southern Command on mobilisation, Sharon was disturbed by the rumours of Egyptian preparations for war. Two days before Yom Kippur he had driven down to Tasa from his ranch at Beersheba. There he was shown intelligence reports, and aerial photographs of bridging equipment close to the west bank of the Canal. Convinced that an attack was imminent, anxious for action, and restless for mobilisation, the forthright views Sharon expressed to his former subordinate were bound to create a furore. 'If I were still in command here', he said, 'you would not have much to do in a war'. Gonen was furious, but said nothing. Thus before even the first shot was fired the scene was set for a quarrel among the Israeli generals on the southern front.

By Saturday night — with the Egyptians pouring across the Canal and many of the observation posts of the Bar Lev line already in Egyptian hands, with Egyptian infantry knocking out tank after tank, and the Israeli Air Force unable to give the close support the Israeli troops had come to expect — an atmosphere of near despair had settled over Southern Command. Gonen was rapidly becoming a nervous wreck and his three ugda commanders — Sharon, Avraham 'Bren' Adan, and Kalman Magen — were disputing his orders or simply ignoring them. Bitter rows developed between Gonen and Sharon over the latter's view that Resheff's tanks were being sacrificed in a holding operation that could not possibly succeed. What Sharon wanted was a concentrated counter-attack to strike across the Canal and turn the enemy's flanks; Gonen, staking his faith on an Alam Halfa type battle in front of the vital passes, insisted that an offensive must wait until more reserves had arrived. Gonen was prepared to fight by the book and obey the directive issued by the Israeli High Command without question, while Sharon could visualise the war being brought to an end by a cease-fire — leaving the Egyptians on the east bank where they were now digging in.

News of the quarrels and discontent in Southern Command Headquarters quickly filtered back to the Ministry of Defence in Tel Aviv. Moshe Dayan realised that something would have to be done quickly; Israelis were already asking why Arab attacks had come as such a surprise and criticism that Dayan's warnings were too muted and too late was mounting. Public opinion would not take kindly to news that the generals were squabbling among themselves. So, on Monday, the third day of the war, Dayan tried to settle the dispute, by suggesting to Elazar that Gonen and Sharon should reverse their roles. The Chief of Staff refused. But he flew down to Sinai to investigate the troubles at Gonen's headquarters, and it did not take him long to decide that someone with a stronger personality than Gonen would have to take charge. Next day an Israeli Government spokesman announced that six senior retired generals had been recalled for active service, and the quiet, highly respected General Haim Bar Lev flew in to Southern Command Headquarters.

All six generals were said to have been recalled for 'Special duties'. And although these duties were never spelled out publicly, it was soon clear that Bar-Lev had superseded Gonen in directing the war in Sinai. Gonen was not displaced officially, but Bar-Lev was in command and the precarious situation was resolved. However, while the quarrelling ceased, the arguments continued as to how the initiative should be wrested from the Egyptians and a counter-strike delivered.

Meanwhile the situation was going from bad to worse for the Israelis in Sinai. Yakouri's regiment had been wiped out and the crews of Resheff's tanks — whittled down to a mere 90, which had been in continuous action for two days — were almost exhausted. They had gone into battle with the ammunition racks inside their tanks filled with armour-piercing shells to fight other tanks, while what they needed was high explosive rounds to use against the Egyptian infantry manning the anti-tank missile screen. Five Egyptian infantry divisions had crossed the Canal and the 500 tanks which General Ismail had held on the west bank of the Canal to protect the rear of his 3rd and 2nd Armies had started to roll over the bridges and concentrate for the next phase of the Egyptian offensive.

As set-back followed set-back Sharon continued to maintain that he could 'make the Egyptians change their tune and throw them off balance'. Not only could he reach the Canal, he claimed, he could cross it and end the war with one audacious stoke. In the four years he had held Gonens job, Sharon had studied and even prepared crossing points along the Canal. Plans for an operation to force a crossing had already been laid, and his argument for resuscitating them now was straightforward: the west bank of the Canal offered a chance to use traditional Israeli

Left: The Israelis reached the Canal bank and came under fire.

Above: Subsequently a second bridge was thrown across the Canal.

Centre right: Egyptians captured near the bridgehead were blindfolded before being ferried across into Sinai and thence to PoW camps in the Negev.

Bottom right: Israeli armour crosses the Canal after Sharon's break through.

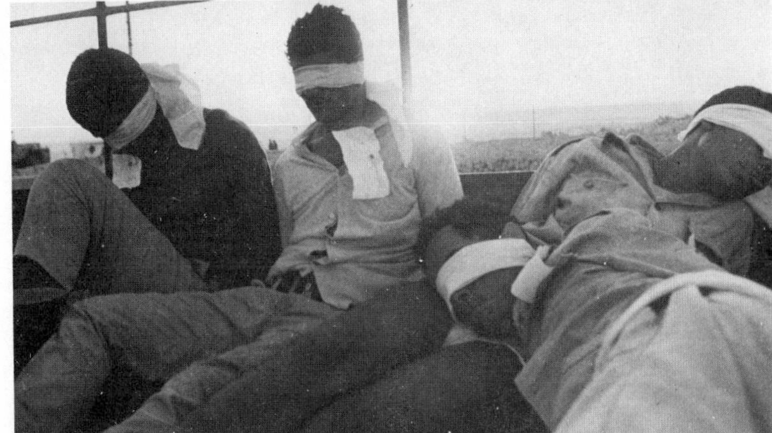

Top and left: Israelis race south down the west bank of the Canal.

Above: An Israeli column passing an Egyptian military installation on the Fayid-Ismailia road.

Right: Briefing for Operation Gazelle.

tactics — the employment of fast moving armour in open, classic tank country. Success within 48 hours was guaranteed, Sharon said, if he was given a task force of tanks and infantry to carry out the operation.

Gonen had refused to listen, Bar-Lev said 'no', and Dayan demurred — pointing out that the only troops that could be spared at that moment was a reservist parachute brigade deployed to stop the Egyptian 3rd Army pushing down towards Sharm-El-Sheikh. Sharon accepted Dayan's verdict, for the time being, but continued to prod Bar-Lev whose views he is reputed to have said were 'typical of the "chicken-soup" thinking in Jerusalem'. Both Dayan and Bar-Lev eventually sanctioned the operation, but there was more quarrelling and much hard fighting before Operation Gazelle was launched across the Canal.

In the plan he had worked out before the war Sharon had selected a spot for crossing the Canal just north of the Great Bitter Lake. Between Lake Timsah and the Bitter Lakes the north-south Canal road runs a mile or two east of the bank. But just above the entrance to the Lake two side roads branch off within a 1,000 yards of each other and link up at the side of the Canal. At this point, some 13 miles south of Ismailia, Sharon had had the high walls of the Canal bank thinned down, and the weakened section marked with easily identifiable red bricks. He had also had the ground nearby bulldozed to provide a parking area, protected by sand walls where vehicles could be marshalled prior to an assault crossing. (Less than a mile away from this point the Egyptians had run into difficulty hosing a passage through the Canal bank. If they had hit upon Sharon's weakened section their task would have been eased, and — deprived of his pre-planned crossing place — the story of Sharon's operation might have been very different.)

Sharon was allotted three armoured brigades whose original strength had been each 90-100 tanks, but which were now depleted by the recent fighting to a total strength of about 200 tanks in all, a mechanised parachute brigade, and a composite force of engineers with bulldozers, assault-craft and bridging equipment. This force concentrated on the high ground between the Khatmia and Gidi Passes on Sunday 14 October, the ninth day of the war. Sharon started to brief his officers at dawn the following day and Operation Gazelle began at dusk. Eight hours later Sharon's troops were across the Canal and fighting a devastating battle which lasted until midday on the Wednesday.

With the Egyptian 21st Armoured Division deployed astride both of the roads leading from Tasa to the Canal, Sharon's problem was to get to the water and establish the bridgehead in the dark. Surprise and speed were essential; otherwise the Egyptians would have tanks waiting on the far side of the Canal. Sharon's plan therefore depended on getting control of the roads leading south from Tasa to the Great Lake. This road joins the main Canal road about a mile and a half short of the southen most of the two junctions leading to the prospective crossing place. Near these junctions was an irrigation project, set up as a prestige experiment by President Nasser shortly before the Six-Day War. Much of the machinery was of Japanese manufacture, and the first Israeli troops had called the area the 'Chinese Farm', when they saw the characters which denoted it origin.

The essence of Sharon's plan was to use one of his armoured brigades to seize control of the road, while another moved north in an offensive feint against the Egyptian 2nd Army. Once control of the road and road junctions had been won the paratroops and engineers,

Left: The 'Treaty' road on the west bank of the Canal.

Below: Blazing oil installations on the western edge of Suez town.

Right: The Battle of the Chinese Farm was one of the bloodiest actions of the war.

waiting near Tasa, would go through to secure a crossing. Some tanks would be ferried across to help the paratroops establish a firm bridgehead behind which the engineers would build a bridge across the Canal. Finally the third of Sharon's armoured brigades would cross to the west bank to sweep down the Canal, sever the 3rd Army's lines of communications and destroy the SAM sites — so restoring freedom of action to the Israeli Air Force. The plan was a bold one promising tremendous dividends if successful; but risky and promising equally tremendous penalties if it failed.

According to the schedule of the operation, the assault crossing was timed for 2300hrs which left five hours for the armour to get down to the Canal and clear a passage for the infantry and engineers. As a large part of the route was through trackless sand dunes, and tanks travelling at night can rarely average more than five miles an hour, any battle which developed round the road junctions would have to be settled quickly.

The diversionary attack against the 2nd Army was launched at 1700hrs when Sharon's second armoured brigade, north of the Tasa-Great Bitter Lake road, started to advance towards Ismailia. The Egyptians reacted as Sharon had expected and the battle which developed gradually drew the main weight of the Egyptian 21st Armoured Division north towards the Tasa-Ismailia road. Meanwhile at 6pm, as nightfall began to shroud the battlefield, the armoured brigade spear heading the assault force crossed the start line and headed due south. Then, as the tanks approached the road skirting the east side of the Great Lake, the brigade turned west and north, making for the juncture of General Maamoun's 2nd Army and General Wassel's 3rd Army. Here, in an area of overlapping command, was the traditional weak spot in the Egyptian front, which had been pinpointed by Israeli Intelligence. Driving through the uncharted dunes and up the road along the lake shore, Sharon's tanks encountered no oposition. Before leaving, this brigade had been divided into three groups and at the 'Y' junction of the Tasa and lake shore road the first of these groups swung north-east to drive back up the road towards Tasa. Its task was to clear the road by attacking the Egyptian forces blocking it from behind.

The tanks of the second group motored on north-east, passed the 'Y' junction, turned left, and followed the road north-west to the projected crossing place. Behind them the third group continued up the main road towards the next junction ('T'): its task was to establish a protective perimeter round the crossing place as far north as possible. Approaching the 'T' junction this group ran into trouble. Heavy Egyptian fire halted the advance, and here, at the Chinese Farm, one of the fiercest and bloodiest tank actions was fought out over the next 48 hours.

The men who bore the brunt of this fighting were, once again, Colonel Resheff's 14th Armoured Brigade. Resheff wanted to be first across the Canal but because he knew the area so well he was given the job of securing the crossing. By the time the battle was over his brigade had suffered nearly 100% casualties — for the third time since Yom Kippur. Fighting in the dark, often at 40 yards range, the Egyptians fought hard to stop the Israelis gaining control of the road-junction area. And their unexpectedly stout resistance delayed the operational schedule, already running late: at a time when they should have been on the far side of the Canal the assault crossing groups were still in Tasa. But the task force which headed back towards Tasa, to clear the Egyptians blocking that road, broke through successfully. And by midnight it was motoring back towards the Canal at the head of a column of paratroops in half-tracks and Egged buses, and trucks loaded with rubber rafts and engineering equipment.

The first Israelis — Sharon among them — paddled across the Canal about 0100hrs (Tuesday, 16 October) and clambered up the west bank. It was a quiet moonlit night and in the plantations and palm trees ahead there was no sign of any activity. Two miles behind them, however, noises and flashes of gunfire, rocket trails and criss-crosses of tracer indicated that a fierce battle was in progress around the Chinese Farm. Gun-flashes further to the north-east showed that the armoured brigade making the feint attack was also in action. As the main assault force of paratroops and engineers had to bypass the Chinese Farm battle it was hardly surprising that they did not start to arrive until 0300hrs, four hours dangerously behind schedule. The barges to ferry the tanks over the Canal did not arrive until 0500hrs, shortly before dawn broke; and there was as yet no sign of the bridging equipment. Nevertheless Sharon, isolated on the wrong side of the Canal, showed no signs of concern. He behaved, said one Israeli soldier, 'like the Angel Gabriel'.

Ignoring the battle going on only a few thouand yards behind them, the Israeli sappers speedily bulldozed a passage through the canal embankment, and eased the barges into the water. By 0600hrs the ferrying operation was under way. But the Egyptians had woken up by this time and their artillery had zeroed in on the crossing place. The first two ferries received direct hits and the two tanks they were carrying sank with their crews. Meantime four Egyptian tanks, which had rumbled up to the Israeli perimeter on the west bank, had been quickly knocked out by Israeli infantry anti-tank weapons. After that there was no further interference from the Egyptian Army at the crossing point, and by 0900hrs 30 Israeli tanks and about 2,000 men had crossed the Canal. Back along the Tasa road, however, the two armoured brigades which had made the operation possible were still fighting savagely to keep open the corridor to the crossing place. Surprise was gone

Above: 'Arik' Sharon at the Israeli bridgehead on the 'African' (western) side of the Canal.

Left: The bridgehead on the west bank of the Canal shortly after the first of Sharon's tanks had been ferried across.

Above right: Casualties.

Right: More Israelis cross the Canal.

and if the Egyptians had put in a determined attack on the bridgehead during Tuesday morning, there can be little doubt that Sharon would have been in a very precarious position. And the risks taken by the flamboyant general now acclaimed as the Israeli Patton might well have been condemned as the Israeli panjandrum.

But the crossing had caught the Egyptians absolutely by surprise and it was 36 hours before they awoke to the seriousness of the incursion. The reason for this can be attributed to the rigid workings of the Egyptian military machine, which functioned well in set-piece situations, less well when suddenly confronted with the unorthodox. During the Yom Kippur war individual Egyptian units showed that they could handle complex equipment competently and fight courageously and tenaciously. Egyptian staff officers also showed that they could plan and cope with the multifarious logistics problems of an elaborate offensive. But communicaion up and down the chain of command was slow, and liaison between flanking formations appears to have been woefully inadequate. General Ismail, directing the war from the Egyptian Army's magnificent underground command and control centre near Cairo, knew nothing about the Israeli crossing until late on Tuesday morning — by which time Sharon had been on the western bank for over 11 hours. Nor amazingly enough, did anyone apparently see fit to inform General Maamoun in Ismailia or General Wassel in Suez that anything unusual was happening at all.

Ismail said later that he only heard about the Israeli operation as he returned to the command centre from a meeting at the People's Assembly (where President Sadat

Left: Knocked out Egyptian armour.

Below: The Israelis established clearing stations in Egyptian houses and schools.

Right: Once across the Canal Sharon's armour tore in behind the Egyptians.

Below right: For the Israelis a bridge across the Canal was vital if Operation Gazelle was to succeed. Because of the battle at the Chinese Farm the equipment arrived four hours behind schedule.

told the Egyptian people that they had won a great victory, and voted that the fighting would not stop until the Israelis had disgorged every scrap of Arab land). It may be that little information had been passed up to the Cairo GHQ. Egyptian reconnaissance patrols were not so active as their Israeli counterparts — or so quick about reporting their contacts. Nor were reports from some units always accepted as reliable, and one explanation for the Egyptians failing to react sooner may stem from the fact that the first Arab troops to clash with Sharon's force on the Egyptian side of the Canal were men of the Ain Jalloud Brigade of the Palestine Liberation Army. Excited reports from these men tended to be dismissed as emotional exaggerations. On the other hand it is possible that senior Egyptian officers, enraptured by the initial Arab successes, just did not want to believe what was happening. Or there may even have been some reluctance to pass the information on to the Minister of War. 'The reports I received', said Ismail, 'indicated that a small batch of amphibious tanks had infiltrated, and it was the conviction of the local command that they would be wiped out quickly...'

Far from being wiped out quickly, Sharon's force on the eastern bank was in fact growing stronger by the hour. But the battle on the east bank was still raging and when Egyptians did eventually mount an attack on the Tuesday evening, it was directed against the eastern approaches to the crossing place. Late as it came this attack nearly succeeded in depriving the Israelis of control of the road junctions and blocking the routes to the crossing point.

With Maamoun's 2nd Army pressing down from the north, and a force from Wassel's 3rd Army throwing their weight on the south, the battle flared up and raged more fiercely than before. Darkness reduced the value of the Egyptian infantryman's anti-tank missiles. But reduced visibility also cut down the Israelis' advantage in long-range gunnery. Slowly and bloodily, however, the outnumbered Israelis gained the upper hand, and Egyptian

resistance at the Chinese Farm started to crumble. As it did so the shelling of the crossing place also slackened, and the Israeli engineers were able to start work on the bridge which should have been in position 24 hours before.

While it had not been possible to put the bridge pontoons in position, the ferries continued to operate throughout the day. It was a dangerous business. Killed by the blast of shells exploding in the water, dead fish littered both banks of the Canal. No casualty figures have been released, but it is believed that about 100 Israelis were killed and another 300 wounded. Yet Sharon was determined to go on — abandoning the crossing place if need be — to sweep southwards and wreak havoc behind the Egyptian 3rd Army. Gonen, still urging restraint, ordered Sharon to stop where he was, dig in, and hold the crossing place until such time as a bridge could be thrown across the Canal. Sharon's radioed response was 'Balls'. To dig in, he maintained, would make his force conspicuous and present the Egyptians with an easy target. With that he split up his tiny force into raiding parties and sent them out to search for SAM sites, fuel and ammunition dumps and anything else that seemed worth attacking. Inevitably much of the damage caused by the raiders was relatively trivial. Nevertheless four SAM sites had been knocked out by midday on the Tuesday. This opened a hole in the SAM umbrella and the Israeli Air Force swiftly moved in to provide Sharon with tactical air support. Alarmed by this development the Egyptians sent up their own air force to challenge the Israeli Phantoms and Skyhawks. In the dog fighting which followed dozens of MiGs were shot down and the Israelis established air superiority in the central sector of the Sinai front.

Sharon's bridge was in position about midday on Wednesday — 30 hours or so behind schedule — and the first of Major-General 'Bren' Adan's three tank brigades started to roll across into 'Africa'. Sharon justly deserves the credit for planning Operation Gazelle and the laurels due to him for leading the Israeli thrust across the Canal. But it was the less publicity-conscious Bren Adan who made the running during the all-important follow-up. After the war Sharon accused the Israeli High Command of being slow to exploit the opportunity with which he had presented them. Thirty-six hours elapsed before reinforcements were sent to his bridgehead, he complained. Nor was he allowed to drive north to encircle the Egyptian 2nd Army; and no senior general visited the bridgehead in the first initial days of the war. No names were mentioned, but clearly those he had in mind were Generals Gonen, Bar-Lev and — to a lesser extent — David Elazar. Elazar responded with a scathing comment on Sharon's conduct across the Canal. 'It may be less glamorous to fight for the holding of a bridgehead than to drive your tanks into Africa', he said, 'but the holding of the bridgehead may be the crucial move of a battle.' This was another sally in the so-called Israeli 'War of the generals'.

Below: Eventually the bridge was built and the Israelis poured across the Canal.

15 Cease-Fire

While the Egyptian leaders continued to play down the dangers posed by what they termed publicity as the 'Israeli commando force' on the western bank of the Canal, the generals in the field were beginning to appreciate the seriousness of the new threat. On Wednesday night (17 October) a stubborn attack against the bridgehead launched by General Maamoun was repulsed with heavy loss. The hand-writing was on the wall, and although General Ismail was beginning to regret having committed virtually all Egypt's first-line armour to Sinai, he did not pull back any of the 500 tanks he had sent across to the east bank. On Ismail's own subsequent admission, 'information was interrupted due to changes of responsibilities which we had made in some commands . . .' during this period. (One such change was the replacement of General Maamoun who was said to have suffered a heart attack. General Wassel was soon to be sacked as well. So too was the Chief of Staff, General Shazli.) Even as Israeli armoured columns were spreading like a giant oil slick across the land on the west bank of the Canal from Ismailia to the Great Bitter Lake, there were no signs of the Egyptians pulling back from Sinai.

Fierce fighting and heavy casulties were reported but the Israeli army in Africa — whose strength had grown to 200 tanks and 8,000 men — continued to advance north and south along the Canal. By the weekend, all the missile sites and gun batteries along a 50-mile stretch of the waterway had been knocked out. (They were terribly vulnerable because the Egyptians had not bothered to protect them.) Fayid and Abu Suweir had been overrun, and the capture of the airfields at these two places gave the Israelis forward landing fields and fuel for their tanks. There was now every prospect of the six Egyptian divisions clinging to their beacheads in Sinai being cut off and trapped between two Israeli armies. Besides threatening to cut their last bridges, Sharon and Adan were moving against their supply lines, and the situation raised the spectre of something worse than the rout which brought the termination of the Six-Day War.

At long last the Israeli Government had some encouraging news to pass on to a dazed and anxious public which had been warned not to expect an easy victory. As the architect of the operation which promised the virtually total annihilation of the Egyptian Army, Sharon became more of a hero than ever. And his image as a front-line fighting figure was further enhanced with news that he had quickly gone back into action after being wounded in the head by a shell splinter. When Moshe Dayan paid a surprise visit to the bridgehead the two generals were photographed. They made a striking pair — Dayan with his familiar piratical eyepatch and Sharon with his head wrapped in a bandage still stained with spots of blood.

Back in Jerusalem the Israeli Minister of Defence announced that 'the decisive moment was near'. 'Israel

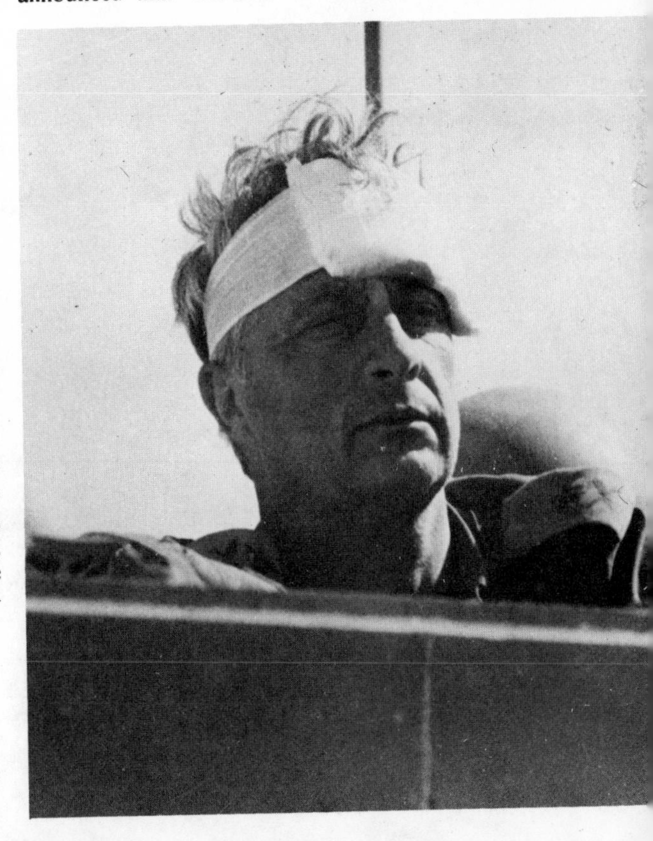

Right: Sharon, the man who is still a focus of controversy. During Operation Gazelle he was slightly wounded in the forehead. Some Israelis suggested that he wore a bandage for effect.

should not be in any hurry for a cease-fire,' he said. 'Every day that passes is to Israel's benefit.' And General Elazar added 'We are now dictating conditions for developing the attack . . . Conditions exist for decision and victory'.

For their part the Arabs also appeared to be in no hurry for a cease-fire. There was no sign that the Syrians — resupplied, reorganised, and bolstered by Iraqi and Jordanian reinforcements — were about to break, and the Egyptian Army seemed determined to fight to the death to keep its foothold on the last bank of the Canal. The fact is the Egyptians did not realise just how serious the situation was and other people were much better informed about what was going on in the field. On 4 October the Russians had launched a Cosmos 'spy in the sky' satellite programmed to watch the military events in the Middle East from on high. An American spy satellite was doing the same, for although both sides were obsessed with the idea of detente the Soviet Union and the US knew they would have to keep a close eye on events if they were to protect the interests of their respective clients.

Since the Israelis had crossed the Canal the Russians had watched with mounting horror the progress of the war in Egypt, and on 16 October Mr Kosygin, the Soviet Prime Minister flew to Cairo for three days of talks with President Sadat. With Israeli troops pouring across the Canal less than 100 miles away the war was at a critical stage. There

Left: Dayan visits Sharon's bridgehead in Africa.

Below left: Egged buses in an Israeli reinforcement convoy approaching the Canal.

Right: Stragglers from the Egyptian Third Army rounded up near Suez.

Below: Israelis manning a post on the western side of the Canal near Suez.

were traffic jams on the Canal roads and a staggering variety of Israeli transport carried about 20,000 infantry across the Canal. Tnuva milk tankers, full of water, giant pantechnicons and Egged buses were conspicuous in the long columns of vehicles crossing the bridge. A few days later the Egged Company proudly announced that it had extended its service into Egypt and Africa. Sadat was still convinced that nothing was seriously wrong: he still had 100,000 troops and 500 tanks on the Israeli side of the Canal, he said, and he wanted to keep the war 'hot', bleed Israel's manpower, erode her resources, tax her ability to remain mobilised. Asked about the Israeli 'commando raid' across the Canal, Sadat told Kosygin that it was just a propaganda stunt — something which Mrs Meir could use to boost the flagging morale of her compatriots. Kosygin then spelt out the Soviet interpretation of the operation and the current state of affair deduced from the Cosmos pictures.

The Russians had already decided that it was high time there was a major effort to stop the fighting, and once Sadat was convinced of the truth of the situation he reluctantly agreed. Meantime, before he returned to Moscow, Kosygin ordered Russian military personnel to be flown in to put muscle back into the Egyptian air defences around Cairo and to take over the ground control of the Soviet airlift. Thus, in the course of the week beginning Friday 19 October some 400 Soviet 'technicians' and 'representatives' returned. Then, when Kosygin went back to Moscow, Mr Brezhnev despatched an urgent note to Washington inviting Dr Kissinger to go to Moscow for discussions 'on means to end hostilities in the Middle East before an irrevocable decision was taken.' While the message was being delivered US Intelligence experts were reporting to the State Department that Israel was considering attacking Soviet ships ferrying heavy equipment to Syria and Egypt.

Even before the Soviet note was sent and the Intelligence reports presented, Washington had already concluded that it was time the war was stopped. The 'irrevocable decision'

Top and left: In the confusion following the Israeli break through across the Canal many small Egyptian detachments were cut off and eventually had to surrender.

Above: Some prisoners had been without water for 48 hours or even longer.

Above right: Syrian pilot in an Israeli hospital.

Right: UN Convoy moving up to the Golan Heights.

to which Brezhnev had referred was a threat of direct Russian intervention in the fighting. The detente might survive confrontation but not the defeat of a client state. Moreover America's allies were expressing alarm not only at the dangers of a Soviet-US confrontation arising out of the escalating airlift of arms to both sides, but also — especially the West Europeans — at the potentially catastrophic effects of cuts in Arab oil supplies. In a broadcast from Radio Riyadh on 18 October King Feisal announced that producion and shipments of oil from Saudi Arabia would be progressively reduced until there was peace in the Middle East. Egypt's and Syria's oil-rich Arab allies had decided to implement their threat to use oil as a geopolitical weapon. Next day President Nixon asked Congress for a supplemental military-aid appropriation of 2.2 billion dollar to pay for war material for Israel. He also announced that the Mediterranean-based Sixth Fleet would be reinforced. King Feisal's response was to cut off all oil shipments to the US. Fearing that the US was being drawn into a vortex, Nixon ordered Kissinger to go to Moscow to try to find some way of moving Middle East problems from the battlefield to a conference table.

So Kissinger made a dramatic early-morning flight to Moscow, where agreement was quickly reached that both superpowers would exert strong pressure on their respective clients to stop the war. They agreed on a cease-fire in situ, and laid down some broad but crude political conditions. The Arabs were handed their sop; that Resolution 242 of the Security Council — demanding Israel's 'withdrawal from occupied territories' — must be implemented 'in all its parts'. However, as another condition stipulated 'immediate negotiations'. the Israelis could interpret the cease-fire terms as requiring no withdrawal in advance of a negotiated agreement on secure and guaranteed frontiers.

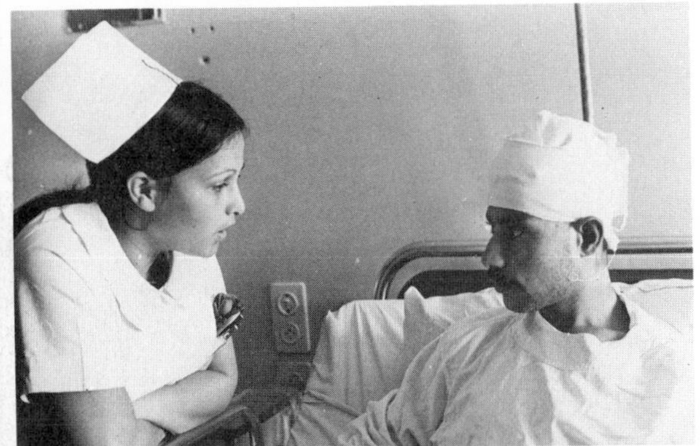

In Cairo President Sadat was ready to accept a cease-fire — although most other Egyptian leaders were still talking in terms of an eventual military victory. 'We will not be sweet-talked into anything this time', said one official. 'We have learned a bitter lesson from the long history of cease-fires.' President Assad of Syria was even less keen. But the Russians had already begun putting pressure on Syria with threats to cut off the supplies. On 16 October three Russian cargo ships loaded with military supplies docked at Latakia only three hours after the Israeli Navy shelled the port. The Syrians, desperate for shells and anti-tank missiles, had trucks waiting to rush the supplies off to the front. But while Syrian officers argued and complained, the Russians refused to start unloading. 'We are waiting for orders', they said. Late in the afternoon orders did come from the Soviet Embassy: 'Put to sea', they said. Ostensibly this was because of the danger of another Israeli attack on the port; in fact it was all part of the pressure on President Assad, and this incident marked the end of the Soviet seaborne re-supply operation. The Soviet Ambassador told Assad that while the Russians would continue to fly in ammunition they were not prepared to send any more heavy weapons as they feared the Israelis might capture them. (Subsequently when the Egyptians and Israelis had accepted the conditions for cease-fire the Russians threatened that if the Syrians were to go it alone they would deliver no more supplies at all and withdraw the

Left: Shattered Egyptian radar in the Canal zone.

Below: One of the 449 lost Arab planes.

Right: UN cease-fire brought relief to the Egyptian defenders.

'technicians' serving with the Syrian air defence missile units. And this brought President Assad to heel.)

Like the Syrians, the Israelis were also reluctant to accept a cease-fire at this stage of war; they too had learned bitter lessons from the history of cease-fires. Moreover the news of the decision reached in Moscow came as a surprise. They realised, of course, that Mr Kosygin's three-day visit to Cairo and Dr Kissinger's hurried flight to Moscow presaged a move to end the war. But the Americans had led them to believe that no immediate plan for settling the war was likely to emerge from the Moscow meeting. There was therefore none of the sense of urgency which had marked the closing hours of the Six-Day War — when Israeli tank commanders had fought their final battles with one ear glued to the tank radio set and the other listening for news bulletins on the UN cease-fire debate in New York. Thus the announcement of the super power agreement in Moscow came as a bombshell to Jerusalem. After a tense session of debate on Sunday 21 October, the Israeli Cabinet reluctantly agreed to accept President Nixon's personal appeal to Golda Meir to comply with the Moscow resolution. Shortly before 0400hrs Israel's ambassador to the UN in New York told the Security Council of his country's acceptance of a cease-fire; and at 0630hrs a similar announcement was made in Jerusalem.

Trouble started at 0730hrs when the leader of the Israeli Government Opposition. Mr Menahem Begin, called on Mrs Meir to register his party's disagreement. A cease-fire in situ, he said, would leave the Syrian and Egyptian armies intact in positions where they could be rearmed by the Russians, and the Israelis would be left with a much longer line to defend. Moreover the second paragraph of the Moscow resolution implied the evacuation of at least a substantial part of the territories occupied in 1967 — to which Begin's right-wing Likud alliance was resolutely opposed.

Mrs Meir telephoned President Nixon for advice, and at midday Kissinger — on his way home from Moscow — arrived at Lod airport to 'clarify' the terms of the Moscow agreement. Whether Mrs Meir even broached the subject or whether there was tacit agreement to let the Israelis go ahead with their plan to cut off Egypt's 3rd Army will probably never be revealed. (The Russians privately accused Kissinger later of going back on what he had agreed in Moscow. In Tel Aviv, they said, he was persuaded into letting the Israelis gain more ground for bargaining purposes — instead of insisting on strict observance of the cease-fire.) Meantime the UN Security Council, after only two hours of debate, unanimously passed the cease-fire resolution, and a truce appeared to be on the way.

The fighting on the Syrian border ended where it had begun, high up on the slopes of Mt Hermon, where the Syrian commandos had stormed the Israeli observation post on the first day of the war. For the Israelis' pride as well as military considerations necessitated its recapture. so paratroops and men of the Golani brigade who knew the ground were given the task. Like the Syrians before them they were helicoptered up to their objective. But the men who manned the position were on the alert in a fashion which the Israelis had not been on Day 1. They fought

Left: Helicopter recovery.

Below: Dayan, the Israeli Defence Minister, visits the Israeli positions in Suez.

Right: Rations for the Egyptian Third Army were checked by the Israelis before being allowed across the Canal or into Suez.

hard, and only after vicious hand to hand fighting and heavy Israeli casualties were they eventually dislodged.

In the desert the cease-fire broke down almost immediately. The Israelis were trying to establish their grip on the Suez-Cairo road — control of which would throttle the supply line to the Egyptian 3rd Army, and the Egyptians were fighting back, genuinely unaware of the strength of the Israeli force on their side of the Canal, and unable to understand why Sadat had agreed to a cease-fire anyway.

And so on the night of 22 October — barely a few hours after the cease-fire was supposed to come into effect — the battlefield erupted once more. The Israelis, trying to complete the encirclement of the 3rd Army, attacked Suez town and raced round the Suez Gulf to capture the port of Adabiya, where much of Egypt's oil supply is unloaded. All the roads and approaches linking Suez with Cairo were severed, and the outer suburbs of Suez town were taken. But the Egyptians stubbornly resisted the Israeli advance into the built-up area and when the cease-fire at last took precarious effect on 25 October the greater part of the devastated ruins of Suez were still in Egyptian hands.

Meantime an international crisis had begun to develop. The Russians, furious at the break-down of the original cease-fire on 22 October, claimed that they had been deceived by the Americans. It seemed, they said, that the latter had made a secret deal with their clients which had resulted in the Israelis seizing another great chunk of Arab territory. The Americans had in fact warned the Israelis of the risk they were taking by breaking the cease-fire as soon as the fighting started again on 22 October. But neither their warning nor a veiled threat from Moscow about 'grave consequences' if cease-fire violations continued, had any effect. The simple fact was that neither of the superpowers necessarily tried to swindle the other; it was just that they had not credited their proteges with having minds and wills of their own.

ALEXANDRIA
MADE IN JAPAN
8007/A1/
2538/14606 GO
C/No.
ALEXANDRIA
MADE IN JAPAN

FK 95

Left: The rations were ferried over the Canal at one of the original Egyptian crossing points.

Below left: UN troops at the cease-fire line on the outskirts of Suez.

Right: The UN Camp at Kilo 101 on the Cairo-Suez road.

Below: Israeli tanks on the outskirts of Suez.

However, when the cease-fire broke down the Russians were in a difficult situation. If they did nothing the Arab world would see their lack of action as merely standing by while the destruction of the Egyptian Army was consummated. So it was inevitable that they should attempt something. First came a proposal to the US for joint intervention in the Middle East. To the Americans this could only mean a force big enough and powerful enough to intervene by fighting — something that was not acceptable. So the suggestion was turned down. And at this point the crisis started to escalate with rapid acceleration. For about five days US Intelligence had been receiving reports that Soviet troops were preparing for operational duty. Now it became clear that the Soviet airlift of supplies to Cairo had dramatically diminished — possibly to free planes as troop transports. The Mediterranean Red Fleet was also known to have a force of marines. Finally the Soviet Ambassador to the US, Anatoly Dobrynin, called on Dr Kissinger to deliver a tough message from Brezhnev. Unless the Israelis were called to heel the Russians would send in airborne troops to protect their Egyptian clients, was the gist of the message.

Fearing a Vietnam style of involvement in the Middle East, but anxious not to give the Russians any cause to believe that they could get away with sending in troops unilaterally, Kissinger and his advisers opted for firm action. President Nixon was advised to put US forces on a worldwide alert, and shortly before 0200hrs (Washington time) on 25 October the preparatory order was issued for a Stage 3 alert in the five stage American Defence Condition (Defcon) order. (During the Cuban missile crisis in 1962 the American forces were put on Stage 2.) At 0300hrs, when Defcon 3 came into operation, 2,300,000 American sevicemen were standing by at bases across the world from Miami to Okinawa; aircraft carriers steamed out to their operational stations, and the Strategic Air Command B-52s returned to the US from Guam. It was the first time since the Cuban crisis 11 years before that such a thing had happened. But Nixon and Kissinger had decided that a world-wide alert — rather than a selective alert to particular air bases, as in the 1970 war between Jordan and Syria — was necessary, because it was vital to convince the Soviet Union of American determination to react if the Russians attempted to interfere on the ground in the Middle East.

The crisis lasted another 24 hours, then both superpowers pulled back and agreed that a United Nations' sponsored emergency force raised from Nations other than the big five should be put into the Middle East, to restrain the combatants. Both Russians and Amerians had decided that their own self interest was more important than the interests of their clients or allies.

Meanwhile an uneasy calm began to settle on the battlefields. In Syria the front had stabilised, and although the Syrians were rapidly rearming the Israelis were confident that they could deal with any new offensive. The Egyptian front continued to simmer. The cease-fire left 20,000 men of Egypt's 3rd Army trapped in Sinai, and the Israelis showed little inclination to let them out of the trap unless the Egyptians surrendered. In response to an appeal from Egypt to the Red Cross, Israeli vehicles crossed No Man's Land to deliver 200 containers of blood plasma for the 3rd Army's wounded. Until international pressure forced them to do so, however, they were not prepared to provide anything else. Eventually senior Israeli officers met their Egyptian counterparts on the Cairo-Suez Canal road and a convoy of 125 United Nations lorries was subsequently permitted to cross the Canal, taking supplies of food and medicine to the beleaguered 3rd Army. These were the only supplies to reach the Egyptian troops since the road to Cairo was cut, and they could only have been or small comfort. Each man's ration brought from Cairo was a few pints of warm water, two pieces of cheese, a packet of biscuits, two vitamin tablets, two aspirins, a sachet of sugar, tea, coffee, one box of matches and three cigarettes.

Whether the majority of the 3rd Army troops trapped in the Sinai pocket realised they were trapped is doubtful, especially as Radio Cairo kept them in the dark. But the Egyptians inside Suez must have seen ample evidence of the strength of the invading army. One example will suffice. On the day the cease-fire finally came into effect three Egyptians were catured while on their way to deliver an Israeli lieutenant, Allon Kaplan, to a prisoner of war camp. Kaplan had been captured on the east bank of the Canal, behind the Bar Lev line, and then taken across the water in a punt to what the Egyptians thought was home ground. To their bewilderment the soldiers they came across, sleeping under Russian tanks, were Israelis, and the Arab captors found themselves prisoners.

In 19 days of fighting the Arabs had shattered the myth of Israeli invincibility, and they had regained their pride. Few of them realised that they would not have kept their pride for long if the Russians and Americans had not insisted on calling a halt. The Arabs produced a miracle when they united against Israel. But the Israelis also produced a miracle when they fought back from the ropes to establish a physical presence in Egypt west of the Canal. They broke the pattern of the war and they were in no mood to give up. 'We intend to crush their armies and kill a hell of a lot of young soldiers', said one senior Israeli officer grimly. 'The essential thing is to plant in the mind of young commissioned Arab officers — those who survive this war and who will be the leaders of the next generation — that war will simply be no solution'. But Israeli hopes of inflicting another crushing military defeat were dashed because the superpowers could not afford to see the Arabs humiliated yet again.

Left: Men of the Egyptian Third Army held these blocks of flats in Suez and resisted stubbornly.

Epilogue

ever a war could truly be described as popular, then the raelis would say it was that of 1967. Even before it was 'er they were dancing in the streets, and the capture of rusalem's Old City brought forth a collective national stasy. But that was back in 1967; six years later Israel's ood was very different. Even during the first dark days of e war there was a firm conviction that their country uld survive, but is was conceded that the cost would be gh — in casualties, material, and the way Israelis would living in the months and years ahead. And the cost in ood and material on both sides was indeed high. The ice paid in human lives by the Israelis for stopping the rab invasion and gaining a few hundreds of square lometres of territory they did not need on the Golan eights and the west bank of the Canal was far higher than e toll exacted in the war of 1967. Egypt and Syria also ffered very heavy casualties and staggering losses of ms and equipment.

But when the war was over both sides remembered only initial stages: the Arabs recalled only their initial gains, e Israelis remembered only their initial set-backs. Despite e fact that they had been defeated President Sadat oclaimed that 'Egyptian forces had performed a miracle any military standard and this restored the honour of e nation'. The Israelis in the immediate postwar period on e other hand thought only of what might have been if the rab attack had been launched along the pre-1967 armistice lines. In such a case it would have been Tel Aviv and Jerusalem — not the Golan Heights and the Bar Lev line that would have had to absorb the initial shock. Thus in the Israeli view tens of thousands of their people could be killed if such an attack were only marginally more successful than that which was launched in October 1973.

So the fifth round of fighting ended with hardened attitudes and unallayed passions on both sides. The Israelis, embittered by the attack on Yom Kippur tended to forget that the Arabs attacked in order to recover the territories they had lost in 1967. The Arabs, equally embittered, were so intent on regaining the lost ground and their prestige that they almost came to believe that they had actually won the war. Paradoxically enough it is because of these attitudes that for the first time in Israel's history a real attempt has been made to follow a war through to its logical conclusion: a negotiated peace. Chastened by five wars it seems that the Arabs may have come to regard the existence of a Jewish state as less repugnant than hitherto, while the setbacks experienced in the initial stages of the October War and its unbearably high cost have made Israel's leaders more receptive to Egyptian and American diplomatic overtures. Whether this means that the world has witnessed the last Arab-Israeli war is unfortunately open to question. Peace in the Middle East may come only when the contestants revert to the old concept of a Palestine shared peacefully between Arab and Jew.

Appendix

Israeli-Arab Conflict 1948-1978
Relative Strengths

	Tanks	*Aircraft*	*Guns*	*Troops*
1948: Israel's War of Independence				
Israel	3	35	5	28,000
Arabs (not including regular Palestinian units)	270	300	150	35,000
1956: Sinai Campaign				
Israel	330	85	150	25,000
Egypt *only*	350	200	600	65,000
1967: The Six Day War—Israel	800	300	800*	260,000*
Arabs (Egypt, Syria Jordan, Iraq, etc)	2,500	1,000	1,560+	550,000
1973: The October War				
Israel	1,700	480	800*	275,000
Arabs (Egypt, Syria, Jordan, Iraq, etc)	5,500	1,160	3,200	1,200,000
Current Situation (End 1978 Estimated)				
Israel	2,800	550	850	400,000
Arabs (not including Saudi Arabia)	6,200	1,300	3,600	1,250,000

* Estimated † at full mobilisation

Below: Funeral of Israeli casualties in Tel Aviv.

Characteristics of Armour in the Middle East in 1974

Type	*Characteristics*
T-62	This was the main battle tank in the Soviet forces. It has a 115mm smooth-bore gun and a top speed of about 30mph. It can cross water up to about 18ft in depth and has night-vision equipment.
T-54/55	Some are still in service with the Soviet Army. It is equipped with a 100mm gun and has a road speed of about 30mph. It can cross water up to about 18ft in depth and has night-vision equipment.
Pt-76	The Pt-76 is a light amphibious tank used by the Russians as the main reconnaissance vehicle. It is capable of operating in a fast-flowing river or the open sea. It is considered mobile but it has limitations as a fighting vehicle. Armour protection is less than that of other light tanks. This vehicle has a 76mm low-velocity gun and a road speed of about 25mph. It apparently has no night-vision equipment.
M-60	The M-60 is currently a main battle tank of the United States Army. It has a 105mm high velocity gun and a top speed of about 30mph. It can cross water up to about 13ft in depth and has night-vision equipment. The M-60's cross-country mobility is said to be inferior to more modern European tanks.
M-48	The M-48 is the main tank armament of the US Marine Corps. It has a 90mm M-41 gun and a road speed of about 30mph. Night-vision equipment can be fitted.
Centurion (Mark 13)	After 25 years this tank is being phased out of the British Army. The most recent version has a 105mm gun and can move at speeds up to about 20mph. It is fitted with night-vision equipment, and can be fitted with water-crossing equipment.
Ben Gurion	This tank is similar to the Centurion, but the Israelis have replaced the original gun with a French 105mm gun.
Super-Sherman	This is the old American Sherman tank modernised by Israel with the addition of French medium-velocity tank guns and new diesel engines. The majority of guns fitted are 105mm, some are 75mm. Road speed is less than 30mph. Comparatively thin armour makes the Super-Sherman vulnerable to the 100mm guns of the T-54/55.
Isherman	This is a rebuilt Sherman tank with a French 105mm gun and new engines for increased speed. It is probably very similar to the Super-Sherman.
TI-67	Equipped with a 105mm gun, this is the Israeli conversion of captured T-54/55 tanks.

Characteristics of Major Aircraft in the Middle East in October 1973

Aircraft Type	*Approximate Combat Radius (miles)*	*Operational Role*
MiG-25	700	This aircraft was probably designed to intercept fast strike aircraft and carries air-to-air guided weapons
MiG-21	350	The MiG-21 is fitted with search-and-track plus warning radar and K-13 Atoll air-to-air missiles with an infrared guidance system similar to the American-made Sidewinder 1A
Su-20	230-400	The Su-20 has been referred to as a variable-geometry fighter version of the Su-11. The Su-11 was probably developed to meet the Soviet requirement for a faster interceptor to replace the Su-9. Normally it carries one radar homing and one infrared homing Anab air-to-air missile. There are provisions for additional weapons or fuel
Su-7	450	Subsequent to 1961, the Su-7 became the standard tactical fighter-bomber of the Soviet air force
Mirage 5	400-805	The Mirage 5 can carry one Matra R530 all-weather air-to-air missile with radar or infrared homing heads, an air-to-surface missile, and two Sidewinder air-to-air missiles. It has air-to-air interception radar with an additional mode for control from the ground and can function as a dive bomber
F-4E	900-1000	The F-4E uses highly sophisticated electronic countermeasures equipment computers, and radar in its role as a long-range all-weather attack fighter
A-4E	400-800	The A-4E fighter-bomber is equipped with an angle-of-attack indicator, ground clearance radar, and a variety of optional sophisticated weapons such as air-to-air and air-to-surface rockets (Sidewinders, infrared Bullpup, air-to-surface missiles and torpedoes)
Mirage IIIC	560-745	The characteristics of the Mirage IIIC are the same as for the Mirage 5, except that different electronic equipment was fitted in the planes supplied to Israel. Israel has developed an infrared homing air-to-air missile with a 'see-and-shoot' capability and has fitted it to its Mirage fighters

Bibliography

Antonius, G.; *The Arab Awakening;* Hamish Hamilton, London 1938

Barbour, N.; *Nisi Dominus;* Harrap, London 1946

Barker, A. J.; *Suez: The Seven Day War;* Faber, London 1964

Beaufre, A. (Gen); *L'Expedition de Suez;* Grasset, Paris 1967

Begin, M.; *The Revolt;* Steimatzky, Tel Aviv 1952

Ben Gurion, D.; *Israel: Years of Challenge;* Holt, Rinehart & Winston, New York 1963

Ben Porat, Y. et al; *Kippur;* Special Edition Publishers, Tel Aviv 1973

Bullard, Sir R.; *Britain and the Middle East;* Hutchinson, London 1951

Burns, E. L. M. (Lt-Gen); *Between Arab and Israeli;* Harrap, London 1962

Calvocoressi, P. (ed); *Suez Ten Years After;* BBC, London 1966

Churchill, W. and R.; *The Six-Day War;* Heinemann, London 1967

Dayan, M. (Gen); *Diary of the Sinai Campaign;* Schocken, New York 1967

Dayan, M.; *Story of my Life;* Weidenfeld & Nicolson, London 1976

Elston, D. R.; *No Alternative. Israel Observed;* Hutchinson, London 1960

Eshel, D. (ed); *Born in Battle;* Eshel Dranit, Israel 1978

Eytan, W.; *The First Ten Years. A Diplomatic History of Israel;* Weidenfeld & Nicolson, London 1958

Glubb, Sir J. B.; *A Soldier with the Arabs;* Hodder & Stoughton, London 1957

Greenfield, R. P. and I. A.; *The Life Story of Menachem Begin;* Manor Books, New York 1977

Henriques, R.; *One Hundred Hours to Suez;* Collins, London 1957

Herzog, C.; *The Yom Kippur War;* Keter, Jerusalem 1975

Hopkins, H.; *Egypt, the Crucible;* Secker & Warburg, London 1969

Howard, M. and Hunter R.; 'Israel and the Arab World. The Crisis of 1967', *Adelphi Papers No 41;* Institute of Strategic Studies, London 1967

Kerr, M.; *The Arab Cold War 1958-64;* Chatham House Essays Series, OUP Oxford 1965

Kinche, J. and D.; *Both Sides of the Hill;* Secker & Warburg, London 1960

Lacqueur, W. Z.; *The Road to War;* Penguin, Harmondsworth 1969

Levin, M.; *The Story of Israel;* Putnam, New York 1966

Lorch, N.; *One Long War;* Keter, Jerusalem 1976

Luttwak, E. and Horowitz, D.; *The Israeli Army;* Allen Lane, London 1975

Nasser, G. A.; *Toute la Vérité sur la Guerre de Palestine;* Direction des Relations Publiques des Forces Armées, Cairo 1955

Nasser, G. A.; *Speeches and Interviews* 1958, 1959, 1960, 1963; Information Dept, Cairo

O'Ballance, E.; *The Sinai Campaign 1956;* Faber, London 1959

O'Ballance, E.; *The Third Arab-Israeli War;* Faber, London 1972

O'Neill, B. E.; *Revolutionary Warfare in the Middle East,* Paladin, Boulder, Colorado, 1974

Rondot, P.; *The Changing Patterns of the Middle East 1919-1958;* Chatto & Windus, London 1962

Royal Institute of International Affairs; *Great Britain and Egypt 1914-1951;* Information Papers No 19, London 1952

British Interests in the Mediterranean and Near East; London 1957

Surveys of International Affairs; Documents on International Affairs

Sadat, Anwar el; *In Search of Identity;* Collins, London 1978

Safran, N.; *From War to War;* Pegasus, New York, 1971

Stephens, R.; *Nasser. A Political Biography;* Allen Lane, London 1971

Schwartz, W.; *The Arabs in Israel;* Faber, London 1959

Sunday Times Insight Team; *The Yom Kippur War;* Deutsch, London 1975

Sykes, C.; *Cross Roads to Israel;* Collins, London 1965

Teveth, S.; *Moshe Dayan;* Weidenfeld & Nicolson, London 1974

Thomas, H.; *The Suez Affair;* Weidenfeld & Nicholson, London 1967

Weizman, E.; *On Eagle's Wings;* Weidenfeld & Nicholson, London 1976

Young, P. (Brig); *The Israeli Campaign 1967;* Kimber, London 1968